PROSECUTING THE SHOPLIFTER

A Loss Prevention Strategy

PROSECUTING THE SHOPLIFTER

A Loss Prevention Strategy

JAMES CLEARY, Jr.

Butterworths

Boston London Durban Singapore Sydney Toronto Wellington

Library of Congress Cataloging in Publication Data
Cleary, James.
  Prosecuting the shoplifter.

  Includes index.
  1. Shoplifting—United States.   I. Title.
KF9352.C58   1986   345.73'0262   85–11342
ISBN 0–409–95116–1   347.305262

Butterworth Publishers
80 Montvale Avenue
Stoneham, MA 02180

10 9 8 7 6 5 4 3 2 1

Printed in the United States of America

Contents

Preface

This book is primarily a result of my six years as a trial prosecutor. Based on that experience, I designed and wrote a set of loss-prevention seminars for merchants entitled "The Dual Legal Aspects of Handling Shoplifting Cases." This book is centered around the approach used in the seminars.

It is important to understand what this book is not. It is not just a collection of statutes and cases on prosecution of shoplifting cases. Nor is it a group of cases where retail employees mishandled a shoplifting situation, resulting in the store's being sued for false arrest type civil actions. It was written to be a learning tool. It is intended to be a practical guide for nonlawyer store managers and security staff persons to use in the store. This book will better equip retail employees to prevent shoplifting by giving them the legal tools they need to prosecute more effectively and do so with minimum exposure to civil liability. By using these tools, any retail merchant in any state can reduce the two types of losses they sustain with regard to shoplifting: the loss of merchandise to shoplifters and the loss of dollars paid out when the store is sued civilly.

My intention is to keep this complicated subject simple yet provide retail employees with specific information they can use in their stores when dealing with shoplifting situations. Awareness is a laudable goal, but it falls short when talking about the dual legal aspects of shoplifting. To be aware that a retail company has a shoplifting problem is one thing. For company employees to possess skills to deal effectively with shop-lifting situations is quite another.

In a word, this book is about *evidence*. Evidence of any offense is found at the crime scene. The crime scene in a shoplifting case is in the store. Thus all the evidence a store manager or security person needs to rely on in court to obtain a conviction for shoplifting is found right in the store. Merchants need the ability to gather the evidence in the store and then, several weeks later, present that evidence at a shoplifting trial. This book will teach retail employees to understand this evidence found in the store and to gather it logically and systematically. Readers will see how to review and evaluate that evidence and then how to make prosecution decisions based on that evidence. The book will show merchants that in some cases the evidence rejects the decision to prosecute and supports the decision to release the suspect without taking the case to court. Contrary to popular opinion, shoplifting cases are not won by dazzling testimony in a courtroom. Shoplifting cases are won because a store manager or security person had the ability to gather evidence in the store. To do a better job of preventing shoplifting, a retail employee needs to improve evidence-gathering skills.

A second key word in this book is *responding*. Store owners, managers, and security personnel can improve their ability to respond to shoplifting situations. What counts is the ability to respond armed with evidence-gathering skills. A retail employee who responds properly first detains the suspect on probable cause. Next, that employee logically and systematically gathers the evidence found in the store. A proper response is one where the retail employee does not violate the civil tort law. The role of the merchant is not just to prosecute shoplifting cases but to do so without unnecessary risk of a "false arrest" suit being filed against the store.

The approach taken in this book is for merchants to learn from other merchants. In chapter 3, for example, a number of shoplifting situations are presented where the retail employees handling the cases responded properly. The result in each of these cases was a conviction for shoplifting. By studying these cases a merchant in any state can learn to improve his ability to prosecute shoplifting cases. By contrast, the cases in chapter 8 and 9 demonstrate shoplifting situations where retail employees responded and made mistakes. These mistakes either directly caused or set the stage for civil actions to be filed against the stores. By studying cases where civil actions resulted the reader will be able to identify these in-store mistakes most commonly made. Once they are brought to light they can be compared, distinguished, and better understood. A retail employee is then better equipped to avoid making these common mistakes during future encounters with shoplifting suspects. A store owner, manager, or security person not equipped with *specific information* about the dual legal aspects of handling shoplifting cases will—sooner or later—respond and make a mistake. That mistake will permit the shoplifting suspect to turn the tables and sue the store civilly.

There are over seventy cases presented in this book, cases dealing with both prosecution of shoplifting suspects and stores being sued civilly. I have edited out the procedural points, leaving the reader with the essential facts having to do with shoplifting prosecution and civil liability. These cases are learning vehicles. They tell a story. Read them, then compare and distinguish them. The cases demonstrate how the courts decide points of law having to do with the dual legal aspects of handling shoplifting cases.

As to the statutes, I have selected ones which are representative of shoplifting prosecution and detention for probable cause statutes. Rather than laundry listing statutes at the end of the book I have explained how these statutes are applied and construed by the courts. In this way, the merchant can get a better idea of how the courts in states where he is operating stores will rule.

Finally, I have tried to keep the material readable, which is no easy task when dealing with legal subjects. It is my intention to help store owners, managers, and security people, because they are the ones who must deal with shoplifting suspects and shoplifting situations in their stores. This book will better equip retail merchants with two things—a vocabulary and a method of analysis. Once merchants can learn to see the problem in legal terms and discuss it in a legal vocabulary, they are well on the way to being more effective in handling a shoplifting situation.

PROSECUTING THE SHOPLIFTER

A Loss Prevention Strategy

1

The Shoplifting Problem

WHO SHOPLIFTS

There is no typical shoplifter. Based on apprehensions there are three categories of shoplifters. The most numerous is the *average citizen shoplifter*. They account for about 75 percent of all persons picked up for shoplifting. The next category is the *full-time amateur shoplifter*, who makes up about 20 percent of the total. The final group is the *professional shoplifter* or *booster* as they are called on the street. This group makes up no more than 5 percent of the shoplifters, and that estimate may be high.

The Average Citizen Shoplifter

An article in the January 1982 issue of *Ladies Home Journal* is a good place to begin discussing the average citizen shoplifter. A photograph at the beginning of the article, entitled "When 'Honest' Women Steal—A Middle-Class Crime Wave," shows an attractive and well-dressed woman standing at a counter in a fashionable department store. She is dropping a $40 gold compact into her purse. The article says that this college-educated woman has two elementary school children. She had her checkbook and eight credit cards, as well as $80 in cash, on her at the time she shoplifted the compact. The article goes on to point out that from 25 to 33 percent of all persons apprehended shoplifting are women between the ages of twenty and fifty. According to the article, the only larger identifiable group of shoplifters is teenagers.

Moving from the world of popular journalism to documented studies

of persons arrested for shoplifting is helpful in answering the question—
Who shoplifts? In Travis County (Austin) Texas, 1,000 persons were
interviewed after being caught shoplifting. None of them had a prior
criminal record so they were placed in a pretrial diversion program by the
prosecutor and the court. Consider some of the findings based on anonymous interviews with these average citizen shoplifters.[1]

Sex: Female, 52 percent; male, 48 percent
Decided to shoplift: before entered store, 32 percent; after entered
    store, 68 percent
Reason Given for Shoplifting:
Convenient, easy mark, won't miss it, 36 percent
Angry, ripoff system, get even, 25 percent
For the thrill, 14 percent
No money but wanted the item, 12 percent
Line too long, did not want to wait, 9 percent
Other reasons (depression, personal problems, mental illness, and
    innocence), 9 percent

Items shoplifted:
Cosmetics, 23.6 percent
Clothing, 16.6 percent
Miscellaneous, 15.9 percent
Food, 14.6 percent
Medicine, 12.7 percent
Tools and hardware, 11.4 percent
Household products, 5.2 percent

Did you have the money to pay? Yes, 88 percent

A similar survey was conducted in Pennsylvania with 1,700 persons
picked up for shoplifting over a five-year period.[2] None had a prior
conviction for shoplifting. Consider some of the more important findings
of this survey:

The average value of a single theft was $26.35.
The average person apprehended had shoplifted 98.8 times before being
    caught.
58.3 percent were female and 41.7 percent were male.
57 percent (or 969 out of 1,700) said they had shoplifted at least once per
    month before being apprehended.

---

[1]Study conducted by Larry A. Lloyd of the National Corrective Training Institute,
Austin, Texas, September 4, 1981.
[2]Study conducted by Lawrence A. Connor, director of Shoplifters Anonymous, Glen
Mills, Pennsylvania, 1982.

The age breakdown was as follows: juveniles, 17.7 percent; persons
   between ages sixteen and twenty, 28.7 percent; persons between ages
   twenty-one and fifty-four, 44.3 percent; and persons over age fifty-
   five, 9.3 percent.
Answer to question "Why did you shoplift?" "Stores write off the losses
   on their taxes." "I've spent plenty of money in that store and I'm
   entitled to get a little of it back."

This well-documented study concluded there are three categories of
shoplifters. The *soft-core shoplifter* is a person who steals for personal use
regularly, even habitually, and has never been prosecuted. This person
has no criminal record and is not considered by society as a thief. They
make up probably 75 percent of the people who shoplift. The *hard-core
shoplifter* is a person who steals for personal use but has a criminal record,
either for shoplifting or for other offenses.

The *professional shoplifter* is a person who steals regularly to resell
the merchandise for money to support a drug habit. The findings thus
uphold the traditional view that from two-thirds to three-fourths of the
people shoplifting on any given day are these soft core or average citizen
shoplifters. The fact that should concern retailers is this—probably 80
percent of these average citizen shoplifters steal with regularity. Of the
1,700 first offenders interviewed, 57 percent said they shoplifted at least
once per month before being caught. The study concluded that shoplifting among a large percentage of the average citizen types is habitual.

What can merchants learn from this information about who shoplifts?
The most crucial fact is that the average citizen types shoplift regularly. Like
the woman in the *Ladies Home Journal* article shoplifting the $40 compact,
these people conceal merchandise in pockets, purses, shopping bags, and
under clothing. Then they walk out of stores without paying. They *do not*
use gimmicks like booster boxes (ones with a false bottom) or booster coats
(ones with pockets sewn inside the linings) and they do not put merchandise between the legs and walk out of stores. I am not saying people do not
shoplift by using these gimmicks because some do. The point is simply
this—the largest number of people shoplifting on any given day are these
average citizen types who do not use gimmicks to steal.

The average citizen type shoplifter steals relatively little each time
(average value only $26) when compared to the professional shoplifter
who steals large amounts of merchandise daily to resell to a fence. The
head of the Retail Bureau of the Washington, D. C. Board of Trade was
recently quoted in a retail industry magazine.[3] He said the average citizen
shoplifters actually steal more merchandise each year than the profes-

---

[3]"When You Least Expect It," *Chain Store Age Executive Magazine*, February
1985, p. 18.

sional and for a simple reason—there are so many more of them. As a group these average citizen type shoplifters will do two things—shoplift from and sue stores. They will do both with success unless the merchants train employees to prevent shoplifting losses.

A large number of cases in this book concern stores that have been sued civilly when a shoplifting situation was mishandled. These false arrest type cases were not filed by the professional or by the full-time amateur shoplifter, not at all. The stores in these cases were sued by the average citizen type shoplifter. Merchants must teach their employees how to handle cases involving the average citizen shoplifter. Because they are so numerous they constitute both a shoplifting and a civil liability threat to the company assets. These people will cost a store merchandise and lost profit. Also, they will cost the store dollars, meaning money paid out to defend and settle civil actions.

The Full-Time Amateur Shoplifter

In most cities the police will circulate a list of "known shoplifters" around the retail community in a good faith attempt to help merchants with shoplifting loss-prevention. There is a problem with these lists. They do not contain the descriptions of average citizen shoplifters, because these people do not have criminal records. The average citizen shoplifter is not known to the police. The lists generally do not contain descriptions of the professional shoplifters, as boosters are rarely apprehended by merchants or their security staffs. The people on these lists are really the full-time amateur shoplifters, people who account for only about 20 percent of those caught shoplifting. In conducting shoplifting awareness training programs, merchants should not rely totally on these known shoplifter lists. The typical shoplifter is much more likely to be the well-dressed woman shoplifting the compact or young adults. Finally, this group of full-time amateurs is not as likely to file a civil action against a store because they have prior criminal records—for shoplifting many times. In a civil action the fact that the plaintiff had a prior conviction for shoplifting will be brought to the attention of the jury. These full-time amateurs will shoplift from but will not sue stores. In others words, the civil liability threat is less with this category of shoplifters.

The Professional Shoplifter

The final type of shoplifter is the professional, or "booster." They are small in number when compared to the average citizen and the full-time amateur shoplifters. The professional is typically a drug addict who has to shoplift daily to support a habit. They shoplift for one reason: money. They sell the goods to a fence (a buyer of stolen merchandise), who in turn sells the store's merchandise to the general public at about one-third or one-half its retail selling price.

Most often boosters work in pairs (a man and woman) although sometimes two women team up to shoplift. They travel from city to city, shoplifting in malls and in freestanding stores as they go. Boosters are well dressed, because they wear clothing they have shoplifted. They shoplift enormous amounts of merchandise, because it is their job. Most professionals have a drug habit which must be supported by stealing merchandise and selling it to a fence. One former professional shoplifter[4] now conducts shoplifting loss-prevention training seminars for merchants all over the country. He made over $100,000 in his first year as a booster. Since the merchandise is sold to a fence for 25 percent of its retail value this means a booster has to shoplift over $400,000 at retail to net out at $100,000 per year. Boosters are in every major city. They are rarely caught by merchants and their security staffs. A booster would never consider filing a civil action against a store.

Merchants, especially security personnel, do not like to be told the professional shoplifter is rarely apprehended. This fact is documented by an article in a national security magazine which said less than 1 percent of the persons apprehended for shoplifting were professionals.[5] The reason so few professionals are stopped is that merchants are looking for the wrong people. Remember, the professional is well dressed and knows a lot about merchandise. Because professionals operate differently than both the average citizen and full-time amateur shoplifters, the information a merchant has about shoplifters does not apply to the booster.

Conclusion

This book is about the merchant's role in preventing shoplifting losses, both the loss of merchandise to shoplifters and the loss of dollars paid out in civil actions. It is important to understand that seven out of ten shoplifters will be the average citizen type. Training programs must take

---

[4]Mr. W. R. (Dick) Deal was a professional shoplifter for many years. He was never stopped for shoplifting, nor was he ever with another professional shoplifter who was stopped. He now presents seminars for retail merchants, telling them how to identify boosters and how to prevent them from shoplifting.

[5]*Security Management Magazine*, July 1978, p. 47. This magazine is published monthly by The American Society for Industrial Security.

into account that many of the people caught shoplifting will also qualify as a credit account customer. These people have jobs, families, and otherwise good reputations. If the shoplifting situation is mishandled these people will sue the store. It is important to understand that young adults and minors shoplift. They too can bring civil actions if mistreated by a store owner, manager, or security person. Since there is no typical shoplifter, the merchant must train employees to watch for people concealing merchandise in pockets, purses, shopping bags, and under clothing because this is the way the average citizen type person shoplifts. Merchants must forget about "shifty eyes" or "furtive gestures" when it comes to identifying shoplifting suspects. Average citizen types, full-time amateurs and professionals all shoplift one way—with their hands.

Handling shoplifting situations is anything but a game of "cops and robbers." Merchants are not peace officers, and most suspects detained for shoplifting are not criminals but average citizens. This book is about the legal tools available to merchants in handling shoplifting situations. Before the merchant becomes too wrapped up in the legal aspects of shoplifting, he should give some serious thought to the subject of *who shoplifts*. The court studies presented above are excellent sources of information—information not previously available to the retail community until the past five years. Study this material and develop a profile of whom may be shoplifting in your stores. Shoplifting is not committed only by poor people—hardly. It is not confined to stores in high crime areas of a city. Shoplifting takes place on malls in the most affluent suburbs of America every day. Understanding who shoplifts is important for any store in formulating policies and procedures.

THE EXTENT OF SHOPLIFTING LOSSES

An article in a recent retail trade magazine said the annual shoplifting loss was $22 billion.[6] The article went on to say that 90 percent of those arrested for shoplifting had cash, checks, or credit cards on their person which could have been used to pay for the merchandise shoplifted. Based on income level 28 percent of those arrested were in the higher category, 45 percent in the middle, and 27 percent in the lower income group. There is no segment of the retail industry that escapes shoplifting losses. Consider some of the types of retail operations where people shoplift.

---

[6]"When You Least Expect It," *Chain Store Age Executive Magazine*, February 1985, p. 18.

Stores generally with a full-time security staff to handle shoplifting

Department
Discount
Food
Drug

Specialty Stores

Where the store manager and sales people handle shoplifting situations

Children's apparel	Toy	Office supply
Women's apparel	Gift	Stationery
Men's apparel	Novelty	Home centers
Family apparel	Hobby	Shoe
Sporting goods	Music and record	
Hardware	Card	
Variety	Convenience	

Groups indirectly involved with shoplifting

Mall security staff personnel
Off-duty peace officers "moonlighting" in security for retail stores
Contract security guard service companies

The amount of merchandise shoplifted nationally is not the primary concern to a retail company. Table 1.1 illustrates typical losses a department store is likely to suffer. This is much more important because it shows exactly where a store can be losing merchandise.

As a general rule, most retail companies will report theft losses as a percentage of sales. Let's examine a shoplifting loss from the viewpoint of making it up with additional sales. Suppose a clothing company is doing business at a 2.5 percent profit level and a $100 sweater is shoplifted. It will take almost $4,000 in additional sales to make up for the profit lost on that sweater. The owner or chief executive officer will be hard pressed to document that this lost profit can be made up with additional sales on a regular basis. Looking at the situation from a loss-prevention viewpoint, it can be said that preventing a $100 shoplifting loss is like finding $4,000 in additional sales. Store owners and retail executives realize they cannot consistently generate additional sales to cover shoplifting losses so they train employees to prevent shoplifting in the first place.

PREVENTING SHOPLIFTING BY SALES EMPLOYEE VIGILANCE

In department and discount stores only security staff members are authorized to prevent shoplifting by detaining persons after they have con-

| TABLE 1.1 | Shortage report—the ABC Store, Anywhere, USA |

Department	Shortage (%)
Cosmetics and beauty aids	3.91
Lawn and garden	1.38
Building supplies	2.34
Auto accessories	1.58
Bras and foundations	1.33
Women's dresses	3.19
Women's coats and suits	1.48
Lingerie, robes, and sleepware	1.35
Outerwear-sportswear	1.97
Costume jewelry	11.33
Jewelry and watches	2.48
Sports, leisure, beachwear	1.59
Handbags and accessories	2.59
Hardware	2.81
Toys and games	2.01
Sporting goods	1.85
Tapes and records	2.95
Photo supplies	2.06
Gifts and flowers	2.09
Candy	1.35
Tobacco	1.89
All other departments	1.61

cealed merchandise and left without paying. By contrast, specialty stores do not employ full-time security people to patrol the selling floor looking for shoplifters. In specialty stores, the owner or manager has the responsibility of detaining persons who have concealed merchandise and left without paying. Most retail companies, whether it is a department store with a security staff or a specialty store without a security staff, do not authorize sales employees to stop shoplifting suspects. Sometimes sales employees feel they can make no contribution to the shoplifting loss-prevention effort. Nothing is further from the truth. The most effective deterrent to shoplifting is a well-trained and alert sales employee.

Consider the comments by a southern California department store manager about the value of sales employees in shoplifting loss prevention:

Tags generally have been a good deterrent but *alert people are better than tags or anything else.* If a customer has not been recognized by a sales person saying "May I help you" or anything else the customer feels more anomyomus and is more likely to try it (meaning attempt to shoplift). (Riverside CA—The Press Enterprise, November 11, 1984).

The essential ingredient in all successful shoplifting efforts is *privacy*. A person needs privacy to conceal merchandise before walking out without paying. This is true whether one is talking about the average citizen, full-time amateur, or professional shoplifter. Nobody can conceal merchandise in a pocket, switch a price tag, if they are being watched. Store owners and retail executives sometimes complain they do not want to make security people out of sales employees. This is a valid comment. A suggestion is this—train sales employees to develop a *shoplifting alertness dimension* to their primary job of selling. Make sure they understand that by approaching a customer and asking "May I help you," they are removing the privacy factor right off the bat. Make sure sales employees understand they are playing a vital role in preventing shoplifting by giving good "customer service."

Sales employees are trained to greet customers and back off so the customer can browse. No sales person wants to be pushy or to be considered a pest. The point is simply this—sales employees cannot neglect customers, nor can they greet customers, back off, and forget about the possibility of shoplifting. They must be taught that the businessman, the teenager, the senior citizen, and even the woman pushing the baby stroller are all possible shoplifting candidates. Sales employees must be taught that the average citizen shoplifter does not use gimmicks to steal. Sales employees must understand that most people simply remove merchandise from a counter, rack, or shelf, conceal it, and walk out without paying. These people—especially the average citizen shoplifter—are successful because a sales employee gave them that needed privacy.

Merchants and their sales employees must remember the average citizen shoplifters are not true criminals. If these people are spoken to or otherwise acknowledged by eye contact, psychologically they are less likely to try and conceal merchandise. On the other hand, if no sales employee makes any kind of contact two things happen. The customer is given the actual privacy plus a feeling of privacy. People feel more anonymous if they are not contacted, so they will be more likely to shoplift. Customer service techniques will vary from company to company. One technique all retailers agree on is greeting the customer and making eye contact. Speaking to and looking at a customer is the best way to remove that feeling of privacy as well as actual privacy.

Since most companies do not permit sales employees to detain shoplifting suspects, there are some basic facts a sales employee needs to know—both about shoplifting and their role in preventing it (see Table 1.2).

Generally sales employee turnover is high in most retail companies. For this reason owners and managers must provide sales employees with shoplifting loss-prevention information which is simple and basic. If nothing else, sales employees should understand that by giving good "customer service" they are playing an important role in shoplifting

TABLE 1.2	Facts sales employees should know to prevent shoplifting

1. Removing the privacy factor is critical. A shopper needs privacy to become a shoplifter. Any person must have privacy to conceal merchandise after removing it from a rack, counter, or shelf with his or her hands.

2. There is just one way in which people shoplift—with their hands. Train sales employees to watch a person's hands and think about where that person could conceal the merchandise if they were going to shoplift it.

3. The most effective way to remove the privacy factor is by greeting the customer and making eye contact.

4. Sales employees must learn to develop a SHOPLIFTING ALERTNESS DIMENSION to their selling function. This shoplifting alertness dimension should center around facts about the average citizen shoplifter such as:
   a. They do not use gimmicks like booster boxes, booster coats, or putting merchandise between their legs. They simply conceal merchandise and walk out of stores, trying to act as normal as possible.
   b. These people are not true criminals. They shoplift because they get away with it. They get away with it in large part because sales employees give them that much needed privacy required to shoplift.
   c. A large percentage of the average citizen shoplifters make the decision to shoplift *after* entering the store. They decide to shoplift because they are being ignored by sales employees—because they have that privacy.
   d. Most of the average citizen type shoplifters will shoplift alone.
   e. Merchants only apprehend one out of ten persons who are shoplifting, and this estimate is probably low. Some estimate that only one in twenty persons who shoplift are caught.

loss-prevention. Even though sales employees generally are not permitted to stop shoplifting suspects, the manager or owner should discuss shoplifting situations with them. Make it clear that the owner or manager will stop suspects, but that sales employees should always maintain an alertness to the possibility of shoplifting.

In my opinion specialty stores—ones without a security staff person on the selling floor—are especially vulnerable to shoplifting. During the years I prosecuted, rarely was a case filed by a specialty store—a book, music, card, gift, sporting goods, apparel, hardware, toy, hobby, office supply, or home center store. Traditionally retailers say they lose more merchandise to dishonest employees than to shoplifters. This sacred assumption has now been effectively challenged by Mr. Peter D. Berlin, the head of Shrinkage Reduction Services at Price Waterhouse. Using a hypothetical 137 outlet specialty apparel store chain, Mr. Berlin concludes that shoplifting accounted for $1,233,000 of the inventory shrinkage, while only \$151,200 was attributable to internal theft. Retail and security executives in specialty stores should pay close attention to the formula Mr. Berlin developed and apply it to their own operations.

Specialty store owners and managers should develop training programs for sales employees. Some will counter by saying their stores use electronic article surveillance (EAS) systems to deter shoplifting. There is a twofold problem with EAS systems. First, not all of the merchandise is generally tagged with the warning devices. Secondly, employees may begin to rely totally on these EAS devices, forgetting all about giving good customer service. A store that uses these EAS systems may begin to neglect sales employee alertness training. EAS systems, assuming they are cost justified, are really only a support system for employees anyway. Since some retailers do not feel they are cost justified or cannot afford the systems, giving good customer service is the only preventive measure available.

Let's compare the role of a sales employee in preventing shoplifting with the role of a security staff member. The sales person prevents shoplifting by removing the privacy factor—by giving good customer service. By contrast, a security person never removes the privacy factor. Security people are taught to take the opposite approach. They roam the selling floor, generally in plainclothes, and watch for people concealing merchandise, switching price tags, or passing merchandise off to accomplices. They never approach a customer until that customer has obtained wrongful possession of merchandise and has left the store. Security people prevent shoplifting by stopping people *after* they have obtained wrongful possession of unpurchased merchandise. Sales employees prevent shoplifting by greeting customers and making eye contact *before* that person tries to obtain wrongful possession of goods.

It is important to remember that statistics on shoplifting apprehensions only show who gets caught. They are not reliable evidence of who shoplifts and gets away with it. For example, the security director of a department store chain with fifteen outlets in the Boston area was quoted as saying his security staff apprehends only one out of ten persons who are shoplifting.[7] One year his staff caught 4,000 persons. This means that 36,000 people shoplifted in those fifteen stores without being caught—even though the store had a full-time security staff. If stores with full-time security staffs catch only one out of ten, what about the number of people who shoplift and get away with it in specialty stores? If a specialty store owner or manager has not stopped a shoplifting suspect in the last thirty days, the chances are the shoplifting losses are high in that specialty store.

---

[7]"Shoplifters Pad Lists," *Kansas City Star*, November 20, 1981, p. 6.

For years the retail community has talked about the "impulse" theory of shoplifting. Retailers are heard to say that people shoplift on impulse. The Pennsylvania study cited above said 57 percent of the first offenders interviewed admitted to shoplifting at least once a month before being caught. It went on to say the average person in the study shoplifted ninety-eight times before being charged with the offense. This appears to be much more than impulse. The study concluded that shoplifting was addictive among a large number of the average citizen types.

Consider an important statistic revealed in the Texas study among people who got caught. Sixty-eight percent of these first offenders said they made the decision to shoplift *after* they entered the store. This means these people thought they had sufficient privacy to conceal merchandise without being spotted. If 68 percent of those who got caught said they decided to shoplift after entering the store, a fair question is this—What percentage of those *who did not get caught* decided to shoplift after they entered the store? It is reasonable to assume that an equal number of successful shoplifters decided to steal after entering the store. This leads us to the question of why they got away with shoplifting? The answer is that the successful shoplifter was given that privacy necessary to conceal merchandise. Simply stated, privacy equals the opportunity to shoplift.

What does all this mean when it comes to sales employees and shoplifting loss-prevention training programs. It means the role of the sales employee is not always well-understood or well-defined. Although sales employees are legally authorized to detain shoplifting suspects, most stores do not allow it. In stores with a security staff the sales employee is always told to "call security" when he sees a shoplifting situation taking place on the selling floor. In specialty stores the sales employee is normally instructed to notify the owner or manager when a person is seen concealing unpurchased merchandise. This means shoplifting loss-prevention skills for sales employees are different than those needed by a store owner, manager, or security person.

The role of the sales employee is to remove the opportunity a person has to shoplift. This means removing the privacy factor by greeting customers and making eye contact. The role of the store owner, manager, or security person is to detain shoplifting suspects. Both are equally important. Shoplifting is an offense against the merchant's lawful possession of merchandise. Sales employees can deter people from obtaining wrongful possession of merchandise in the first place. Owners, managers, and security personnel prevent shoplifting by detaining people after they have obtained wrongful possession of merchandise and have left the store. By clearly defining the role of the sales employee, the retailer will make those sales employees more effective in preventing shoplifting losses.

PROSECUTION OF SHOPLIFTING CASES DETERS FUTURE SHOPLIFTING ATTEMPTS

Chapter 7 discusses a famous California shoplifting case where a female teenager was stopped for palming some costume jewelry. When the security employee asked why she failed to pay for the jewelry she told him her friends said the store was "an easy place to shoplift." Stores that do not prosecute quickly earn the reputation of being an easy mark when it comes to shoplifting. Remember the studies have found shoplifting is not impulsive but habitual or addictive. Each time a person shoplifts without being caught it is easier psychologically for that person to come back to the store and shoplift again.

Most retailers feel that prosecution is a deterrent to future shoplifting attempts. I agree, especially when it comes to the average citizen shoplifter category. Many merchants tell the press they prosecute 100 percent of the people stopped for shoplifting in their stores. The facts of life are that stores prosecute some suspects and release others. In other words, many merchants follow a selective prosecution approach, because they do not take all their cases to court. The two studies which follow show many merchants use a selective prosecution policy.

Each year a national retail trade association publishes a survey of its members on a variety of loss-prevention subjects.[8] Consider their statement about prosecution of shoplifting cases— "Strong prosecution policies continued to be a major factor among retailers." The following statistics show these merchants prosecuted cases because they felt it was a deterrent to future shoplifting attempts. Note that they followed a selective prosecution approach in that not all persons detained for shoplifting were taken to court.

	Percentage of cases prosecuted	Percentage of cases where suspect was released without formal prosecution
1982	56	44
1983	66	33

Note: In both survey years these mass merchandise, discount, and specialty stores obtained convictions in 90% of the cases they prosecuted.

[8]National Mass Retail Institute—Security & Shrinkage, 3rd Annual Study of Inventory Shrinkage Control and Security Procedures in Retailing. Conducted by Arthur Young & Co., released January 15, 1982.

A study of west coast retailers also demonstrates that merchants use a selective prosecution approach.

Type of store	% of cases prosecuted	% of cases not prosecuted
Discount	53	47
Food	42	58
Drug	26	74

Selective Prosecution Is Authorized by the Merchant's Privilege

Sometimes merchants think that all persons stopped for shoplifting must be arrested and prosecuted. This is not true. The legislatures of all states have passed laws known as detention statutes which have incorporated the "merchant's privilege" into their provisions. The privilege permits a merchant to detain a shoplifting suspect and investigate the facts without declaring the stopping to be a citizen's arrest. If the detaining merchant conducts an investigation of the facts which is legally reasonable in manner, method, and time, the retailer has complied with the privilege. If the suspect later sues the store civilly, the merchant can plead compliance with the privilege as a defense to the civil action.

Most people think of these statutes as granting merchants conditional immunity from false imprisonment actions, which of course is what they do. There is another aspect of these statutes which permits the merchant to selectively prosecute. No detention statute in any state requires that all shoplifting suspects detained under the merchant's privilege be prosecuted. The privilege is one to detain, investigate the facts, and recover the unpurchased merchandise. A retail employee who detains a suspect under authority of the statutory privilege has a choice in the way he or she handles the shoplifting situation. The merchant can:

1. Detain, recover the unpurchased merchandise, warn, and release the suspect without involving the police at all; or
2. Detain, recover the unpurchased merchandise, call the police, and cause the person's formal arrest and prosecution.

In either situation a store owner, manager, or security person has prevented shoplifting by detaining suspects under authority of the merchant's privilege.

These detention statutes are the legal authority by which any retailer can adopt a selective prosecution approach. Under a selective prosecution policy, each retail company is free to prosecute as many or as few cases as the merchant feels will serve as a deterrent to future shoplifting attempts. As the west coast survey cited above clearly demonstrates, discount, drug, and food stores each prosecute a different percentage of persons detained for shoplifting. This flexibility in taking cases to court is the reason retailers should base their policy on the merchant's privilege. Understanding these detention statutes is an absolute necessity for any store in any state. This is true whether the store has a full-time security staff to handle shoplifting situations or whether shoplifting cases are handled by the store owner or manager. These statutes are the key to more effective prosecution with minimum risk of having a civil action filed against the store.

Merchants often complain that prosecution of shoplift cases is expensive in terms of payroll costs. It may take two or three trips to court before a case is over. In most states a person found guilty of misdemeanor shoplifting has the right to appeal the case and have tried all over again— this time in front of a jury. This means more trips to court. It means the merchandise cannot be returned to stock because it is prosecution evidence needed at the trial. Merchants look at payroll costs for the employee time spent in court and often conclude prosecution is not cost justified. By using a selective prosecution approach the merchant can warn and release suspects in the inexpensive item cases, thus saving the payroll costs they complain about. In situations where the suspect shoplifted expensive merchandise, or shoplifted multiple items, the case could be prosecuted as a deterrent. These detention statutes, all containing the merchant's privilege, were passed to make it easier for merchants to stop suspects and recover unpurchased merchandise without being sued civilly. Always remember by using the merchant's privilege the store can prosecute as many or as few cases as it wishes. An effective prosecution policy generally means a selective prosecution policy.

The cost of prosecuting shoplifting cases is not always justified from another point of view. Court dockets in all cities are clogged with both civil and criminal cases. A businessman was convicted of shoplifting for eating a $.79 bag of nuts in a New York supermarket. He said he routinely spends $100 per week on groceries in that store. After the trial the Nassau County, New York authorities said the prosecution costs so far were $10,000 after the six-day jury trial.[9] Each shoplifting case must be dealt with on its merits but this case seems to be an excellent example of a store not considering a selective prosecution approach.

Merchants are fond of complaining about prosecutors and the court system as part of their shoplifting dilemma. They must remember that crimes against persons are always high priority with prosecutors, courts,

---

[9]"The Nut Muncher Case," *Kansas City Star*, May 11, 1982, page 7.

and the general public. The Nassau County authorities were not overjoyed to spend $10,000 and tie up a judge for six days over a $.79 package of nuts, especially when the merchant had another legal option. All property offenses take lower priority in any court system and with the public. Shoplifting is an offense against property.

A merchant, like any other citizen who is the victim of crime, has the right to use the court system. The legislatures have given retailers a legal tool in these merchant's privilege statutes. Some court systems have a pretrial diversion program for first offender shoplifting cases. A well-thought-out shoplifting loss-prevention program will consider all options available, as well as how the courts and prosecutors view shoplifting cases. Many retail security people only show up around a prosecutor's office when they have a problem rather than maintaining any regular liaison. Do not get the reputation of the "mystery security director" in your city. Set up an appointment to discuss shoplifting and internal theft cases with the district attorney, because cost-effective prosecution is a two-way street.

The beauty of the merchant's privilege is that besides giving the store a defense to a civil action if one is filed, it also authorizes selective prosecution of shoplifting cases. Store owners, managers, and security personnel must understand the provisions of these detention statutes because they are the ones who must make decisions based on evidence. Effectively handling shoplifting situations involves three factors: (1) deterrence of future shoplifting attempts, (2) cost effectiveness of taking cases to court, and (3) keeping the civil liability exposure to a minimum in each shoplifting situation. When store policy is based on these merchant's privilege statutes, a retailer in any state is using the best legal tool available.

Evidence-Gathering Skills Needed
to Prosecute Shoplifting Cases Selectively

Without the ability to produce, investigate, and evaluate evidence found in the store, the merchant's privilege will be of little value. As the trade association survey above showed, merchants who did prosecute selectively obtained convictions in 90 percent of the cases filed. They also saved payroll costs because not all persons detained for possible shoplifting were taken to court. These stores had effective prosecution policies because their employees understood the evidence needed to obtain a conviction in court for shoplifting. They also knew when the evidence produced in the store told them a prosecutable case did not exist and should not be filed.

In all states, a merchant will present two types of evidence in court when seeking a conviction for shoplifting—eyewitness evidence and physical evidence. Eyewitness evidence is the observations made of the person concealing merchandise or switching a price tag. The physical evidence is the recovered merchandise and its price tag. This evidence is produced, reviewed, and evaluated in the store. If the retail employee decides to file the charge this evidence is presented some weeks later in court at the trial to establish the elements of the offense found in the shoplifting prosecution statute.

The fact that shoplifting prosecution statutes have different names from state to state often confuses retailers, especially those with stores in several states. A retail or security executive could validly be heard to comment as follows:

> We have 31 stores located in four states. In Illinois the law is called Retail Theft, in Tennessee it is named Shoplifting/Concealment, in Texas they call the statute Theft and in Missouri the shoplifting prosecution statute is called Stealing. How can we write an effective policies and procedures manual when the laws are different in each state where we are doing business?

The answer is to teach employees to produce the two types of evidence—the eyewitness and physical evidence. In each state a merchant can obtain a conviction by presenting those two types of evidence in court. Training programs should teach employees how to produce evidence in the store they need later in court to prove the elements of the offense as found in the shoplifting prosecution statute. A person can be found guilty of retail theft in Illinois, of shoplifting/concealment in Tennessee, of theft in Texas, or of stealing in Missouri on the basis of eyewitness and physical evidence. Only evidence convicts a persons of shoplifting, not the name of the shoplifting prosecution statute.

There are five basic evidence-gathering skills a store manager, owner, or security person needs to acquire in order to prosecute shoplifting cases more effectively. Remember that shoplifting cases are won because a retail employee had the loss-prevention skills needed to gather evidence in the store.

1. *Logically and Systematically Gather Evidence.* When cases are lost in court, it is usually because of insufficient evidence. This means the store manager or security person overlooked some facts in the store, facts now needed as evidence at the trial. The ability to produce facts logically and systematically in the store that can be relied on at trial as evidence to prove the elements of the offense is a necessary skill. The *Sources of Evidence* chart in Chapter 4 presents a format that retail employees in any state can use to gather the evidence.

2. *Make Decisions Based on Evidence Produced in the Store.* The essence of selective prosecution as authorized by the merchant's privilege is the ability to make decisions based on evidence found in the store. A

retail employee must learn to see when the evidence supports the decision to prosecute a case. Sometimes the evidence will reject the decision to prosecute and support the decision to release the suspect. Simply stated, not all persons detained should be prosecuted because there is not always sufficient evidence to justify filing the formal charge. The cases presented in Chapters 4 and 8 demonstrate situations where the decision made by the merchant was wrong. The suspect in these cases should have been released rather than prosecuted.

Sometimes merchants make decisions about how to handle shoplifting cases based on suspicion or opinion rather than on the basis of evidentiary facts (evidence). *Suspicion and opinion are not evidence in any court in any state.* No retail employee will be permitted to take the witness stand and testify, "Your Honor, *in my opinion* the woman is guilty of shoplifting." No retail employee will obtain a conviction by testifying that the suspect had shifty eyes or was exhibiting furtive gestures. Shifty eyes and furtive gestures are not facts that show the shoplifting suspect obtained wrongful possession of any merchandise and then left without paying for it. No retail employee can testify about suspicion and hope to win shoplifting cases. Retail employees must make the decision to detain shoplifting suspects and the decision to prosecute shoplifting cases on the basis of facts.

3. *Produce the Two Types of Evidence Needed to Obtain Convictions.* Merchants must learn how to produce the two types of store prosecution evidence needed to obtain a conviction for shoplifting in any state. Eyewitness evidence is produced by watching the suspect on a sales floor conceal merchandise or switch a price tag or assist a companion who is concealing merchandise. The physical evidence is *always* produced after the suspect has first been detained on probable cause. This two-step-evidence-gathering procedure is illustrated by the *Sources of Evidence* chart found in Chapter 4 (Figure 4.1).

4. *Understand the Legal Meaning of the Suspect's Explanation.* Even veteran security people sometimes forget the suspect's explanation is also evidence: defense evidence. Merchants must become good listeners. They will see that store managers and security people produce evidence with their ears, as well as with their eyes. As all with even slight experience in dealing with shoplifting suspects know, very rarely will the person admit guilt. Most of the time people deny they are shoplifting. This is particularly true with the average citizen type shoplifting suspects. They will say, "I forgot to pay," or "I intended to pay," "I bought the merchandise at another store," "I bought it earlier at your store," or "I was returning the merchandise for a refund [or an exchange]." These explanations have specific legal meanings, both in the store and later in court if a case is filed. The merchant will be taught to understand these explanations for what

they really are: defense evidence. The retail employee will see that in making the decision to prosecute the case, these explanations must be evaluated. In court a judge or jury will listen carefully to the defendant's explanation (called the *formal courtroom defense to the charge*) before making a decision about guilt. Retail employees must learn to do the same in their stores as part of the evidence-gathering process authorized by the merchant's privilege. Retail employees will see that these explanations are also important in making the decision not to prosecute. If a suspect is detained and says he is returning merchandise, a store manager or security person should think twice before deciding to prosecute that case. The proper decision could well be to release the suspect because the explanation is true or because the merchant cannot prove it is false. The suspect's explanation is often the key piece of evidence used in deciding whether to prosecute the case or to release the suspect.

5. *Speak the Language of Evidence.* In France, people speak French. In court, people speak evidence. Judges, prosecutors, and defense lawyers all speak evidence. Thus store managers and retail security persons must learn the language of evidence in their stores while they are handling the case and deciding whether to file a formal charge. Merchants will be shown how to discuss a shoplifting case in their stores in terms of what the evidence will prove in court. If the store manager or security person is speaking the language of "suspicion" or "opinion," the chances of filing a nonprosecutable case and losing it are much greater.

Making a decision to warn and release the suspect or to prosecute the case is a process. First, the merchant must know what facts found in the store will become evidence in court to prove the elements of the offense. Next, the retail employee must discuss the case in language that will count in court if the case is filed. That discussion must be in the language of evidence rather than in the foreign tongues of suspicion or opinion. Training programs must teach employees to review and evaluate their cases by speaking the language of evidence.

Dealing with Shoplifting Situations
from a Position of Strength

Retail merchants are not sworn law enforcement officials. They do not have the duty to prosecute any shoplifting suspect; they have the option of prosecuting or warning and releasing shoplifting suspects. Experience has taught merchants that prosecution can mean an employee is out of the store, often for several hours on two or three occasions, while the case is going through the court system. In many instances, the value of the recovered merchandise is small so prosecution seems not to be cost justified. But, if persons are not prosecuted—especially the average citizen shoplifter who steals habitually—the store is branded as an easy place to shoplift, and losses increase.

What counts is the ability to deal with *all shoplifting situations* from a position of strength. A position of strength means understanding the evidence and the options. It means having the ability to make decisions based on evidence. It means having the ability to systematically gather evidence before making a decision. A store owner, manager, or security person who understands the evidence and the prosecution options under the merchant's privilege is in the legal driver's seat. Strong cases can be prosecuted to deter future shoplifting attempts. Weak cases will be recognized as such along with the evidence reasons that make them weak cases. The ability to recognize the existence of a nonprosecutable case is an essential skill in shoplifting loss-prevention. Making the decision to release and understanding the evidence reasons why that decision is made is part of a selective prosecution approach.

There are three basic shoplifting situations a merchant in any state will encounter. The key to effectively handling all three depends entirely on the merchant's ability to understand evidence. Consider the three situations:

1. When a prosecutable case exists and should be filed.
2. When a prosecutable case exists but is not filed because the value of the recovered merchandise is small. Here the decision is to release without formal prosecution even though the case could have been taken to court.
3. When a nonprosecutable case exists because there is not sufficient evidence to establish the elements of the offense at trial. Here the suspect is released. Said another way, the decision made is not to prosecute.

The retailer's normal reaction when talking about training programs is wanting to know *how to prosecute shoplifting cases?* This overlooks the fact that some cases should not be prosecuted. It overlooks the fact many retail companies follow a selective prosecution approach. The other side of a selective prosecution policy is understanding when the evidence supports the decision *not to prosecute.* Making this decision not to prosecute is one which must be included in all training programs. As will be demonstrated in this book, when a merchant files a nonprosecutable case there is a strong possibility the store will be sued civilly after the wrongfully charged suspect is acquitted.

There are three basic situations where the evidence tells the merchant the proper decision is not to prosecute. First is the *returning merchandise* situation which is demonstrated by the Vest Case in Chapter

8. The second situation is where the suspect is detained before passing the last cash register and explains that he "intended to pay" for the merchandise. This situation is demonstrated by the $1.97 Bra Case in Chapter 4. The third situation where a nonprosecutable case exists is when the suspect claims ownership after being detained on probable cause. The Toothpaste Case and Socket Wrench Case in Chapter 4 are excellent examples of situations where the proper decision was not to prosecute. Selective prosecution is a valuable tool in shoplifting loss-prevention. It is effective only if merchants know when to prosecute and when to release suspects.

REDUCING THE CIVIL LIABILITY RISK FACTORS WHEN HANDLING SHOPLIFTING CASES

This book will provide retailers with specific information about how to reduce the chances of having a civil action filed against the store by a shoplifting suspect. For several decades the insurance industry has taught its claims adjusters about the law of negligence as it applies to automobile accidents. It is time for the retail industry to teach itself about the law of false imprisonment, false arrest, malicious prosecution, slander, and assault and battery as it applies to handling shoplifting cases.

Reducing the civil liability risk factor in shoplifting cases is a neglected part of loss-prevention training programs. Generally merchants have concentrated on preventing shoplifting attempts by purchasing expensive electronic article surveillance and closed circuit television systems. They have spent some training time learning to prevent shoplifting losses by prosecuting cases as a deterrent to future shoplifting attempts. This is generally called "apprehension" to distinguish it from prevention. Actually detaining is a prevention tool. If the person was not detained under the merchant's privilege the store will suffer a loss. Now the retail community is realizing the value of teaching itself a set of loss-prevention skills which center around reducing the civil liability risk. Preventing and prosecuting are not sufficient. It is the ability to prevent, prosecute, and do so with minimum exposure to false arrest type civil actions that make a shoplifting loss-prevention program complete.

There is good reason for merchants to learn about reducing the chances of having the store sued out of a mishandled shoplifting situation. In the fall of 1984, a university-based survey about civil law suits over crime and security was released.[10] The authors state that retailers are the

---

[10]Lawrence W. Sherman and Jody Klein, "Major Lawsuits Over Crime and Security: Trends and Patterns 1958–1982," The Institute of Criminal Justice and Criminology, University of Maryland, College Park, MD, September 1984, p. 28.

TABLE 1.3	Primary defendants in security lawsuits			
Rank	Defendant	Number	Percent	Cumulative percent
1	Retailer	50	27	27
2	Other business*	45	24	51
3	Residential landlord	33	18	69
4	Hotel/Motel	20	11	80
5	Common carrier	12	6	86
6	Municipality	6	3	89
8	State agency	4	2	91
8	Bank	4	2	93
8	All other	4	2	95
10	Office landlord	2	1	96
13.5	Public schools	1	—	—
13.5	Private schools	1	—	—
13.5	Private college/University	1	—	—
13.5	Hospital	1	—	—
13.5	Shopping center	1	—	—
13.5	Federal agency	1	—	

most common defendants in successful security type civil law suits, suffering one-fourth of the major awards. Consider Table 1.3.

The study went on to break down the types of civil actions filed against retailers. The number one ranking was false arrest type cases filed by business invitees, which means customers. Table 1.4 is very informative.

Many of these false arrest actions *are preventable.* One loss-

TABLE 1.4	Types of civil actions filed against retailers			
Rank	Type of case	Number	Percent	Cumulative percent
1	False arrest-invitees	19	38	38
2	Inadequate security-invitees	13	26	64
3	Other improper security act	5	10	74
4	False arrest-employee	3	6	80
5	Improper investigation/polygraph	3	6	86
6	All other	7	14	100
	Total =	43	100	100
	Missing cases =	0		

prevention goal for any store is to prevent the loss of dollars paid out in these false arrest civil actions filed as a result of mishandled shoplifting situations. Learning about the civil liability aspects of shoplifting is the way to reduce preventable losses.

Make no mistake about it—if a shoplifting situation is mishandled, a civil action can be the result. Remember, over 70 percent of the persons encountered are the average citizen type shoplifting suspect. They make excellent plaintiffs in civil actions against stores because they do not have prior criminal records. Instead, they have families, jobs, and otherwise good reputations in the community. If these average citizen types are improperly detained and mistreated or if they are wrongfully prosecuted and acquitted they will hire a lawyer and sue the store. The following table lists the most common types of civil actions filed against stores and the reason the civil action can be filed.

Types of civil actions commonly filed	Reason the civil action can be filed
False imprisonment False arrest Malicious prosecution	The retail employee handling the case made an evidence-gathering mistake
Slander Assault and battery	The retail employee handling the shoplifting case mistreated the suspect in a legally unreasonable manner

As demonstrated, there are two basic types of mistakes merchants make which permit persons to sue the store civilly out of a mishandled shoplifting situation. First is where the retail employee makes an evidence-gathering mistake. Second is where the retail employee mistreats a suspect either at the time of the detention or while conducting an investigation of the facts. Both types of mistakes are preventable.

An example of an evidence-gathering mistake led a national department store's security personnel to wrongfully charge a woman with shoplifting. This thirty-five-year-old woman and her son were accused of leaving the department store without paying for a snowmobile suit. Outside the store she was handcuffed. The snowmobile suit was stripped off the boy while adult family members watched in terror. The woman said when they put the handcuffs on her she urinated. Before being arrested and charged with shoplifting she pointed out that the snowmobile suit was not new. She said it had been purchased some eleven days earlier. She said, "Anybody with eyes could see the suit was not new. It was filthy dirty and had a hole in it." The family members verified her explanation that the garment had been previously purchased.[11]

Notwithstanding her corroborated claim of ownership, a shoplifting charge was filed. After several trials she was found not guilty; then she filed the civil suit for false imprisonment and malicious prosecution. The jury awarded the mother $15,000 and her son $10,000 on the false imprisonment count. On the malicious prosecution count the jury awarded her $325,000. Under Michigan law the trial judge was required to triple all jury awards in malicious prosecution actions, making the total $975,000. When combined with the $25,000 awarded on the false imprisonment count, the total was a staggering 1 million dollars. The jury award was large, but the evidence-gathering mistake made by store security personnel was a common one. They filed a shoplifting case where the evidence to prove store ownership of merchandise was lacking. Under the merchant's privilege they had the choice of releasing or prosecuting the woman. If she had been released rather than prosecuted the only civil action possible was one for false imprisonment, an action to which the national department store had a defense under the merchant's privilege statute. This case is an excellent example of where a selective prosecution policy would have prevented loss—the loss of dollars.

Cases where stores have been sued civilly are clear on one point. Retail employees mistreat shoplifting suspects because store policy has not taught them how to systematically gather evidence to decide if a prosecutable case exists. Effectively handling shoplifting cases requires two sets of loss-prevention skills: (1) the ability to gather evidence, and (2) understanding how to avoid mistreatment of the suspect while gathering the evidence. The case law indicates that retail employees get in a hurry because they are afraid of making mistakes. Getting in a hurry is a mistake itself, one that leads to mistreatment which leads to civil liability exposure. Table 1.5 lists the most common ways a store owner, manager, or security person mistreats a shoplifting suspect. These mistakes are made either at the time the suspect is detained or while the retail employee is attempting to investigate the facts.

If retailers detain and make one of the following mistakes the courts will most likely find the employee's conduct violated the merchant's privilege statute. The store will then lose its immunity from false imprisonment liability granted by the statute and have to pay out money.

Training programs must consider one simple fact—shoplifting is predictable. The studies show that 70 percent or more of the persons detained will be concealing merchandise in a pocket, purse, shopping bag, or on their person. There is no great mystery about how people shoplift. The merchant's training goal is to teach employees how to avoid evidence-

---

[11]Walker v. J. C. Penney and Co., *The Detroit Free Press*, September 5, 1984, p. 5A.

TABLE 1.5	Mistreatment of shoplifting suspects

1. Use of excessive force

2. Making an accusation of shoplifting

3. Searching a suspect without first obtaining consent or permission

4. Making threats of prosecution to obtain a civil liability release

5. Making threats of prosecution to obtain a confession type statement

6. Fingerprinting or photographing a shoplifting suspect

7. Handcuffing a suspect who has not tried to escape or not become violent

8. Conducting an investigation of the facts on the selling floor

gathering and mistreatment of suspect mistakes when they respond to these predictable shoplifting situations. Merchants must learn to play the percentages when setting policy and when conducting training programs. Concentrate on these cases involving concealment first. In about 30 percent of the shoplifting situations, people will shoplift by some combination of price tag switching, container stuffing, by shoplifting in fitting rooms, or by passing merchandise off to an accomplice. In these miscellaneous shoplifting situations, a merchant must also avoid making both the evidence-gathering and the mistreatment of the suspect type mistakes to minimize civil liability exposure.

Suppose we are in a department store equipped with surveillance cameras and an electronic article surveillance system. Suppose further that this department store knows the value of employee alertness and has trained sales employees in high-shoplifting-incident departments. There will come a time—most likely each day—when the average citizen type has not been deterred by expensive cameras or antishoplifting tags. A security employee has just seen a well-dressed woman drop a $40 compact into her purse and head toward the mall exit. Suppose the setting is an apparel specialty store, one with an EAS system. The manager has just seen that same well-dressed woman remove a silk scarf from its place of display, tear off the price tag, throw the tag behind the counter, put the scarf around her neck, and head toward the mall exit. Neither the compact nor the scarf will activate the EAS system. Now the only way to prevent shoplifting is to detain that woman because she is in wrongful possession of unpurchased merchandise. In the department store situation, the compact is concealed. In the specialty store situation, the scarf is at all times visible to the store manager.

The retail employee cannot rely on devices to prevent shoplifting. The effectiveness of the store's shoplifting loss-prevention program boils down to one thing: the *specific information* about the dual legal aspects of shoplifting possessed by that retail employee. The crucial tool for that security person or store manager is knowledge of the merchant's privilege. The security person or store manager can detain on probable cause and either prosecute the case or recover the unpurchased merchandise, warn and release the suspect. Reducing the civil liability risk factor means reducing the chance of making a mistake when detaining this woman concealing a compact in her purse or when detaining the woman walking out of the specialty store with the scarf around her neck.

In a civil action, store policies and procedures are actually on trial. A jury decides if that department store security person or that specialty store manager used reasonable care in three respects: (1) in detaining the woman on probable cause, (2) whether the investigation of the facts after detaining her was legally reasonable in manner, method, and time, and (3) whether the decision to prosecute the case was based on evidence rather than on suspicion or opinion. If store policy is not specific in all three areas, mistakes will be made. Store policy and procedures must be based on the civil tort law requirement to use reasonable care before and during the encounter with a shoplifting suspect.

Some retail and security executives are reluctant to develop a loss-prevention manual that is specific. They like the guideline approach. Some even think that having no written loss-prevention manual at all is the best approach. These merchants feel that a person suing the store (the plaintiff) will subpoena the manual and then show that a security employee or a store manager violated company procedure. These retailers reason that it will be easier for a plaintiff to establish liability against the store by using its own loss-prevention manual against the company.

The problem with the "guideline" or the "no manual at all" approach is this: the civil tort law duty to use reasonable care when dealing with a shoplifting suspect exists whether the store has a loss-prevention manual or not. Stores that do not train employees about the specifics of the duty to use reasonable care will find employees violating the civil tort law. The result will be a civil action, one alleging false imprisonment, false arrest, slander, assault and battery, malicious prosecution, or some combination of them. As a practical matter, store manuals contain procedures that are well within the civil tort law as found in the merchant's privilege anyway. The fact that an employee did not follow procedures to the letter in a case will not be evidence by itself that the employee acted outside the scope of the merchant's privilege.

Employees in these no manual or guideline manual stores are more likely to mistreat a suspect or make an evidence-gathering mistake. Mistakes lead to civil actions. Training is the way to reduce the possibility of making mistakes. Training programs are evidence of a good faith effort by retailers to prevent the loss of goods and to comply with the merchant's privilege statutes. The security director or retail executive who testifies in court (or at a deposition) that his store conducts no regular shoplifting loss-prevention training programs is making it easier for a plaintiff to establish civil liability and recover damages. The absence of training programs is evidence that the store has made no effort to learn about the civil tort law duty to use reasonable care when handling a shoplifting case. Merchants can no longer afford the luxury of simply prosecuting shoplifters. They must learn to prosecute shoplifting cases and do so with minimum exposure to civil liability exposure. The civil liability risk will not go away by pretending it does not exist. The chance of being sued civilly is inherent in all attempts to handle shoplifting situations.

This book contains over forty cases where merchants either mistreated a suspect or made an evidence-gathering mistake. By reading these cases store owners, managers, and security personnel can see exactly where other merchants made mistakes that caused the civil actions to be filed. More importantly, they can learn to avoid making these common mistakes during future encounters with shoplifting suspects. Chapter 6 is devoted to explaining the merchant's privilege statutes and how to comply with them. The essence of more effective prosecution with minimum civil liability exposure is understanding evidence-gathering and the merchant's privilege statutes. This book will give merchants that specific information they need to better understand the dual legal aspects of handling shoplifting cases.

A final word about training programs is necessary: merchants spend too much time studying shoplifters. They love to show films about shoplifters, ones with shifty eyes or ones exhibiting furtive gestures. But shifty eyes and furtive gestures are not elements of the offense of shoplifting in any state. People shoplift with their hands, not with their eyes or their gestures. These films put the emphasis on the wrong persons. There is nothing in a film about shoplifters that will help a store owner, manager, or security person learn to gather evidence or to comply with the merchant's privilege. Sometimes these films even throw retail employees off the track about who shoplifts and how they do it.

Too often films show people using gimmicks to shoplift. A film show a person using a booster box or putting merchandise between legs. This film is interesting but misleading. Most people conc chandise in pockets, purses, shopping bags, and under clothing— not use gimmicks. These films are justified—in the budget a under the banner of awareness. Awareness does have some valu ability to gather evidence and comply with the merchant's pri the information which prevents shoplifting and reduces exposure to civil liability.

If films are of little value, merchants can validly ask what they should concentrate on in training programs. My answer is, concentrate on yourselves, on the way you respond to shoplifting situations. Examine the mistakes you make, and learn from them. Stores with a full-time security staff have a wealth of information right in their own file cabinets. Files about cases in which the store was sued civilly because of a mishandled shoplifting situation can be used in training programs. Stores can learn from past mistakes and not make the same ones in the future. Stores without a security department that do not have old files can begin with the cases and material found in this book.

THE BOTTOM LINE

Retail and security executives like to talk about preventing shoplifting. Some accomplish this goal by spending large sums of money on closed circuit television systems and electronic article surveillance systems. Merchants who use these preventive devices justify the cost by saying things like this: "We would rather prevent four thefts than apprehend one shoplifter." Retail and security executives who use these expensive systems do not claim to prevent shoplifting by stopping it entirely. They may be able to reduce the shoplifting shrinkage numbers, which, of course, is a loss-prevention goal. The fact remains that people shoplift everyday in department and specialty apparel stores that have installed these devices.

Monitoring cameras and antishoplifting devices may be part of the answer for some stores. For other stores, these devices are too expensive to be cost justified. The problem with devices is the same as the problem with showing films about shoplifters with shifty eyes: both concentrate on the wrong people. Devices are aimed at deterring shoplifters rather than directed toward improving an employee's loss-prevention skills. My suggestion is to consider devices only as support systems. The first line of defense is always the alert sales employee. In some stores these sales employees will be backed up by a security staff. In specialty stores, the sales employee is backed up by a store manager who is authorized to detain shoplifting suspects and investigate the facts.

Store owners and retail executives are coming to see the value of training employees to prevent shoplifting. Traditionally, the retail community has been content to ride along with the inventory shrinkage figures at about 2 percent of gross sales each year. They consider it a "cost of doing business," passing it along to the customer. Now store owners and retail executives are coming to see that time, effort, and money spent in training pays off at the bottom line. If somebody shoplifts the merchandise, it cannot be sold at a profit. If the merchandise is shoplifted, it takes a large amount of additional sales to make up for the profit lost on the shoplifted item. When sales projections are flat, this means preventing shoplifting is even more important for a retail company at the bottom line.

Preventing shoplifting losses means protecting profit margins. Merchants should teach sales employees one set of shoplifting loss-prevention skills centering around removing the privacy factor by giving good customer service. They should teach security personnel and store managers (in stores without a full-time security staff) another set of shoplifting loss-prevention skills, ones centering around gathering evidence and complying with the merchant's privilege statutes.

Forget about shoplifters with shifty eyes and forget about antishoplifting devices for a while. Instead, concentrate on developing a set of shoplifting loss-prevention skills, ones that can be used by store owners, managers, security personnel, and sales employees.

2

The Shoplifting Prosecution Statutes

One evening Archie Bunker was talking about why the courts tossed out a recent criminal conviction. Everybody in New York "knows" the guy was guilty, he explained to Edith. Archie continued, "The problem with the courts is they need evidence." Archie was right. A store owner, manager, or security person can easily say to himself, "I know that customer is shoplifting." The problem with thinking this way is that opinions about guilt are not evidence of guilt that can be used in court. An opinion about guilt coming from the merchant, the arresting peace officer, or the district attorney prosecuting the case is *not* evidence. As Archie Bunker said so well—"the courts need evidence."

The trial of a lawsuit, civil or criminal, is a contest based on evidence. As in another contest—there is just one winner. If a merchant makes that trip from the store to a courtroom with insufficient evidence to prove the elements of the offense at trial, the result will be an acquittal. After the store loses the shoplifting case, there is a good chance the person found not guilty will file a civil action for false imprisonment and/or malicious prosecution. Since merchants may not rely on suspicion or opinions in court to establish guilt, a retail person involved with shoplifting cases must learn to produce evidence.

Evidence of any crime is always found at the crime scene. In shoplifting cases the crime scene is in the store. All the evidence a merchant needs to use later in court to obtain a conviction is found in the store. Shoplifting cases are not won because of brilliant testimony presented at trial. They are won because a store owner, manager, or security person knew how to produce, investigate, and review evidence found in the store. Said another way, merchants produce facts (not suspicion or opinions) in their stores. Later in court these facts are presented to a judge or jury as evidence to establish the elements of the offense. To improve the ability to prosecute while at the same time reducing exposure to civil liability risk, a merchant needs to learn about gathering evidence in the store.

In any state the trial of a shoplifting case starts out the same way. A security officer for Sears could be testifying that in the hardware department he saw a man remove a set of wrenches from the display rack. As he continued to watch, the man put the wrenches in his jacket pocket, walked around casually for a few minutes, then left the store without paying for them. Next, the witness would describe what happened when he detained the man just outside the door in the mall. The man told him he was looking for the lay–a–way department and when he could not find it he just "forgot" the wrench set was in his pocket. After testifying about the suspect's explanation, the witness then produced the wrench set he recovered, identified it as belonging to the store. He stated the item sold for $9.99 and pointed to the price tag as evidence of the value. Both the wrench set and price tag are then offered into evidence as a store prosecution exhibit.

The store witness could be a security person for Saks Fifth Avenue in New York, from the store on Michigan Avenue in Chicago, or the one on the South Coast Plaza Mall in Newport, California. That employee is testifying that she saw a well-dressed woman remove a price tag from a scarf, throw the tag under a display counter, put the scarf around her neck, and walk out without paying for it. The witness then testifies as to what happened once the woman was detained just outside the door. The woman explained that she just "forgot to pay" for the scarf because of personal problems (a pending divorce for example). The woman then offered to pay for the scarf, saying she had cash and two valid credit cards in her purse. The Saks employee then identifies the scarf, the price tag she recovered, and states the selling price of that scarf. Both the price tag and scarf are offered into evidence as a store prosecution exhibit.

The names of the stores are all hypothetical. The point is that in all states shoplifting cases begin the same way—with a store employee describing what he saw and then telling about the investigation of the facts he conducted once the suspect was detained. After hearing the store's prosecution evidence and the defendant's evidence, a judge or jury will make a decision. That decision cannot be based on opinions or on suspicion offered by the store witness. The finding—guilty or not guilty— is based 100 percent on facts gathered in the store and presented later in court at the trial.

In both cases, the stores would have obtained convictions for shoplifting of the wrench set and scarf. The man and woman could have been found guilty of retail theft in Illinois, shoplifting in Rhode Island, theft in Texas, or stealing in Missouri. The reason is that the facts produced in the stores later in court became store prosecution evidence to prove the elements of the offense. Even though the names of the shoplifting prosecution statutes are different from state to state, the evidence used to obtain a conviction is the same. If merchants know how to produce evidence to prove the elements of the offense of shoplifting, they can obtain convictions in any state where the company is doing business. The name of the game is proving the elements of the offense with evidence found in the store. Forget about the actual name of the shoplifting prosecution statute and learn to gather evidence.

AUTHORITY TO STOP A SHOPLIFTING SUSPECT

The authority to stop a shoplifting suspect is not found in the shoplifting prosecution statute itself. The shoplifting prosecution statute only sets forth elements of the offense that must be proven in court with evidence gathered in the store. Before stopping suspects and investigating the facts a store owner, manager, or security person must know by what source of legal authority the suspect is stopped. The word "stop" has no legal meaning. Merchants also like to use the word "apprehend" which, like the word stop, has no legal definition. If a shoplifting stop or apprehension is made by a private citizen retail employee, it is either a citizen's arrest or a detention. If the stop is made by an off-duty peace officer or a special peace officer it is an arrest—a warrantless arrest to be specific. The following discussion deals with whether a stop by a private citizen merchant is a citizen's arrest or a detention on probable cause under the merchant's privilege.

In discussing shoplifting stops, both merchants and courts are sometimes careless. They use the word arrest when they actually mean "detain for investigation of the facts." Since there is both a criminal law and a civil liability consequence when a merchant stops a shoplifting suspect, store policy must be specific. Employees must known whether the stop is a citizen's arrest (under the arrest by private person statute) or a detention for investigation (under the merchant's privilege). This book suggests that merchants have their employees (those not holding any type of commission) detain shoplifting suspects for investigation of the facts under the merchant's privilege rather than to make a citizen's arrest.

In any state, the possibility of a civil action begins the instant a retail employee stops a shoplifting suspect. For this reason, merchants must consider both the authority by which they stop people and any possible defense that may be available later in the event the person stopped files a civil action against the store. In most states, the only defense available to a private person who makes a citizen's arrest is to show that the person arrested was guilty of the offense for which the citizen's arrest was made. This means that the retail employee making a citizen's arrest would have to prove guilt in court in each case or otherwise be liable for false arrest. Simply stated, the only defense available when a store manager or security person makes a citizen's arrest for shoplifting is to prove guilt in court. It is often said with much truth that a private citizen arrests another private citizen at his civil liability peril. If the arresting merchant cannot prove guilt for shoplifting, the store can be easily sued successfully for false arrest and probably for malicious prosecution.

By contrast, a retail employee who deems the stopping of a shoplifting suspect a *detention for investigation of the facts* (under the merchant's privilege) has a statutory defense available if the store is later sued. A second advantage to detaining for investigation of the facts under the merchant's privilege is the store does not need to prove guilt each time. Under the merchant's privilege the retailer may detain, investigate the facts, recover the unpurchased merchandise, and release the suspect without taking the case to court. The merchant does not have to involve the police and does not have to formally prosecute all persons detained. Succinctly stated, under the merchant's privilege, actual guilt is no longer the only defense available to a store in a civil action. Table 2.1 shows the two different sources of authority by which a merchant can stop a shoplifting suspect and the two defenses available to the store in a civil action. As the table shows, under the merchant's privilege, the test for a detention is not knowledge of the suspect's actual guilt but rather a reasonable belief that guilt exists based on probable cause evidence. It is an obvious legal advantage for merchants in any state to have their store managers or security people detain for investigation of the facts pursuant to authority of the merchant's privilege rather than to make a citizen's arrest. A merchant's policy must make it abundantly clear to employees whether they detain on probable cause under the merchant's privilege or make a citizen's arrest under authority of the law of citizen's arrest.

As will be seen in Chapter 6, the merchant's privilege is incorporated into detention statutes in each state. These detention statutes do not grant merchants any type of police power. At all times a store owner, manager, or security person who is detaining a suspect, investigating the facts, and deciding if a prosecutable case exists is a private citizen. Suppose the store detective in the Wrench Set Case above stopped his suspect and said, "You are under arrest for shoplifting those wrenches in your pocket." This store detective has just made a citizen's arrest. To avoid a false arrest suit the store would have to prove the man's guilt in court. Suppose the store detective stopped the man and said, "Pardon me, sir, did you forget to pay for those wrenches in your pocket?" In this situation, the man could be prosecuted or released depending on the evidence produced and also

TABLE 2.1	Sources of authority for stopping
Source of authority by which a shoplifting suspect is stopped	*Defense available to store if later sued civilly by person stopped*
Law of citizen's arrest as found in a statute or in decisional law	Actual guilt of person arrested must be proved in court
Merchant's privilege as incorporated into detention statutes	Probable cause for reasonably believing the person detained has committed or is committing shoplifting of store property

upon store policy. If the man was released and later sued the store, his cause of action would not be for false arrest but for false imprisonment because no citizen's arrest was made. The store could successfully defend a false imprisonment action by showing its detective had probable cause to justify the detention and conducted a legally reasonable investigation of the facts as authorized by the detention statute.

In setting policies and procedures for handling shoplifting cases, merchants must learn to think these situations through to the possible civil liability consequences. It is more difficult for a person to successfully sue a store that can plead compliance with the merchant's privilege as a defense than to sue a store that has only the defense of actual guilt available to it. If store owners, managers, and security personnel detain suspects on probable cause, they have more flexibility regarding prosecution of the case and they have less civil liability risk. As a general rule, merchants will instruct their employees to detain on probable cause and investigate the facts as authorized by the detention statute rather than to make a citizen's arrest. Such an approach makes good sense from both a prosecution and a civil liability reduction standpoint.

The Oregon Statutes

Two statutes are presented here to remind merchants that a private citizen stops a shoplifting suspect under one source of authority or the other. The shoplifting suspect is either arrested (under the arrest by private person statute) or detained for investigation (under the detention statute). All retail employees, including retail executives, store managers, and security personnel, must know whether they are making a citizen's arrest or detaining on probable cause.

Not all states have codified the law of citizen's arrest into a statute such as found in Oregon. In Missouri, for example, there is no arrest by private person statute. In states like Missouri, the merchant must consult judicial decisions to find the circumstances under which a private citizen can make a warrantless arrest. Merchants with stores in several different states will have to formulate different policies depending on the state if they use the law of citizen's arrest as the legal basis by which shoplifting suspects are stopped. On the other hand, if the merchant has employees detain under the merchant's privilege, the test in all states is the same. Detention statutes permit the merchant, his agent (a contract guard service), or his employee to detain on probable cause and investigate the facts.[1] It is much easier for stores doing business in several states to set policy and conduct training programs if they have employees detain under the merchant's privilege.

| STATUTE | Oregon arrest by private person statute |

1. Arrest by Private Persons
(§§ 133.225, 133.255, Oreg. Rev. Stats.)

(1) A private person may arrest another person for any crime committed in his presence if he has probable cause to believe the arrested person committed the crime. A private person making such an arrest shall, without unnecessary delay, take the arrested person before a magistrate or deliver him to a peace officer.
(2) In order to make the arrest a private person may use physical force as is justifiable . . .

(1) Except as provided in subsection (2) [below] of this section, a private person acting on his own account is justified in using physical force upon another person when and to the extent that he reasonably believes it necessary to make an arrest or to prevent the escape from custody of an arrested person whom he has arrested . . .
(2) A private person acting under the circumstances prescribed in subsection (1) of this section is justified in using deadly physical force only when he reasonably believes it necessary to defend himself or a third person from what he reasonably believes to be the use or imminent use of deadly physical force.

This statute is typical of most others. Note that it permits a private person to arrest for "any offense," so it does not apply just to shoplifting. It does not authorize an investigation of the facts but says the arrested

---

[1]In Chapter 4, the merchant is given an evidence-gathering chart that shows how to establish probable cause to detain a suspect in a case involving concealment of merchandise. This chart or some form of it can be used by any merchant in any state to teach employees how to establish probable cause to justify a detention.

person, *without unnecessary delay*, shall be taken before a magistrate (a judge) or turned over to a peace officer. This statute does not provide the person making the arrest with a defense to use if later sued for false arrest. The only defense available when a citizen's arrest has been made is to show the person arrested was actually guilty of the offense.

STATUTE	Oregon detention statute

2. Detention
(§ 131.655, Oreg. Rev. Stats.)

(1) Notwithstanding any other provision of law, a peace officer, merchant or merchant's employe who has probable cause for believing that a person has committed theft of property of a store or other mercantile establishment may detain and interrogate the person in regard thereto in a reasonable manner and for a reasonable time.

(2) If a peace officer, merchant or merchant's employe, with probable cause for believing that a person has committed theft of property of a store or other mercantile establishment, detains and interrogates the person in regard thereto, and the person thereafter brings against the peace officer, merchant or merchant's employe any civil or criminal action based upon the detention and interrogation, such probable cause shall be a defense to the action, if the detention and interrogation were done in a reasonable manner and for a reasonable time.

It is important to note that this statute, like all other detention statutes, does not use the word *arrest*. Instead it says that the merchant or his agent who has established probable cause "may detain" and interrogate the person in a reasonable manner and for a reasonable period of time. Second, this statute does not apply to any offense but only to shoplifting. Finally, the statute says that if the detention was supported by probable cause and the investigation of the facts was legally reasonable, the merchant shall not incur civil liability.

Merchants in any state must realize the advantage of having employees detain on probable cause rather than to make citizen's arrests. A store manager or security person about to stop a shoplifting suspect should know whether the restraint of the person's freedom of movement is a detention or an arrest. Store policy must be absolutely clear on the authority by which employees stop shoplifting suspects.

There are three distinct advantages to stopping persons under the detention statute:

1. The retail employee can detain, investigate the facts, and release the suspect without declaring the stopping a citizen's arrest.

2.   The retail employee may conduct a legally reasonable investigation of the facts rather than having to take the suspect before a judge or to summon a peace officer to the store immediately.
3.   If later sued civilly by the suspect, the store can defend the conduct of its employee by showing the store manager or security person established probable cause to justify the stopping rather than having to show the person was actually guilty of shoplifting.

Detention statutes permit a merchant to stop a suspect who has been seen concealing unpurchased merchandise and leaving without paying. The stopping is called a detention rather than an arrest. This means that the retail employee can detain temporarily and investigate the facts without having the store automatically become subject to false arrest liability. This is a distinct advantage over the older common law rule, which said that the only defense available to a person making a citizen's arrest was actual guilt. Since merchants have the constant problem of stopping persons and since they do not prosecute all persons stopped, it is less risky from a civil liability standpoint to detain rather than to make a citizen's arrest.

Because a detention statute is on the books does not mean that a merchant is precluded from making a citizen's arrest. The private citizen retail employee can stop a shoplifting suspect under either source of authority. It is always advisable to research both the law of citizen's arrest and the law of detention on probable cause when setting store policy. In this way, each merchant can see the advantage of declaring the stopping a detention.

The Illinois Retail Theft Act

This well-thought-out statute is set forth in its entirety. Unlike most states, the Illinois legislature has combined the shoplifting prosecution and the detention-immunity provisions into one statute, placing it in the criminal code. Pay particular attention to Section 16A-5 entitled Detention.

STATUTE	Illinois Retail Theft Act

§Section 16A-3. Offense of Retail Theft

A person commits the offense of retail theft when he or she knowingly:

(a) Takes possession of, carries away, transfers or causes to be carried away or transferred, any merchandise displayed, held, stored or offered for sale in a retail mercentile establishment with the intention of retaining such merchandise or with the intention of depriving the merchant permanently of the possession, use or benefit of such merchandise without paying the full retail value of such merchandise; or

(b) Alters, transfers, or removes any label, price tag, marking, indicia of value or any other markings which aid in determining value affixed to any merchandise displayed, held, stored or offered for sale, in a retail mercantile establishment and attempts to purchase such merchandise personally or in consort with another at less than the full retail value with the intention of depriving the merchant of the full retail value of such merchandise; or

(c) Transfers any merchandise displayed, held, stored or offered for sale in a retail mercantile establishment from the container in or on which such merchandise is displayed to any other container with the intention of depriving the merchant of the full retail value of such merchandise; or

(d) Under-rings with the intention of depriving the merchant of the full retail value of the merchandise; or

(e) Remove a shopping cart from the premises of a retail mercantile establishment without the consent of the merchant given at the time of such removal with the intention of depriving the merchant permanently of the possession, use or benefit of such cart.

§ 16A-4. Presumptions
If any person:

(a) conceals upon his person or among his belongings, unpurchased merchandise displayed, held, stored or offered for sale in a retail mercantile establishment; and

(b) removes that merchandise beyond the last known station for receiving payments for that merchandise in that retail mercantile establishment such person shall be presumed to have possessed, carried away or transferred such merchandise with the intention of retaining it or with the intention of depriving the merchant permanently of the possession, use or benefit of such merchandise without paying the full retail value of such merchandise.

§ 16A-5. Detention

Any merchant who has reasonable grounds to believe that a person has committed retail theft may detain such person, on or off the premises of a retail mercantile establishment, in a reasonable manner and for a reasonable length of time for all or any of the following purposes:

(a) To request identification;

(b) To verify such identification;

(c) To make reasonable inquiry as to whether such person has in his possession unpurchased merchandise and, to make reasonable investigation of the ownership of such merchandise;

(d) To inform a peace officer of the detention of the person and surrender that person to the custody of a peace officer;

(e) In the case of a minor, to inform a peace officer, the parents, guardian or other private person interested in the welfare of that minor of this detention and to surrender custody of such minor to such person.

A merchant may make a detention as permitted herein off the premises of a retail mercantile establishment only if such detention is pursuant to an immediate pursuit of such person.

§ 16A-6. Affirmative Defense

A detention as permitted in this Article does not constitute an arrest or an unlawful restraint, as defined in Section 10-3 of this Code, nor shall it render the merchant liable to the person so detained.

Section 16A-5 does not use the word "arrest." It says a merchant may detain if he has reasonable grounds to believe a person has committed retail theft. In Section 16A-6 the statute says a detention as authorized herein does not constitute either an arrest or an unlawful detention as those terms are defined elsewhere in the Illinois code. The section ends by saying the merchant shall not be civilly liable to the person so detained if the merchant has complied with the provisions of the statute. The Illinois legislature has done an excellent job of codifying the basic merchant's privilege, clearly stating that a shoplifting suspect does not have to be arrested but can be detained for investigation of the facts without calling the detention a citizen's arrest.

Section 16A-5 goes on to say the merchant may detain the shoplifting suspect for "any or all" of the listed purposes set forth in subsections (a), (b), (c), (d), and (e). The most important purpose is found in (c) which is to inquire (ask questions of the suspect) and investigate the question of ownership. This statute recognizes that determining ownership of merchandise lies at the heart of the merchant's evidence-gathering task, once the suspect is detained on probable cause (called reasonable grounds in Illinois).

Subsection (d) says the detaining merchant may inform a peace officer about the detention and surrender of the person to the custody of the officer when that officer arrives at the store. It is very important to note that the detention section does not require the merchant to call the police once the investigation of the facts has been completed. As pointed out in Chapter 1, merchants can use a selective prosecution approach to handling shoplifting cases because the authority to do so is found in these detention statutes. If the store owner, manager, or security person investigates the facts and decides a prosecutable case exists, a peace officer is then called to the store. Based on the evidence presented to the officer by the merchant the officer makes the formal arrest, and custody of the suspect is transferred to that officer. The private citizen merchant does not make a citizen's arrest but causes an arrest to be made by a peace officer following the detention of the suspect on probable cause.

Merchants will encounter several types of shoplifting situations. A person may shoplift by concealing merchandise, by switching price tags, by stuffing unpurchased merchandise in a container, by passing goods off to a companion, or by walking out with the unpurchased merchandise in plain view. In any of these shoplifting situations, the merchant may detain that suspect (or suspects) for investigation of the facts under authority of a detention statute in the state where the store is located. All stores should base shoplifting stops on these detention statutes rather than having their employees make citizen arrests.

The cases where merchants have been successfully sued civilly demonstrates one point very clearly. Many retailers do not know how to gather evidence once a suspect has been properly detained on probable cause. Simply stated, they do not realize the purpose of detaining a shoplifting suspect is to gather evidence and decide whether a prosecutable case exists. In Chapter 4 the reader is given an evidence-gathering guide, one which can be used by any merchant in any state. The guide presents a step-by-step procedure to follow when a suspect is detained for investigation of the facts under authority of a detention statute. The guide shows merchants how to investigate and review both prosecution and defense evidence which must be evaluated before deciding how to handle the shoplifting case.

Shoplifting Prosecution Statutes of Texas, Missouri, Pennsylvania, and Georgia

Shoplifting prosecution statutes call the offense of shoplifting different names. This should not cause merchants confusion if they understand one simple fact. All shoplifting prosecution statutes set forth the elements of the offense, elements which must be proven in court with evidence gathered in the store when a suspect is detained under authority of the merchant's privilege. Said another way, the merchant detains on probable cause (under a detention statute), to produce evidence to use later in court in order to prove the elements of the offense as found in the shoplifting prosecution statute.

The two hypothetical cases involving the wrench set inside the man's jacket pocket and the scarf around the woman's neck could be filed under any shoplifting prosecution statute in any state. One involved concealment, while the other involved no concealment at all. In each shoplifting situation the store employee produced evidence in the store which, later in court at trial, established the elements of the offense. The name of the statute under which the suspect is prosecuted is not so important as the fact that these retail employees produced the evidence they needed to establish a prosecutable case.

As will be seen, the four statutes which follow all give the offense of shoplifting a different name. Some of these statutes (Texas and Missouri for example) are short and sweet. Others (Pennsylvania) are long and wordy. The one thing that they all have in common is that the merchant must prove the elements of the offense under each one to obtain a conviction in court. Proving the elements of the offense is accomplished by acquiring evidence-gathering skills and by using the evidence gathering guide in Chapter 4.

| STATUTE | Texas shoplifting statute |

3. Theft
(Art. 31.03, Tex. Code Ann.)

(a) A person commits an offense if he unlawfully appropriates property with intent to deprive the owner of property.
(b) Appropriation of property is unlawful if:
(1) it is without the owner's effective consent; or
(2) the property is stolen and the actor appropriates the property knowing it was stolen by another.

| STATUTE | Missouri shoplifting statute |

3. Stealing
(§ 570.030, Mo. Stats. Ann.)

A person commits the crime of stealing if he appropriates property or services of another with the purpose to deprive him thereof, either without his consent or by means of deceit or coercion.

| STATUTE | Pennsylvania retail theft statute |

3. Retail Theft
(Tit. 18, § 3929, Pa. Stats. Ann.)

(a) A person is guilty of a retail theft if he:
(1) takes possession of, carries away, transfers or causes to be carried away or transferred, any merchandise displayed, held, stored or offered for sale by any store or other retail mercantile establishment with the intention of depriving the merchant of the possession, use or benefit of such merchandise without paying the full retail value thereof;
(2) alters, transfers or removes any label, price tag marking, indicia of value or any

other markings which aid in determining value affixed to any merchandise displayed, held, stored or offered for sale in a store or other retail mercantile establishment and attempts to purchase such merchandise personally or in consort with another at less than the full retail value with the intention of depriving the merchant of the full retail value of such merchandise.

(3) transfers any merchandise displayed, held, stored or offered for sale by any store or other retail mercantile establishment from the container in or on which the same shall be displayed to any other container with intent to deprive the merchant of all or some part of the full retail value thereof; or

(4) under-rings with the intention of depriving the merchant of the full retail value of the merchandise.

Amounts involved in retail thefts committed pursuant to one scheme or course of conduct, whether from the same store or retail mercantile establishment or several stores or retail mercantile establishments, may be aggregated in determining the grade of the offense.

Any person intentionally concealing unpurchased property of any store or other mercantile establishment, either on the premises or outside the premises of such store, shall be prima facie presumed to have so concealed such property with the intention of depriving the merchant of the possession, use or benefit of such merchandise without paying the full retail value thereof . . . , and the finding of such unpurchased property concealed, upon the person or among the belongings of such persons, shall be prima facie evidence of intentional concealment, and, if such person conceals, or causes to be concealed, such unpurchased property, upon the person or among the belongings of another, such fact shall also be prima facie evidence of intentional concealment on the part of the person so concealing such property.

To the extent that there is other competent evidence to substantiate the offense, the conviction shall not be avoided because the prosecution cannot produce the stolen merchandise.

| STATUTE | Georgia theft/shoplifting statute |

3 Theft/Shoplifting
(§ 26-1802 and 1802.1, Ga. Code Ann.)

A person commits theft . . . when he unlawfully takes or, being in lawful possession thereof, unlawfully appropriates any property of another with the intention of depriving him of said property, regardless of the manner in which said property is taken or appropriated.

(a) A person commits the crime of theft by shoplifting when he, with the intent of appropriating merchandise to his own use without paying for the same or to deprive the owner of possession thereof or of the value thereof, in whole or in part, does any of the following:

(1) conceals or takes possession of the goods or merchandise of any store or retail establishment; or

(2) alters the price tag or other price marking on goods or merchandise of any store or retail establishment; or

(3) transfers the goods or merchandise of any store or retail establishment from one container to another;

(4) interchanges the label or price tag from one item of merchandise with a label or price tag for another item of merchandise.

(c) In all cases involving theft by shoplifting, the term "value" means the actual retail price of the property at the time and place of the offense. The unaltered price tag or other marking on property, or duly identified photographs thereof, shall be prima facie evidence of value and ownership of such property.

All of these statutes make it an offense for a person to remove merchandise from the store with the intention of not paying the full retail value for it. These statutes express the same idea in a different way. Texas simply says that the suspect "unlawfully appropriates" (meaning physically removes) property from the store with the intent to deprive the owner of the property. The Missouri statute says that a suspect appropriates either merchandise or services belonging to the owner with the purpose (meaning intent) to deprive the owner of the property. The removal can be accomplished in three different ways: (1) without consent of the owner being given, which is the most common; (2) by deceit; or (3) by coercion being practiced upon the owner. Pennsylvania says the suspect must be seen taking possession of merchandise and carrying it away with the intention of depriving the merchant of the possession, use, or benefit of the merchandise without paying the full retail value. This statute also sets forth several specific ways people shoplift, such as switching price tags, stuffing containers, or underringing cash registers. The Georgia statute says that the person commits shoplifting by unlawfully appropriating property of another with the intention of depriving him of the property regardless of the manner in which the property is removed.

Suppose a man dropped a bottle of cologne in his coat pocket and left the store without paying for it. When detained outside, he handed it back to the security officer and said he forgot to pay for it. This case could be prosecuted as theft in Texas, retail theft in Pennsylvania, stealing in Missouri, or shoplifting/theft in Georgia. The man did the same thing in each state: he concealed merchandise and left without paying for it. When detained, he denied he intended to shoplift. The name of the shoplifting prosecution statute is not as important as the merchant's ability to gather evidence in the store. This cologne case is a garden variety shoplifting situation, one that merchants in stores across the country encounter every day. By learning to produce evidence that later in court will establish the elements of the offense (regardless of the name of the shoplifting prosecution statute), the merchant will be more effective. Retailers should not become frustrated because statutes have different names. It is the ability to prove the elements of the offense—which are the same in all states—that counts.

In any state shoplifting is a criminal offense involving wrongful possession of merchandise. A person commits theft in Texas, stealing in Missouri, or retail theft in Illinois in one way—by obtaining wrongful possession of goods offered for sale by a merchant. Consider the most common shoplifting situations merchants encounter in their stores:

1.   Concealment of merchandise
2.   No concealment involved
3.   Fitting room shoplifting
4.   Container stuffing
5.   Passing goods to a companion
6.   Price tag switching

In each shoplifting situation the suspect obtains wrongful possession of merchandise and leaves without paying or without paying the true selling price. Even in a price tag switching situation, the suspect's possession is wrongful because he obtained possession by paying for the goods at the lower or switched price.

When reading shoplifting prosecution statutes and ordinances always remember they all make wrongful possession an offense. The title or wording of the statute will be different from state to state, but wrongful possession is always the heart of the offense. In the popular mind shoplifting is equated with concealment, but of course concealment is not necessary to make a person's possession wrongful. The lady putting the scarf around her neck and leaving without paying for this item has obtained wrongful possession of it just the same as if it were concealed in her purse. Shoplifting prosecution statutes and ordinances all make wrongful possession an offense, they just use different language to accomplish the same purpose.

There are other criminal prosecution statutes merchants must understand because they too apply to shoplifting. The most common one is shoplifting by unauthorized use of a credit card. Two examples of theft by credit card statutes are presented and discussed in Chapter 5. These types of shoplifting cases are relatively few in comparison to cases prosecuted under the statutes discussed above. Merchants must learn to prove the elements of the offense under shoplifting prosecution statutes first because most of the cases will be filed under them.

Filing Misdemeanor Shoplifting Cases
Under a City Ordinance

For a case to be prosecuted as a felony (under a state statute) the value of the shoplifted goods must reach a certain level, such as $50 or $100. Some states may say any case where the value of the merchandise is less than

FIGURE 2.1	Sample shoplifting charge: misdemeanor case under ordinance

In The Municipal Court of Kansas City, Missouri			Summons #G123-456
1-15-85	1234 Blueview Mall	1430 Hours	SMITH, MARY JANE

4321 Main   Anywhere USA   Age 30   Date of Birth: 2-16-54

DID WITHIN THE CITY LIMITS COMMIT THE FOLLOWING OFFENSE:

Did intentionally steal property of value belonging to the ABC Discount Store, to-wit; one pair of panty hose valued at $1.49.

In violation of Revised Ordinances: Chapter 26 Section 26.50
Penalty Section 26.50

Bond: $25	Court Date: 2-15-85	Time: 8:30 AM	Division #108

COMPLAINANT: /s/ Store Security Officer   Arresting Officer: /s/ Police Officer

$200 or $250 must be prosecuted as a misdemeanor, so always consult the statute on this point. Since most shoplifting cases involve merchandise valued at less than $100, they are filed as misdemeanor violations under county or city ordinances. Typically, the ordinance is patterned after the state shoplifting prosecution statute, but this is not always true.

A retail company may have four stores in a metropolitan area. Each one could be located in a different city. For example, a company in the Kansas City, Missouri area might have stores in Kansas City, Missouri and in Independence, Missouri. Both cities are in Jackson County, Missouri. A shoplifter at stores A and B would be prosecuted under the Kansas City stealing ordinance while stores C and D file charges against shoplifters under the Independence city ordinance. The point is that store owners, managers, and security personnel must be familiar with the city shoplifting prosecution ordinance where the store is located as well as the state shoplifting prosecution statute. A good suggestion is to xerox copies of both the state statute and city ordinance, putting both in the loss-prevention manual. In this way if there is a difference between the name of the ordinance and statute, this fact will be known. Training programs can then teach employees to prove the elements of the offense under either city ordinance because they will be the same, regardless of the name of the city ordinance. Figure 2.1 presents a sample shoplifting charge, one filed as a misdemeanor under a city ordinance.

Notice that a store employee must sign as the *complainant*, which means the party who owns the merchandise in question, as well as the party who is initiating the prosecution. By signing the *summons* (sometimes called a *complaint* or even a *warrant*), the merchant is saying (1) that the allegations are true and (2) that the store has produced evidence that will establish each element of the offense in court. This charge alleges that Mary Jane Smith intended to steal property (the panty hose) belonging to the store and the panty hose had a value of $1.49. It has alleged all the elements of the offense. It is always time well spent for merchants to study these formal allegations in the charge, whether it alleges felony or misdemeanor shoplifting. By studying the language of the formal charge, a merchant can better understand what evidence must be produced in the store to prove each element of the offense later at trial.

ELEMENTS OF THE OFFENSE OF SHOPLIFTING

In any state, whether filing the case under a city ordinance or a state statute, the prosecuting merchant must prove all the elements of the offense. They are as follows:

1.   The suspect obtained possession of the merchandise
2.   The suspect intended to shoplift the merchandise
3.   The store was the owner of the merchandise
4.   The value of the merchandise was $____(a specific dollar amount)

The most commonly encountered shoplifting situation is one where the suspect conceals merchandise then leaves the store without paying. For this reason the discussion about proving the elements of the offense will deal with concealment shoplifting situations.

Sometimes a loss-prevention manual will contain only guidelines about how to handle a shoplifting situation. A store owner, manager, or security person does not need a guideline but rather needs to know how to produce evidence to establish the elements of the offense. No person was ever convicted of shoplifting under a guideline in a loss-prevention manual sent out from the corporate office. Merchants who use this guideline approach will lose shoplifting cases because their employees will not know how to determine if a prosecutable case exists and should be filed. The loss-prevention manual and training programs should teach employees how to produce evidence to establish the elements of the offense of shoplifting.

Element 1: The Suspect Obtained Possession of Merchandise

This element is established by watching a person. There is just one way people shoplift—with their hands. Merchants often talk about shifty eyes or furtive gestures as if they had some value as evidence in a shoplifting prosecution. They have nothing to do with a suspect obtaining possession of merchandise. People do not obtain possession of goods with their eyes or gestures but with their hands. At best, shifty eyes and furtive gestures are circumstances indicating a person may be intending to obtain possession of merchandise with his hands. As any experienced security director will tell his staff or tell sales employees, "If you want to prevent shoplifting losses watch a suspect's hands."

The first rule in establishing possession is to see the suspect remove the goods from a rack, counter, or shelf with his hands. Too often a retail employee will only see the suspect conceal goods and jump to the conclusion that shoplifting is in progress. This could be an evidence-gathering mistake if the store employee did not first see the suspect remove that merchandise from its place of display. That person could have brought previously purchased merchandise into the store and taken it out of a shopping bag for example. If all the security person sees is the lady dropping her merchandise back into the shopping bag, then possession is not wrongful. Always ask yourself the question— "Did I see my suspect remove the merchandise from a rack, counter, or shelf with his hands?" If the answer is "no" then think twice because that person may have every right to put the goods in a purse, shopping bag, or a pocket.

In most shoplifting cases the suspect will conceal goods immediately after removing it from the place of display. In other situations, particularly in supermarkets, the actual concealment may be delayed for a few minutes. Typically, a woman will place three packages of steaks in her cart. When she is an aisle or two away from the meat counter she then will transfer one package to her purse, paying only for two meat items at the checkout counter. In a department or discount store the suspect may move merchandise before concealing it. A man may remove a leather wallet from the display and carry it around while looking at shirts or cufflinks. When back in the corner of the men's furnishings department, he will put the wallet in his coat pocket. Sometimes suspects will take merchandise into a restroom and then conceal it. Plastic shopping bags are very popular among shoplifters. Some will bring a second bag into the store inside the one they are carrying. After moving merchandise to a corner, they pull out the second bag, drop merchandise in it, and then leave carrying two shopping bags. Women have been known to drop merchandise down the back of baby strollers they are pushing. In one case, a man in a wheelchair was placing items underneath the blanket over his lap as he was being pushed around the store by a friend.

There is an old adage in the retail business: "If you want to stop shoplifting, open your store in a nudist colony." This tongue-in-cheek comment is a way of saying that people shoplift by concealing merchandise in some way after they have obtained possession of it with their hands. Employees should be told to watch more closely those with shopping bags, purses, briefcases, other types of bags, and with coats not buttoned. A woman wearing a belted raincoat and not carrying a purse is an unlikely shoplifting candidate because there is no easy place to conceal merchandise. The same is true of a teenager wearing jeans and a T-shirt. Each store must train employees to identify those who are most likely to shoplift. It all begins with watching a suspect's hands.

Possession of the merchandise must become *wrongful*. In a concealment case, possession becomes wrongful when the item is concealed. A store manager or security person who sees a person remove the item from a rack and conceal it has just established the element of *wrongful possession*. The suspect should not be detained at this point because evidence must be produced to establish the second element of the offense: intent to shoplift. Concealment alone does not best prove intent to shoplift later in court. The suspect must move past the last checkout counter or cash register with the item still concealed and fail to pay before the element of intent to shoplift is established.

After the merchant has seen the suspect conceal goods, his next step is to keep that suspect in view until he is detained. Sometimes a person will realize he has been spotted and ditch or dump the merchandise. A person who has gotten rid of concealed merchandise should not be detained for the obvious reason that he is no longer in wrongful possession of it. Even if the suspect did conceal the goods then dump it, the best approach is to recover the merchandise without detaining. Filing of attempted shoplifting charges is not recommended. Recover the goods and remember the suspect. The merchant's job is loss prevention, which has been accomplished when the item is dumped. If the suspect does not get rid of the merchandise, keep him under constant and unbroken surveillance until he passes the last cash register and fails to pay. Merchants want to detain only persons who still are in possession of concealed and unpurchased merchandise.

Element 2: The Suspect Intended to Shoplift

Sometimes merchants think that seeing a person conceal merchandise on the sales floor automatically establishes guilt in court. This is not true.

Possession of merchandise starts to become legally wrongful when it is concealed. Removal of goods from their place of display and concealment is solid evidence that the suspect has begun the process of shoplifting. In court what happens *after* concealment best proves the suspect intended to shoplift. What happens after concealment is that the suspect walks out of the store without paying for the concealed goods. Only when the suspect passes that last cash register— still in possession of concealed and unpurchased merchandise—is the evidence strong enough to establish that he intended to shoplift.

If the suspect is permitted to continue the concealment past that last cash register and does not pay, this is the best evidence to use in court to convince a judge or jury the person intended to shoplift. Remember that many people who are stopped will deny they intended to shoplift by saying things like, "I forgot to pay." In court, a merchant's evidence must convince a judge or jury that the suspect intended to shoplift and did not just forget to pay. The suspect must be given an opportunity to pay and fail to pay. In court, the store witness will then testify to these objective facts: the suspect was seen (1) removing merchandise from its place of display with his hands, (2) the merchandise was concealed, (3) the suspect continued past the last cash register, (4) the suspect was given the opportunity to pay, (5) the suspect failed to pay, and (6) the suspect was detained at or just outside the door.[2] This type of testimony paints an objective word picture for a judge or a jury. They can more easily see just what happened several weeks earlier in the store. People seldom admit they intended to shoplift. A judge or jury typically has to infer that the defendant intended to shoplift based on the person's conduct and the surrounding circumstances. In cases where the person's concealment of merchandise continues past the last cash register without paying, it is easier for a judge or jury to conclude the person did intend to shoplift and did not just forget to pay as many will claim.

The Wisconsin statute is an excellent example of how a state legislature has incorporated the continuing concealment and last cash register rules into a definition of intent to shoplift. This statute makes it clear that concealment is not enough. It is what the suspect does after concealing the merchandise that best proves intent to shoplift later in court.

---

[2]In court, the strongest evidence of intent to shoplift is where the suspect was detained outside the store. Many have heard the "outside the store" rule. The legal reason for waiting until the suspect is outside the store is to best prove that person intended to shoplift and did not just forget to pay. Many retail security directors tell staff members and store managers to detain only after the suspect is outside the store rather than after the suspect has passed the last cash register. I agree with this approach. The strongest case is one where the suspect continued the concealment past the last cash register, failed to pay, and was detained outside the store.

| STATUTE | Wisconsin |

Section 943.50 Wisconsin Penal Code—Shoplifting-(1981)

(2) The intentional concealment of unpurchased merchandise which continues from one floor to another or beyond the last station for receiving payment in a merchant's store is evidence of intent to deprive the merchant permanently of possession of such merchandise without paying the purchase price thereof. The discovery of unpurchased merchandise concealed upon the person or among the belongings of such person or concealed by a person upon the person or among the belongings of another is evidence of intentional concealment on the part of the person so concealing such goods.

Concealment indicates to a judge or jury that the suspect's possession of merchandise is wrongful—but concealment is not always conclusive evidence that the suspect intended to shoplift. It is concealment coupled with movement past the cash register and failure to pay that establishes probable cause to detain under the detention statutes. As the Wisconsin statute says so well, it is concealment and movement past that last cash register that demonstrates the suspect intended to permanently deprive the store of possession of the goods. Do not jump the gun and detain suspects immediately after they conceal merchandise.

| CASE | Wrench set case |

A female security officer at a department store testified she saw a male suspect conceal several wrench sets inside his jacket. She watched him walk past eighteen cash registers, never stopping to talk with a cashier or offer to pay for the concealed wrench sets. She detained him at the double doors to the street. He told her the reason he made no effort to pay was because he intended to put the wrench sets in layaway. The wrench sets still had the store's price tags on them when they were recovered. In court, the man said the same thing to the judge: he was going to put them in layaway. This explanation was a denial that he intended to shoplift. By her testimony that he walked past eighteen cash registers after concealing the wrench sets, she presented powerful evidence to establish the element of intent to shoplift. Based on this evidence, the jury had no difficulty concluding he intended to shoplift wrench sets and did not intend to put them in layaway.

People v. Martin, 407 N.E.2d 999 (Illinois, 1980)

In summary, five crucial factors must be established to prove the suspect intended to shoplift.

1.   The suspect concealed the merchandise after removing it from the place of display on a rack, counter, or shelf.
2.   The suspect continued to remain in possession of the concealed goods.
3.   The suspect was in possession of the concealed goods when he passed by the last cash register for making payment.
4.   The suspect failed to pay when he had the opportunity to pay.
5.   The suspect was detained after passing the last cash register.

Some shoplifting prosecution statutes have a section that creates a legal presumption that the suspect intended to shoplift. They say that either concealment or the finding of concealed and unpurchased merchandise on a suspect (or among his belongings) is evidence the suspect intended to shoplift. This statutory device is a way some legislatures have tried to make it easier for merchants to prove intent to shoplift. If a shoplifting prosecution statute has this "presumption of intent" section, do not be lulled into a false sense of security. It is not a license to detain suspects before they pass the last cash register and leave the store. Do not rely on a page in a statute book to prove the case. Instead, rely on the fact that the suspect was seen passing the last cash register with the item still concealed in a pocket, purse, shopping bag, or under clothing.

Let prosecutors, defense attorneys, and judges argue over these presumption of intent to shoplift sections where they exist. Retailers should concentrate on producing the strongest possible evidence in the store to use in court to prove intent. Count the number of cash registers the suspect passes as was done in the wrench set case. Show the judge the suspect had a chance to pay and failed to do so. The merchant who is in a hurry and detains immediately after concealment is the merchant who will lose shoplifting cases because of insufficient evidence to prove the element of intent to shoplift.

Element 3: Store Ownership of the Merchandise

The strongest evidence a merchant can present in court to prove its ownership is the merchandise itself. All shoplifting prosecution statutes require the charge to be initiated by the victim-owner of the property. Most merchants have employees put the date and their initials on the merchandise in some way—normally on the price tag. The item is brought to court, identified by the witness, and then offered into evidence as a prosecution exhibit. Some states by statute permit the prosecuting merchant to photograph the goods and bring the picture to court in lieu of the merchandise. Always check the statutes on this point, and ask the prosecutor about photographing merchandise.

The shoplifting prosecution statutes only tell a merchant what constitutes the elements of the offense. They do not tell merchants how to gather evidence in the store to prove the elements of the offense later at trial. Below is set forth the Kentucky detention statute. The legislature has clearly told the merchant what to do after detaining on probable cause. The statute says in Section 1(c) to make an investigation about the ownership of the merchandise. In section 1(d) it says to recover or attempt to recover the unpurchased merchandise. Consider the language of this well-drafted detention statute. It leaves no doubt that the merchandise is to be recovered. If a charge is filed, that merchandise should be brought to court to establish the element of ownership.

| STATUTE | Kentucky detention statute |

433.236. Detention and arrest of shoplifting suspect.

(1) A peace officer, security agent of a mercantile establishment, merchant or merchant's employe who has probable cause for believing that goods held for sale by the merchant have been unlawfully taken by a person may take the person into custody and detain him in a reasonable manner for a reasonable length of time, on the premises of the mercantile establishment or off the premises of the mercantile establishment, if the persons enumerated in this section are in fresh pursuit, for any or all of the following purposes:

(a) To request identification;

(b) To verify such identification;

(c) To make reasonable inquiry as to whether such person has in his possession unpurchased merchandise, and to make reasonable investigation of the ownership of such merchandise;

(d) To recover or attempt to recover goods taken from the mercantile establishment by such person, or by others accompanying him,

(e) To inform a peace officer or law enforcement agency of the detention of the person and to surrender the person to the custody of a peace officer, and in the case of a minor, to inform the parents, guardian, or other person having custody of that minor of his detention, in addition to surrendering the minor to the custody of a peace officer.

(2) The recovery of goods taken from the mercantile establishment by the person detained or by others shall not limit the right of the persons named in subsection (1) of this section to detain such person for peace officers or otherwise accomplish the purposes of subsection (1).

(3) Any peace officer may arrest without warrant any person he has probable cause for believing has committed larceny in retail or wholesale establishments. (Enact. Acts 1958, ch. 11, § 2; 1968, ch. 49, § 2; 1978, ch. 75, § 1, effective June 17, 1978.)

In some situations when a suspect is detained, that person may claim ownership of the merchandise. In Chapter 4 the merchant is given six commonly encountered explanations where a suspect is claiming ownership of merchandise. In these situations the detaining merchant may want to check store records or check with other employees as part of investigating the facts. This checking may take some time which raises the question of completing the investigation in a legally reasonable time. The New York detention statute, another well-drafted and well-thought-out one, addresses the time factor and conducting an investigation of the facts concerning ownership.

STATUTE	New York general business laws

Detention (Section 218)

As used in this section "reasonable grounds" shall include, but not be limited to, knowledge that a person has concealed possession of unpurchased merchandise of a retail mercentile establishment, and a "reasonable time" shall mean the time necessary to permit the person detained to make a statement or to refuse to make a statement, and the time necessary to examine employees and records of the mercentile establishment relative to the ownership of the merchandise.

The Kentucky and New York statutes make it clear that legislatures authorized merchants to detain and investigate the question of whether the store or the suspect owns the goods in question. Refer back to Figure 2. 1 (sample ordinance charge) to see it alleges theft of a $1.49 pair of panty hose. The charge says "property of and belonging to the ABC Discount Store." A charge must always plead that ownership of the merchandise is by the store. This element must be proven in court, using the merchandise itself as the prosecution exhibit.

Element 4: Value of the Merchandise

The general rule is that the value of the merchandise controls whether the case is filed as a felony or a misdemeanor. Consider the Kansas theft statute on this point.

STATUTE	Kansas theft statute

21–3701

Theft of property of the value of fifty dollars ($50) or more is a Class D felony.

Theft of property of the value of less than fifty dollars ($50) is a class A misdemeanor.

The question may arise as to whether "value" means the selling price or the merchant's cost. Decisional law in each state may be the key to answering this question. Suppose $50 is the felony level and a specialty apparel store files a charge against a woman for shoplifting a $60 sweater. Based on its fact, that is a felony, but the sweater may have only cost the store $42. Prosecutors may want to file this as a misdemeanor case. It could be an advantage for the merchant. If the case goes to court as a felony, the store may have to produce the buyer to testify as to the $42 cost. If the case is filed as a misdemeanor, the store manager or security person can most likely establish its value. Proving value may seem simple at first blush. Do not overlook this retail price or merchant's cost problem because the rule will differ from state to state.

In some states, the legislature is specific about the term *value*. The language of the Georgia statute says value means the retail price.

STATUTE	Georgia theft statute

Sec. 26–1802(c)

In all cases involving theft by shoplifting the term "value" means the actual retail price of the property at the time and place of the offense. The unaltered price tag or other marking on property, or duly identified photographs thereof, shall be prima facie evidence of value and ownership of such property.

Suppose a woman is seen placing a $40 dress in her shopping bag. She is followed out to the mall parking lot and detained at her car. The store detective looks in the back seat and sees assorted merchandise, not in shopping bags but just laying on the seat. Investigation reveals there is $580 in merchandise from four stores in that mall. The total value of merchandise is over the felony limit ($100 in that state), but the dress coming from the detective's store is the only priced at $40. This store can only file a misdemeanor shoplifting charge because only $40 has been stolen from it.

In most states this woman could be prosecuted for felony shoplifting under a statute like that found in Pennsylvania which provides for adding up the value of all recovered merchandise. If no statute such as this one exists the subject may be controlled by decisional law. Experienced security personnel know many people will shoplift from several stores in a mall, taking the unpurchased merchandise to their cars each time. Merchants must know whether the case can be filed as felony or misdemeanor shoplifting, so always check with local prosecutors. Consider the Pennsylvania statute which talks about retail thefts committed pursuant to one scheme:

> Amounts involved in retail thefts committed pursuant to one scheme or course of conduct, whether from the same store or retail mercantile establishment or several stores or retail mercantile establishments, may be aggregated in determining the grade of offense.

CONCLUSION

The prosecuting merchant must produce evidence to prove each element of the offense. Shoplifting cases are lost most often (and in any state) because the store's prosecution evidence fails to establish the element of 1) intent to shoplift, or 2) store ownership of the merchandise in question. Remember, the defendant does not have to testify at a trial. His lawyer can simply point out to the judge that the store's evidence is lacking on one or more of the elements and ask for an acquittal. The ability to determine if a prosecutable case exists before filing it is the skill that store owners, managers, and security personnel need to develop. Suspicion and opinion are not evidence to prove an element of the offense in any state. Training programs must teach employees to detain under the merchant's privilege, then investigate the fact, and decide if a prosecutable case exists. A prosecutable case exists when the detaining merchant has produced evidence which will establish each element of the offense as found in the shoplifting prosecution statute.

3

Shoplifting Situations Encountered by Merchants

To prevent shoplifting a merchant must first have the ability to recognize shoplifting situations. The following is a list of the five shoplifting situations that merchants most frequently encounter on the selling floor. The common denominator of each one is that the suspect obtains wrongful possession of unpurchased merchandise.

Five shoplifting situations most frequently encountered by merchants

    I. Suspect conceals merchandise
   II. No concealment involved
  III. More than one person involved—aiding and abetting
     A. The lookout situation
     B. The diversion situation
  IV. False representation involved
     A. Cash refunds
     B. Price tag switching
     C. Container stuffing
   V. Circumstantial situations
     A. Fitting room shoplifting
     B. Suspect not seen removing merchandise from its place of display

The cases which follow came from the law books and demonstrate these five commonly encountered shoplifting situations. In Chapter 4 the reader is given an evidence- gathering guide to use in producing evidence in situations involving concealment of merchandise, because concealment situations are the most common. In any shoplifting situation the suspect obtains wrongful possession of merchandise. In a concealment case wrongful possession means putting the item in a pocket, purse, shopping bag, or under clothing, then leaving without paying. It is no secret that most people detained for possible shoplifting have concealed the goods. The point to glean from the list above is that there are other ways in which people obtain wrongful possession of unpurchased merchandise. Training programs should concentrate on recognizing concealment situations first, but they should also make store managers and security personnel aware of other shoplifting situations.

DIRECT EVIDENCE CASES INVOLVING CONCEALMENT OF UNPURCHASED MERCHANDISE

In court a direct evidence case is one where the retail employee actually saw the suspect obtain wrongful possession of the merchandise and walk out without paying. Direct evidence is eyewitness testimony presented by the store's witness who saw the suspect remove merchandise from its place of display and leave without paying for it. In the six cases which follow, the prosecuting merchants had direct evidence (or eyewitness evidence) to present in court to prove the elements of the offense.

| CASE | Two shopping bags case |

A security officer saw the suspect pick up two shopping bags and walk randomly through the department store placing various items in them. The officer waited to detain until the suspect was starting to leave and was about to reach the door. As the suspect pushed open the door, he was detained. The merchant recovered some men's socks, a lamp, two key chains, several boxes of bras, and a woman's pant suit. The total sale price of all the merchandise was $84.69.

In affirming the man's conviction, the appellate court discussed *continuing concealment* and the *place of detention* by saying the following about the evidence:

Rarely will there be found a stronger case of criminal intent to steal property of another than here. The defendant was seen depositing various merchandise in a shopping bag, attempted to leave the store without paying for the merchandise, but was stopped by the security officer as he was pushing open the door of the store to leave.

As the words of the judge clearly show, the court considers what happens after concealment as evidence to show intent to shoplift. This is true in multiple item concealment cases. It is even more important in a single inexpensive item.

Most shoplifting prosecution statutes require the merchant to prove the suspect intended to deprive the store *permanently* of the merchandise. Failing to pay and heading for the door with concealed merchandise is the best way for merchants to demonstrate in court that the suspect did not forget to pay but intended to remove the merchandise permanently from the store.

State v. Ahern, 546 S.W.2d 20 (Missouri, 1976)

| CASE | Slacks in the car trunk case |

This case demonstrates how a department store obtained a conviction by using facts produced by a nonsecurity employee, the store tailor. The tailor saw a man and a woman standing next to the rack where the men's slacks were displayed. She was carrying what the tailor described as a large purse, which she handed to her male companion. He held it open while she removed two pairs of slacks from the rack, folded them, and put them in the purse, which he handed back to her. Never losing sight of the pair, the tailor watched them leave the store immediately after concealing the slacks and walk directly to a car in the mall lot. The man opened the trunk, removed the slacks from the purse, and placed them inside the trunk. The couple then walked back toward the mall. The tailor notified store security, who in turn called a police officer working mall security.

About ten minutes later, the couple was seen again in the department store, this time in the woman's sportswear department. On this occasion, no store employee saw either of them conceal any merchandise. Based on the facts supplied by the tailor, the police officer detained the couple as they were going back to the car. Because this warrantless arrest made by the officer was supported by probable cause supplied by the tailor, the officer could search the trunk of the car incident to the warrantless arrest, which he did. The slacks were recovered and used in evidence to prosecute the couple. Both convictions were upheld by the appellate court as being based on sufficient evidence. The search of the trunk was also found to be proper, being made incident to a warrantless arrest supported by probable cause.

Neither suspect made any statement or explanation to the police officer when detained. But suppose they had said they "forgot to pay" for the slacks? No judge or jury would accept this defense denying intent to shoplift as the truth after hearing the tailor testify to the facts he observed in the store and in the parking lot. If the couple had said they purchased the slacks at another store, the merchant could have proved its ownership because both pairs of slacks still had the price tags affixed. The observed and investigated facts were so overwhelming that the only conclusion possible was guilty, one that the jury made and the appellate court affirmed as being correct.

State v. Wiley, 442 S. W.2d 1 (Missouri, 88)

| CASE | Two Flair pens case |

A female security officer saw a lone male enter the drugstore. He removed a blister pack containing two Flair pens from the rack. Leaving the school supplies section on the main floor, he then went to the basement, holding the blister pack in his right hand all the time. At the rear of the store, he removed the two pens from the cardboard container, put them in his shirt pocket, and threw the blister pack behind some kitchen gadgets. Next, he selected a can of shoe polish and started back upstairs with the two pens still in his shirt pocket. After recovering the blister pack (which had the price tag on it), the officer used the intercom to obtain assistance. She and the assistant manager detained the suspect at the door, after he had paid for the shoe polish but not for the pens. Both watched him go through the checkout line. He voluntarily returned to the security office with the two drugstore employees.

He explained that the two pens were in his shirt pocket when he entered the store, setting up an ownership defense in an effort to avoid being prosecuted. But he was convicted and fined $50. The recovered blister pack was a crucial piece of prosecution evidence to prove store ownership and disprove his claim of ownership by a prior purchase. Because the investigated facts (the recovered blister pack) supported the security officer's testimony about what she saw in the basement of the store, the judge had little difficulty in finding the suspect intended to shoplift the two Flair pens owned by the discount drug store. The question of guilt turned on whether the store could prove ownership (which it did), thereby disproving his claim of a prior purchase. This store properly supported its decision to file charges by recovering the blister pack that the suspect had discarded in the basement.

A case prosecuted by the author in the Municipal Court of Kansas City, Missouri on June 7, 1981.

Intent to shoplift was clearly shown in this case. The suspect was given the opportunity to pay, he failed to pay, and the concealment of the pens in his shirt pocket continued past the cash register to the point where he was detained at the door. If he had denied intent to shoplift by saying he forgot to pay, the store would have had an equally strong case. The actions of this suspect after placing the pens in his shirt pocket demonstrated his intention was not to pay but to shoplift. This drugstore produced facts that in court showed that the suspect intended to shoplift two pens owned by the store.

CASE	Radio case

A sales clerk in a midwestern department store saw a lone male shopper drop a $39.95 radio into a bag he was carrying. The suspect was permitted to leave the store, being detained just outside. After obtaining consent to examine the contents of the bag, store employees found, in addition to the radio, four dresses ($14.99 each) and two pair of slacks ($8.99 each). No store employee saw the man place the dresses or the slacks in the bag. All six pieces of merchandise had the department store tags attached to them. The total retail value of the merchandise was $117.99. The man was prosecuted and convicted for felony shoplifting under a Tennessee statute that made theft of merchandise valued over $100 a felony.

On appeal, the defendant contended that the merchant did not prove the value was over $100 because of the possibility that some of the merchandise may have been on sale. The appellate court held that the evidence presented at trial (the retail price of the six items of merchandise) was sufficient to prove the value of the merchandise was $100 or more.

State v. Saylor, 618 P.2d 1166 (Kansas, 1980)

When merchants encounter this type of situation, they should always check with local prosecutors to see if the value is the retail price or the merchant's cost. Some jurisdictions may require value to be proved by having the merchant's cost exceed the statutory limit, and others will follow this case.

CASE	Two cartons of cigarettes case

The suspect entered a discount and redemption center, where the co-owner saw him remove two cartons of cigarettes from the shelf and place them under his shirt and pants. He then walked to the front of the store directly across from the checkout counter. The co-owner informed her husband about the concealment of the cigarettes. He confronted the man and asked him three times whether he had taken any cigarettes. Each time, the suspect denied having taken cigarettes. The husband then lifted the suspect's shirt and removed the two cartons of cigarettes from his person. At no time did the suspect open the cigarettes nor did he ever attempt to leave the store with the cigarettes in his possession. The two owners made the decision to prosecute the case. The suspect was convicted and appealed.

On appeal the suspect-defendant argued that the elements of common law larceny as incorporated into the Vermont statute were not properly proved by the merchant's evidence at trial. The defendant said the evidence showed that he never attempted to carry the cigarettes away from the store premises. Therefore he said that an essential element of "carrying away" was not proved by the store so the conviction could not stand. In affirming the conviction, the court cited an older case, holding as follows:

> It is well settled that the elements of a taking and asportation [carrying away] are satisfied where the evidence shows the property was taken from the owner and was concealed or put in a convenient place for removal. The fact the possession was brief or that the person was detected before the goods could be removed from the owner's premises is immaterial. (Groomes v. United States, 155 A2d 73 (DC Mun. App. 1959) (59)

The appellate court concluded that the defendant purposively removed the cigarettes from the shelf, that he secreted them under his clothing, and that he walked to the front of the store. In view of these facts, the court said there was sufficient proof that he was in possession of the cigarettes, carried them away with the intent of depriving the owner of them, and did so with the intent of leaving without paying. In short, this court affirmed the conviction even though both owners violated the last cash register rule.

State v. Grant, 373 A.2d 847 (Vermont, 1977)

| CASE | Twenty-one LP record albums case |

About noon the manager of a variety store was coming down the escalator when he saw a man at the rear of the music department with a green satchel. This man was stacking record albums on top of the counter and then placing them in the satchel. The manager watched this man for a few minutes. When their eyes met, the suspect walked away from the record department cash register where a sales clerk was on duty. He left the music department.

The manager notified a security officer that there was a man in the rear of the store with a green satchel containing record albums he had not paid for. When joined by the security man, the manager pointed to the suspect. He was now at the lunch counter. To get there, he had passed the record department cash register and the register in the stationery department, where a clerk was also on duty. The security man detained the suspect at the lunch counter and asked to look inside the satchel. He found twenty-one LP record albums, all marked with the store's price tag when the contents was examined in the back room of the store. The man was convicted on stealing over $50 (a felony in the state at that time). His conviction was affirmed.

State v. Van, 543 S.W.2d 827 (Missouri, 1976)

TABLE 3.1	Method of concealment (percentage)*		
	Supermarkets	*Drugstores*	*Discount stores*
Pocket	21.5	28.5	12.3
Purse	34.1	27.8	29.2
Under clothing	23.7	13.1	11.3
Shopping bag	2.8	3.4	15.7
Other bag	3.8	4.9	2.9
Total	84.9	77.7	71.4
Label switch	2.1	4.2	6.7
Accomplice	3.2	4.7	4.1

*Commercial Service Systems, Roger Griffin, Van Nays, CA, 1984.

These cases may seem simple, especially to those experienced in retail security. They will not seem so simple in the chapters on civil liability. There it will be seen that national and regional merchants, those with full-time security staffs, made evidence-gathering mistakes in these concealment cases. The mistakes in gathering evidence in the store directly permitted or indirectly set the stage for false imprisonment and malicious prosecution actions to be filed against the stores. What is simple and easy to understand is how the suspect shoplifts. What is more difficult to understand is how a merchant responds to these concealment situations, gathers evidence and decides if a prosecutable case exists.

Table 3.1 is a study based on actual detentions of 16,946 persons by 853 discount, drug, and food stores located primarily on the west coast. It shows the overwhelming majority of cases find retailers watching people removing merchandise from its place of display, then walking out after concealing the item. A training suggestion is to compile a similar chart based on detentions made in each store. Most retailers will find that at least 60 percent of the persons detained will be those concealing merchandise.

DIRECT EVIDENCE CASES INVOLVING NO CONCEALMENT

A shoplifter does not have to conceal items to commit the offense. The possession is legally wrongful if a man puts a hat on his head and walks out of the store without paying for it. He is just as guilty of shoplifting as any of the defendants in the first six cases who concealed merchandise and left without paying. In these *no concealment cases* a store employee watches the man put the hat on his head and leave without paying. Like

his counterpart who concealed the goods, the suspect in the no concealment situation first obtains possession of merchandise with his hands. In
each of the three cases which follow, the merchant produced evidence in
the store that in court established the elements of the offense. The result
was a conviction in each case.

| CASE | Scarf case |

Discount store security people saw a woman take a scarf from a rack, remove
the price tag, and put the scarf through a loop on her purse. Her hands were
full of other merchandise at the time. An employee recovered the price tag
from the floor of the millinery department where she dropped it. The woman
then went through the checkout line, paying for the $66 in other merchandise
but not for the scarf, which at all times remained in plain view through the
loop of her purse. When detained outside the store, she told the female
security officer, "Oh, I must have forgotten to pay for it."

The store elected to prosecute. It obtained a conviction, which was affirmed
on appeal of the case by the woman who claimed she did not understand her
Miranda rights when given to her by the security officer. The appellate court
held that under the Illinois Retail Theft Act, store security people were not in
the same category as law enforcement personnel for the purpose of the
Miranda warning. The court said it was not confronted with a situation where
store security people were acting in a coordinated effort with the police. The
court permitted the use of the "I forgot to pay" statement given by the woman
to the security officer into evidence.

People v. Raitino, 401 N.E.2d 278 (Illinois, 1980)

The facts of this case show that the store detained on probable cause
for the purpose of investigating facts relevant to ownership of the scarf and
the woman's intent (or lack of it) to shoplift. The store detained in order
to conduct its own independent investigation and was not in league with
the police in this detention-investigation effort. The woman's answer to
the question was not an incriminating statement but a denial of intent to
shoplift. She was saying her failure to pay for the scarf was the result of
an accident or a good faith mistake. She was not admitting or confessing
that she intended to shoplift. The court said that as a general rule, when
merchants act under this Retail Theft Act statute, their actions do not
convert the detention and investigation into state action.

If the merchant had notified the police to come and make a shoplifting arrest and then conducted the investigation, the court would most
likely have found that *Miranda* warnings should have been given. Since

the store detained on probable cause, investigated the facts, and then decided to prosecute, there was no state action and hence no need to give *Miranda*. Only after conducting an investigation, as the store was entitled to do under the Retail Theft Act, did this discount store decide to inform a peace officer of the detention. The store detained and conducted an investigation independently of the police and then, based on the result of the investigation, made a decision. The decision was to prosecute, but it could have been to release the woman without taking the case to court.

| CASE | Leather jacket case |

Two department store detectives testified that they saw the suspect rip off a price tag and a sensor warning device from a leather jacket. He then put the coat on and wandered about this large department store for a few minutes, passing several cash registers in the process. He made no effort to pay for the coat at any of the registers and was detained on the stairs near the exit. In court, the two officers said they recovered both the price tag and sensor warning device, but for reasons not disclosed in the case neither pieces of valuable prosecution evidence were brought to court. In affirming the conviction, the court said that under these circumstances, the oral testimony of the two officers was sufficient to sustain the conviction.

At trial, the suspect denied removing either the price tag or the sensor warning device from the jacket. The evidence was in direct dispute. The court elected to believe the two store detectives even though they did not bring the price tag and sensor warning device to court and introduce them into evidence along with the leather jacket. The best procedure is always to bring price tags, garment labels, removed sensor devices, and other such physical evidence to court along with the recovered merchandise and introduce all into evidence

People v. Gaoparik, 425 N.Y.S.2d 425 (New York, 1980)

| CASE | Vaulting the rail case |

Two young men entered the men's department. A security officer saw the suspect remove a leather jacket from the rack, take off his jean jacket, and try on the leather garment. While he looked at himself in the mirror for several minutes, his companion engaged the sales clerk in conversation, requesting something that required her to leave the selling floor. When she left the floor, the man wearing the leather coat left the department, using a circuitous route to get near the exit, where he vaulted the rail and left the store. Outside the store, he realized the security officer was following him, so he began to run but was overtaken. When the police arrived, the suspect said he had only taken the coat outside to show someone, this being his way of denying intent to shoplift.

He was convicted because the jury believed he intended to permanently deprive the store of lawful possession of the coat. The jury found that his companion maneuvered the clerk off the sales floor to give him an opportunity to leave without paying. The fact that he vaulted the rail and once outside broke into a run combined to support the belief that he intended to shoplift the coat rather than to show it to an unidentified person, as he claimed. After hearing both the store's prosecution and the suspect's defense evidence, the jury believed the young man intended to shoplift the leather coat owned by the department store.

State v. Moore, 563 S.W.2d 122 (Missouri, 1978)

AIDING AND ABETTING SITUATIONS

There are four commonly encountered situations where more than one person is involved in the shoplifting attempt: (1) the lookout, (2) diversions, (3) joint participation in concealment, and (4) a cashier "sliding" merchandise by the register to a customer accomplice. In any of these situations where more than one person is involved, a merchant can successfully prosecute the suspects for shoplifting the *same* merchandise. In *lookout* and *diversion* cases, the evidence typically will show that only one of the suspects has actual possession of the unpurchased merchandise. The companion (the aider and abettor) did not physically handle, touch, or conceal the merchandise. In these two situations, store policy must be specific about whether a charge will be filed against one or both suspects. The strongest case obviously is against the person in possession of the goods.

In *joint concealment* and *sliding* cases the evidence shows that both suspects physically handled the merchandise. It is easier to obtain a conviction in these cases because a store employee witnesses both parties in possession of unpurchased merchandise at some point. Training programs should decide in advance how these cases are to be handled. In sliding cases the merchant normally is better prepared because a cashier is put under surveillance. Joint concealment situations can come up at any time, so planning ahead will be of benefit.

| CASE | Grocery shoppers case: A classic "lookout" situation |

The assistant manager of a food store observed two men shopping, one carrying an overcoat on his arm. It was later discovered that this coat had a slit in the lining so grocery items could be dropped inside it. As the man with the overcoat pushed the cart, he dropped items into it—and into the coat. During the forty-five minutes in which the pair shopped, the companion never touched any grocery items and never pushed the cart. The companion stood in front of the man with the coat, acting as a shield while merchandise was concealed inside the overcoat. From a catwalk above the selling floor, the assistant manager saw the companion warn the man with the coat that somebody was coming, and the two would pretend to be shopping. The assistant manager watched the companion act as a lookout at several locations in two or three different aisles while the two shopped.

When they were detained at the checkout counter, employees found several grocery items inside the overcoat, still over the one man's arm. The companion said he did not know his friend was shoplifting. He said it was his intention only to buy a package of cigarettes when they reached the checkout counter. No store merchandise was found on the companion. But both were convicted of shoplifting the items concealed inside the coat. The man with the coat did not appeal his conviction, but his companion did, contending that the evidence did not show he was ever in actual possession of any merchandise, that he did not conceal any grocery items on his person, and that he did not intend to carry away merchandise without paying for it. The appellate court affirmed his conviction, saying that all who participate in the commission of a misdemeanor can be found guilty as principals.

In affirming the companion's conviction, the court said that the observed evidence must show more than mere presence at the scene, which in this case it surely did. The evidence showed active participation in the shoplifting offense by the companion. The court said the words *aid and abet* are well defined in the law, citing authority on the point as follows:

> In order to aid and abet another to commit a crime it is necessary that a defendant in some sort associate himself with the venture, that he participate in it as in something he wishes to bring about, that he seek by his action to make it succeed.

The court found that the evidence presented by the assistant manager showed that the companion definitely participated in shoplifting, even though he never physically was in possession of any merchandise. His conduct of acting as a shield and warning the man with the coat about the presence of other persons was evidence he wanted the acts of shoplifting to be successful. He did, no doubt, associate himself with the shoplifting venture of his friend, who was concealing unpurchased grocery items inside the overcoat lining. By this evidence, the suspect's words, gestures, and signs clearly showed he was aiding and abetting the man with the overcoat in shoplifting, so the conviction was affirmed.

Kansas City v. Lane, 391 S.W.2d 995 (Missouri, 1965)

| CASE | Tan dress case |

A security officer observed the defendant and her female companion enter the department store and go directly to the area where the more expensive dresses were displayed. From a secluded spot in this area, the guard observed the woman standing behind her companion so as to obscure the view toward the latter, who was standing next to a rack of dresses. The companion removed a $90 tan dress from the rack, rolled it around the hanger, and placed it under her own clothing, between her legs. The guard and store manager stopped the pair as they were about to leave the store. The defendant's statement to her companion was to cooperate with the store personnel as she wanted "to get it over with." Both women were searched at the store, and one tan dresss, valued at $90, was recovered from between the legs of the companion. No merchandise was found on the defendant. At the police station, a second search was made, and a $279 ultrasuede suit was found on the companion, also under her clothing and between her legs.

In affirming the conviction of the lookout, the court said her conduct was to screen or block the view of others while her companion removed the dress from the rack and concealed it on her person. The court went on to say that under this type of evidence, the accomplice is legally accountable for the conduct of the principal who actually and physically committed the acts of shoplifting. In reviewing the evidence produced by the security officer and store manager, the court left no doubt the lookout was properly convicted of shoplifting by making the following comments:

> The evidence in this case places appellant in the category of accomplice. She and the other woman entered the store together and went to an area where there were few other customers. Appellant stood facing her companion while the latter concealed the dresses. Appellant knew what her companion was doing, as is made evident by her comments to her friend when apprehended after they had begun to walk out together. There is no doubt from the evidence that appellant was an accomplice of and active participant with the one who actually took possession of the stolen dresses. The conduct of appellant, resulting as it did in promoting the commission of the crime by her companion, makes appellant equally responsible for the criminal activity.

People v. Sabri, 362 N.E.2d 739 (Illinois, 1977)

In both the Grocery Shoppers and the Tan Dress Cases, the lookouts were convicted even though the testimony of store personnel showed neither physically touched, removed, concealed, or carried away any merchandise. In both cases, the evidence did show the lookout was an active participant and desired to bring about the removal of the merchandise without its' being paid for by the companion. The evidence in both cases supported the reasonable belief that the lookout intended to aid and abet the principal in shoplifting merchandise owned by the store.

| CASE | Three teenage girls case: A typical diversion situation |

The following case is an example of diversion tactics used against specialty stores on malls across the country. Most specialty stores do not have a security person on the sales floor looking for shoplifting situations. Thus they are more vulnerable than department and discount stores, which typically have full-time security people roaming the selling floor. This case demonstrates the need for specialty store managers to work closely with mall security people. If management has not taken time to set policy for sales personnel, they will not be equipped to produce evidence in shoplifting situations. As shown by the inexpensive merchandise these three girls took, they are not professional shoplifters. The merchandise shoplifted in this case was for personal use and not for resale to a fence.

In a midwestern city, the mall security officer (an off-duty police officer) was summoned to the Flowerama Store about 6:00 P.M. one June evening. The manager informed him three girls had entered the store. While one distracted a sales clerk, a second girl picked up a red rose floral arrangement and placed it in a black and white sack held open by the third girl. The manager was sure about this, especially about the black and white plastic bag, because it belonged to another specialty store on the mall.

Acting on this information, the officer picked up surveillance of the trio as they entered another specialty store. One of the girls was carrying a black and white plastic bag, coming from the Gap stores. When he approached the three girls, the one with the plastic bag in her hand placed it on the floor and tried to walk away from it. Based on the probable cause supplied by the manager at Flowerama and his subsequent observation, the officer detained and took the suspects to the mall security office to investigate the facts. All three said they did not know where the black and white plastic bag came from when asked about it. The bag contained the following merchandise from six specialty stores on that mall:

Store	Merchandise	Value
The Gap	Three shirts	$24.00
Fashion Conspiracy	Terry cloth top and bottom	14.00
Foxmoor Casuals	Two pairs of slacks	40.00
5-7-9 Store	Green sleeveless shirt	8.99
Worths	Shirt and slacks	32.98
Flowerama	False red rose flowers	11.95

The investigated evidence revealed that none of the three had a sales receipt for any of the merchandise. All recovered items still had the price tags from the respective stores still affixed to them. In checking with the five other stores, the officer found the girls had been seen together in each store earlier that afternoon. Although employees in the five other specialty stores remembered seeing the girls, none had seen them conceal unpurchased merchandise and leave without paying. The employees at all five stores could positively identify the recovered merchandise as coming from their respective establishments. Each girl was charged with six counts of shoplifting.

Kansas City, Missouri, Police Report R20183, June 6, 1981

The fact that none of the five specialty stores spotted the young women shows how effective diversion tactics can be, particularly in specialty stores without a full-time security person. Specialty store owners must train employees to look for various types of shoplifting situations, just as department and discount stores teach security staffs to be alert to possible shoplifting. Suppose the three girls had split up after leaving the Flowerama store. It would have been difficult for the officer to have detained them once they separated. Seeing one woman with a black and white plastic bag alone on the mall was not consistent with the information provided to him by the manager of the flower shop. This case demonstrates the necessity for specialty store merchants to work out a policy with the mall security staff covering specialty store detentions and investigations.

Conclusion

Lookout cases are particularly tricky to prosecute for the obvious reason that the lookout is never seen in possession of merchandise. As the Grocery Shoppers and Tan Dress Cases demonstrate, the lookout normally shields the concealment activities by his companion. They may split up immediately after merchandise is concealed by the companion. It is more difficult (but not impossible) to convict the lookout than it is to prosecute the companion who is in actual physical possession of merchandise when detained. When detained, the lookout will almost always deny knowledge of any concealment by his companion. Since no merchandise is recovered from the lookout, the store's prosecution evidence is inherently weaker. The lookout also can more easily claim the merchant violated the detention statute in a subsequent false imprisonment action against the merchant. For these reasons, store policy must be specific about the circumstances under which the lookout will be charged with shoplifting. If there is any doubt, merchants should file a charge only against the one who is in physical possession of unpurchased merchandise.

The same rules apply to the diverter. In many diversion cases the diverter is never in close physical proximity to the companion who will obtain possession of the goods and leave with them. The diverter may enter the area or department first and separate from his companion. It is much easier for a diverter to claim he had no knowledge of what the companion was doing or can even deny knowing the companion at all. Merchants must set policy carefully and thoughtfully about under what circumstances the diverter will be detained and prosecuted. If a shoplifting charge is filed against either the lookout or the diverter, that person is charged with shoplifting the identical merchandise as found in the possession of the companion. It is best to check with local prosecutors about how to file the charge in these two shoplifting situations.

JOINT PARTICIPATION IN CONCEALMENT

In these cases, the retail employee witnesses both persons becoming involved in the actual concealment of merchandise. As the Slacks in the Car Trunk Case demonstrated, both persons can be charged with shoplifting the same merchandise, although only one of the two physically removes it from the store. The evidence in these types of cases is generally stronger than in lookout and diversion cases because the merchant has witnessed both suspects in actual possession of merchandise.

CASE	Companion's purse case

A security officer saw two women enter the discount store together and then split up. The first woman removed two jackets and a pair of pants from their place of display. She neatly folded the garments and placed them in a shopping cart on top of her purse. Shortly after, she rejoined the second woman in the housewares department. After shopping together for a few minutes, the first woman removed the two jackets and pair of pants from the shopping cart and placed them in her companion's purse. The security officer testified he was about twenty-five feet away and had a clear view of the two women at the time of the transfer of the merchandise from the shopping cart to the second woman's purse. He detained the pair outside the store. A search of the purse revealed the three garments plus two pair of women's undergarments, which apparently had been put there by the second woman when they split up after entering the store.

The companion admitted placing the items in her purse and leaving the store without paying for them. The first woman, the one seen placing the jackets and pants in the shopping cart, disputed the security officer's account of what happened. She denied ever placing the three garments in the shopping cart in the first place. She said that on reaching the housewares department, her companion asked her for a $40 loan to purchase the items as a gift. She testified that she did not have the money to loan her friend and told her so. The woman said her companion then left the store and she did not know if the companion had been shoplifting. Her defense was to deny possession of the two jackets and to deny transferring them to her friend for concealment in the purse.

The courtroom evidence was in direct conflict. It either happened as the security officer said it did or as the woman testified. The trial court in convicting and the appellate court in affirming the woman's conviction accepted the store's version. The basis of the conviction was the observed and the investigated evidence, produced by the security officer in the store and relied on later in court. The trial court concluded that this woman did act with the intention of permitting her companion to conceal and remove the three garments from the store without paying for them. Both the trial and the appellate court rejected the woman's defense that she did not actively participate and that she did not know her companion was shoplifting.

People v. Willard, 414 N.E.2d 504 (Illinois, 1981)

| CASE | Five Banlon shirts case |

A discount store security officer saw a man and woman enter the store and go to the wig counter, where the wife purchased a wig. She placed the wig, which was in a box, into a large paper bag. The couple was next seen going to the men's department where the husband was seen removing five shirts from the rack. After removing the price tags, he put the shirts in the large bag his wife was carrying. The couple was stopped in the vestibule between the double doors. Neither was able to produce a sales receipt when the security officer inquired about ownership of the shirts. The wife claimed she had paid for both the wig and the shirts, saying she must have left the receipt in the car.

At trial, the couple again asserted ownership by prior purchase defense. They were convicted of shoplifting the same five shirts, the conviction being affirmed by the appellate court as being supported by the evidence produced by the security officer in the store.

Kansas City v. Stoner, 424 S.W.2d 768 (Missouri, 1968)

"Sliding" means a cashier teams up with a friendly customer to shoplift. Until the companion reaches the cashier, the situation appears to be a normal transaction. At the register, the cashier can do one of two things to help his companion shoplift. The cashier may underring the register—for example, ring a $9.99 item at $2.99. A cashier may also slide merchandise by the register, meaning failing to ring it up at all. For example, the friendly customer could have nine items to purchase and the cashier rings up only six of them. Of course, a cashier could underring and slide in the same situation. Merchants in all states will encounter this type of theft in both forms.

| CASE | Friendly cashier case |

The Friendly Cashier Case demonstrates both sliding and underringing. The cashier and the customer had been lifelong friends. By prearrangement, the cashier was to give her friend "breaks," as she called it. The cashier had been under observation for some time because of continued shortages at her register. As a practical matter, this is normally how a merchant is alerted to the fact a cashier may be underringing. On the day in question, the security officer made observations of the transactions from about twelve feet away from the checkout counter. His observations established probable cause to detain the customer and cashier to investigate the facts about both sliding and underringing.

In addition to sliding some items through without ringing them on the register, the cashier was underringing others. She charged her friend only $2 for a dress with a $12 price tag. The customer handed the cashier her paycheck ($78.52) and received as her change $54.52. The security officer and store manager could see she was charged only $24 for merchandise valued at $52.51. After the sale had been completed, the parties were detained and an investigation conducted. The investigated evidence consisted of the recovered merchandise and price tags, the paycheck, the detail tape from the cash register, and the explanations offered by the two women.

State v. Boyd, 260 A2d 618 (Connecticut, 1967)

As the Friendly Cashier Case demonstrates, these situations may involve both theft of merchandise and theft of cash. Security people and merchants have a tendency to use the word *loss* as a catchall in describing theft situations. All merchants are well advised to be sure they know *before* setting up the surveillance of a cashier whether the charge will be theft of merchandise or theft of cash. Since these sliding and underringing cases are common in retail operations, deciding which charge can be filed is essential. It is also important to recover the cash register detail tape or other documentary evidence produced by point-of-sale devices. A good sliding or underringing case can become a nightmare if the merchant does not have the supporting documentary evidence to introduce as prosecution evidence at trial. These cases also involve the legal concept of aiding and abetting. Both the cashier and customer can be charged with theft of the same cash and/or merchandise.

Conclusion

In most jurisdictions, the statutory and decisional law is clear that two persons can be convicted for shoplifting the same merchandise. This is true in the joint concealment situations as demonstrated by the Companion's Purse and by the Five Banlon Shirts Cases. In the sliding and underringing cases, the merchant is confronted with having to prosecute both the employee and a customer. Since merchants generally prefer to terminate rather than prosecute dishonest employees, they should have their policy worked out in advance in these situations. It might not be wise to prosecute only the customer-companion while firing the cashier and obtaining restitution for past losses the employee may admit to. Store managers and security people should consider how these cases are going to be handled before they act.

CASES INVOLVING A FALSE REPRESENTATION

In the typical concealment, no concealment, fitting room, or circumstantial evidence shoplifting situation, the suspect does not make any representation to a store employee. Quite to the contrary, the suspect obtains possession of merchandise and walks out of the store without saying anything to anybody. As the following cases show, price tag switching, container stuffing, and cash refund schemes are situations where the customer makes a false representation to the merchant. In price tag switching cases, the suspect represents that the altered or switched price is the actual or full retail price when purchasing it. In a container stuffing situation, the suspect offers to pay the purchase price of the container (a clothes hamper, for example) but does not tell the cashier it is stuffed with other—unpurchased—merchandise. In a cash refund scheme, the suspect tells the store employee the merchandise has been lawfully purchased (which is not true) and then seeks to obtain cash in exchange for giving the store back its own merchandise, which has been shoplifted earlier.

In the following case, a man was prosecuted and convicted twice: once before a judge and the second time by a jury. The facts of the case were not in dispute, which means the question was totally one of law—to be decided by the courts in each state. The charge was filed as an ordinance violation entitled "Obtaining Money, Goods or etc. by False Pretense." At the time, it was the ordinance that should have been used by the merchant under the cash refund scheme set of facts. The ordinance was in all respects identical to the state statute. The state statute read in part as follows: "every person who, with intent to cheat or defraud another shall designedly, by color of any false token or writing, or by *any other false pretense* obtain . . . from any person any money . . . shall be guilty of a mis-demeanor" (emphasis supplied). This statute (and the identical city ordinance) required a defendant to make some type of false representation, one the victim-merchant then relied on in parting with goods or money. The essence of theft by false pretense in any state is that a victim relies on the representation as true (when it is not) and as a result of such reliance parts with property, either merchandise or cash.

| CASE | Curtains case |

A lone male entered a department store. He was not carrying any merchandise, shopping bag, briefcase, or other container. A security officer for the national department store started watching him because he resembled a man the officer had been trying to locate for other reasons. He observed the suspect enter the drapery department, kneel on the floor, and tear open the corner of a package of curtains. He then took the package to a department clerk, offered an explanation about why he was returning the package, and requested a cash refund. The clerk prepared the refund voucher, giving it to him with instructions to take it to the customer accommodations counter to obtain the refund. She told her supervisor she was suspicious of this man. The supervisor contacted the security officer who had witnessed the entire transaction. The security man told the supervisor he was aware of what the man was doing and would handle the situation. He followed the suspect to the accommodations counter and watched as he received the $46.85 in cash called for by the refund voucher. He then identified himself and asked the man to accompany him to the security office, which the man did without incident. Following an investigation of the facts, the suspect was charged with obtaining money by false pretense under the ordinance.

After being convicted the second time, the man appealed his case. The higher courts discussed the principles of law applicable to these false representation theft situations as follows:

> The false pretense need not be the sole nor even the paramount cause of the delivery of the goods or the money. It is sufficient if they are a part of the moving cause, and without them the prosecutor would not have parted with his property. As necessarily implied by the last sentence of the above quotation [from a prior case] . . . the person from whom the money was obtained *must have relied at least in part on the False representations.* [Emphasis supplied]

With these principles of law in mind, the Missouri court went on to examine the facts of the case.

The appellate court found the store did not rely on the representation made by the suspect and reversed the conviction. This meant the defendant won, and there was no chance of another trial. The court said the following:

> Applying the above rules to the facts in this case, it is apparent that the representation that Fritz [the defendant] made that he had purchased

the curtains from Ward's was not relied on even in part by Ward's. For the reason that Ward's knew from the very beginning that Fritz had not in fact purchased the curtains but had simply removed them from the shelf. Thus at *no time did Ward's rely in any part or in any degree on the representation* of Fritz when it fully knew of all the facts. [Emphasis supplied]

The court concluded that the merchant's evidence failed to prove its employees relied on the representation of the suspect in paying out the $46.85 as a cash refund. The security officer knew from the beginning that the suspect was trying to obtain the refund on merchandise he had just removed from a shelf in the drapery department. Therefore the department store as the owner did not rely on this representation. Absent evidence of reliance on the false representation, the conviction could not stand and was reversed.

Kansas City v. Fritz, 607 S.W.2d 837 (Missouri, 1980)

The irony of this case is that the merchant properly gathered all the evidence in the store and then caused the charge to be filed under the appropriate ordinance. This merchant did not make any type of evidence-gathering mistake as shown by the fact that the man was twice convicted under the evidence. This case cited a California case and a Kansas decision involving price tag switching on dresses to support its result. This means that merchants in other states could encounter the same reversal of a conviction as found in the Curtains Case. The Curtains Case was the first time the Missouri appellate courts had considered one of these false pretense cases under a retail theft set of facts. Merchants in all states should check with local prosecutors when filing cash refund scheme, price tag switching, and container stuffing cases because the existing law in the state may not be clear. By calling this situation to the attention of the local district attorney, the merchant may be doing a service to all merchants in the state, as well as helping the DA decide just how to properly file these types of retail theft cases.

CASE	Chicken and gloves case

A food store manager watched a customer switch price tags on a pair of gloves and some packages of chicken. He stood five or six feet behind the suspect as he went through the checkout line paying for the items at the lower, or switched, price. He could hear the conversation between the checker and customer. The customer-suspect said nothing about the price of any of the items in question. The man was detained outside in the parking lot. He was prosecuted for theft by false pretense and appealed his conviction.

The appellate court found the merchant-owner did not rely on the representation because the manager (like the security man in the Curtains Case) knew what was taking place. Rather than reversing this conviction outright, as done in the Curtains Case, the court modified it to find the defendant guilty of attempted theft, a lesser included offense of the one originally filed. In modifying the conviction, the court said, "We are of the view, however, that the evidence amply establishes the Defendant's attempt to commit theft. Reliance is not an element of that offense."

To avoid having to prove reliance in these cash refund scheme and price tag switching cases, the merchant may want to consider using an attempted theft or attempted theft by deceit approach. In Kansas City, Missouri (where the Curtains Case originated), merchants were instructed to file these cases as attempted theft by deceit. As the California court said in the Chicken and Gloves Case, reliance is not an element of the offense that alleges only attempt. The sample ordinance in figure 3.1 shows how merchants were told to allege attempted theft by deceit (under another ordinance) after the Curtains Case was handed down. This approach may work in other jurisdictions. Consider the sample charge now used in price tag switching and cash refund scheme cases in Kansas City, Missouri.

People v. Lorenzo, 135 Cal. Rptr. 337 (California, 1976)

| CASE | Cooler case |

In this case a man was convicted of attempted theft. The conviction was affirmed on appeal. The man was seen placing two tape decks (selling for a total of $147) in an inexpensive cooler. At the checkout counter, he held the cooler under his arm, pointing to the $6.99 price tag, which was clearly marked and not altered in any way. The cashier had been alerted by store security, who had been watching the man as he stuffed the unpurchased tape decks inside the cooler. After ringing up the $6.99 cooler, she asked to check its contents. The man denied knowing how the two tape decks got inside. On closer examination, the cooler was found to be sealed with clear tape. This discount store always used brown tape to reseal opened containers. The evidence clearly established attempt to shoplift and avoided the problem of having to prove reliance.

State v. Finch, 572 P.2d 1048 (Kansas, 1978)

| CASE | Plastic toy chest case |

A discount store security officer saw the male suspect make numerous trips through the store. He always ended up in the hardware department, where he left his shopping cart—empty. He left the store after making a few minor purchases. Investigation by security personnel revealed a cardboard box in the hardware department, one that should have contained a plastic toy chest for children, selling for $13.97. When the man returned, he went directly to the hardware department, retrieved the cardboard box, and paid the $13.97 purchase price. The cashier knew nothing about the investigative work completed by the security people. The suspect made the purchase of the toy chest and was detained in the parking lot by store security and the police. The cardboard box was found to contain several chain saws, metal rules, cigarettes, heavy-duty staple guns, and record albums, with a total selling price of over $500. This case shows the extent to which people will go in stuffing containers if they know cashiers will not check ones left in shopping carts or held under arms as they pass through checkout counters.

Kansas v. Saylor, 618 P.2d 1116 (Kansas, 1980)

Most attempted theft statutes are not contained in the general theft, larceny, shoplifting, or stealing sections under which most shoplifting cases are prosecuted. The merchant must look elsewhere to find them. The Illinois Retail Theft Act is a statute generally and correctly regarded as a good one, but even it omits an attempted theft provision. Several years ago, some interest groups and some retail trade associations put together a document called The Model Shoplifting Code, but it also failed to

FIGURE 3.1	Attempted theft by deception

In The Municipal Court of Kansas City, Missouri			Summons #G123-456
1-15-85	1234 Eastside Mall	1115 Hours	JONES, JOHN A.
3456 Main Street Anywhere USA		Age 35	Date of Birth: 3-18-49

DID WITHIN THE CITY LIMITS COMMIT THE FOLLOWING OFFENSE: Did intentionally attempt to steal property of value from and belonging to the ABC Department store by means of deceit, to-wit; did change price label on a sweater from $29.95 to $19.95 and attempt to pay the lower price, knowing this was not the offered price.

In violation of Revised Ordinances: Chapter _____ Section _____
                                  Penalty Section _____

Bond: $25	Court Date: 2-18-85	Time: 8:30 AM	Division #108

COMPLAINANT: /s/ Store Security Officer   Arresting Officer: /s/ Police Officer

contain an attempted theft provision in the final draft. Clearly even merchants can overlook the fundamentals of the problem.

Merchants in any state with questions about when and how to file price tag switching, container stuffing, and cash refund cases should check with the local prosecutor. If there is a change in the law in a particular state, it will come from the appellate court. The prosecutor's office will be the first to know about it. Part of the prosecutor's job is to keep up with changes in the state decisional law as they relate to criminal prosecutions.

CIRCUMSTANTIAL EVIDENCE CASES

In a direct evidence case, a store employee actually sees the suspect obtain wrongful possession of unpurchased merchandise. For example, a woman may conceal panty hose in her purse and leave without paying, or a man may place a hat on his head and walk out of the store. The heart of the store's prosecution case is this observation of the suspect obtaining wrongful possession and leaving without paying. What about a fitting room case? A store detective does not witness the woman concealing the garment in her purse, because she is in the fitting room. Probable cause to detain is then established by the "circumstances" surrounding the woman's entry and exit from the fitting room. Here the circumstances lead to the reasonable conclusion that the woman obtained wrongful possession by concealing the item while out of view in the fitting room.

As a general rule, circumstantial evidence cases are not as strong as ones that involve direct evidence. In circumstantial cases, the store must produce evidence to prove all the elements of the offense just like in a direct evidence case. A conviction can be obtained by presenting circumstantial evidence, and merchants will encounter these situations. Training programs should devote some time to understanding how to establish a prosecutable case with circumstantial evidence.

CASE	Two dresses case

This case shows where store witnesses were present at various stages while the observed facts were being produced on the sales floor. Although the second officer did not see the woman enter the fitting room, her testimony in court was used to prosecute the case. A female security officer saw a female suspect, carrying a shopping bag, select three dresses from the rack and enter a fitting room. While the woman was in the fitting room, the first security officer was joined by the second one. Both watched as the woman exited, now with only two dresses in her hand. She placed both back on the rack. Still carrying the shopping bag, she left the area. A fitting room check by one of the officers revealed no dress or price tag and garment labels. The circumstances supported the reasonable belief that the woman had placed the missing dress in the shopping bag. Based on this evidence, the security officers were justified in detaining the woman for investigation. The woman voluntarily went to the security office, setting the shopping bag on a table. The store employees recovered the missing dress from the bag. They asked her if she had any more merchandise she had not purchased. The suspect then removed a second dress from inside her panty hose. Both dresses still had the store's price tag affixed to them. By observations and by this investigation, the two security officers produced evidence to justify the decision to detain and to prosecute without ever seeing their suspect actually conceal the dresses.

People v. Jablonskis, 381 N.E.2d 774 (Illinois, 1980)

The circumstances surrounding the woman's entry-exit from the fitting room, coupled with the fitting room check, supported the decision to detain. After completing the fitting room check, these retail employees had seen and investigated enough to justify a belief that the woman intended to shoplift dresses owned and offered for sale by the store. Just as in a case involving concealment or no concealment, the next step was to detain and investigate by obtaining her explanation and recovering the merchandise.

In the following fitting room situations, the circumstances always include a fitting room check after the suspect leaves and support the reasonable belief the suspect is in possession of merchandise owned by the store and does not intend to pay for it.

A woman is seen taking some blouses from the rack and entering the fitting room. When she leaves she places all of them back. A check of the blouses on the rack reveals one is not store merchandise but the blouse she wore into the fitting room. A check of the fitting room shows no merchandise, price tags, or garment labels. This suspect has removed her blouse, put it on the hanger and returned it to the rack, wearing the store's blouse.

In another situation, a man takes a pair of $11 swim trunks into the fitting room. He leaves with nothing in his hands and a bulge in the front of his pants. A fitting room check reveals no swim trunks.

A woman takes a pair of jogging pants into the fitting room. When she leaves, the security officer sees part of the yellow jogging pants sticking out from under the bottom of the slacks the woman is wearing. A fitting room check reveals no jogging pants.

The following case is hypothetical. On a warm fall day, a cosmetics clerk working on the first floor of a fashionable department store saw a woman enter the store. She was not wearing or carrying a coat. The woman went to the second floor to the better coats department. With the assistance of a female sales clerk, she tried on several expensive coats. The clerk did not actually see this woman leave the department, but she noticed after the woman left an empty hanger in the area where the woman had been trying on coats. No other customers had been in the department during the time the woman was there.

Back on the first floor, the same observant cosmetics clerk saw the woman, now carrying a black coat over her arm. By this time, the sales clerk in the coat department had notified the manager about the empty hanger. The manager checked with the cosmetics clerk, who verified that the woman had not been wearing or carrying a coat when she entered earlier. A further check revealed that no coat of this type or description had been sold that day.

None of the employees (store manager, cosmetics clerk, or sales clerk in the better coats department) had actually seen the woman remove the coat from the rack. No employee had seen her put it over her arm, leave the second floor, and take the escalator to the first floor. This is a classic circumstantial evidence case. The circumstances showed a coat was missing and was not purchased. The woman suspect was present in the coat department. The facts had reasonably eliminated the possibility that another customer had removed the coat from the rack and left the hanger. The cosmetics clerk's observations indicated the woman had come in without a coat and now was in possession of a coat. The store manager was now confronted with deciding whether probable cause existed to detain the woman and investigate the situation.

The collective circumstances here would justify detaining to investigate. The crucial facts were her presence in the department, the missing coat, the hanger still on the rack, the time element, and the observations of the cosmetics clerk. In this situation, it was reasonable to conclude the woman was in possession of unpurchased merchandise. No concealment was involved. The manager, upon detaining the woman, would, of course, ask her to explain the circumstances and listen intently as she did. He would have to translate her explanation into either a claim of ownership or a denial of intent to shoplift. If the case is prosecuted, a key piece of evidence would be the hanger. All three employees would be required to testify in court about their respective observations. The woman's explanation to the manager would most likely determine whether the case was prosecuted or she was released—after recovering this $700 coat.

CASE	Green leather coat case

A department store obtained a conviction in a case where no employee saw a woman remove a leather coat from the rack. About 5:00 P.M., a security officer saw this woman leaving the store with a leather coat, folded inside out, over her arm. About fifteen minutes later, he saw the same woman reenter the store neither carrying nor wearing a coat. He followed her to the second floor women's sportswear department, leaving the sales floor for several minutes to notify the security director about the situation. When the two returned to the floor, the woman was seen standing a few feet away from a circular rack containing leather coats. She had a green leather coat, turned inside out, over her arm. They checked with the department manager, who said she had not seen the woman remove any garments from the rack or even try on any leather coats. As the suspect moved out of the department, the manager checked the coats on the rack, finding one empty hanger and one leather coat missing.

This incident took place at the store's west side branch, the other store being on the far east side of the city. The woman was detained after going down the escalator from the second floor just as she was about to leave by the mall exit. She said she had bought the coat at the store's east side branch but did not have a sales receipt with her at the time. An off-duty police officer working mall security was summoned. Based on the facts supplied to him by the store employees, he made the warrantless arrest. The woman was convicted of felony shoplifting, the conviction being affirmed on appeal. The store did have to bring in the buyer at trial to establish that this particular model of coat was never carried at the east side store.

State v. Garner, 538 S.W.2d 937 (Missouri, 1976)

As this case demonstrates, it often takes the observations and investigative activity of several employees to establish probable cause to detain in circumstantial cases. The Green Leather Coat Case is also an example of how evidence is produced by the store employees rather than by the responding police officer. The department store employees had produced all evidence necessary to make a decision when they summoned the police officer.

Detention statutes make no distinction as to whether the suspect is detained on direct or circumstantial evidence. The only requirement is that the evidence establish probable cause. The same is true in court. A person can be convicted of shoplifting based on either direct or circumstantial evidence. The only requirement is that the evidence establish all the elements of the offense. In a direct evidence case, there is no question that the suspect is in possession of merchandise because a store employee watched it being concealed. In circumstantial evidence cases, the fact that a suspect is in wrongful possession of merchandise is less obvious. Obtaining convictions in circumstantial evidence cases is always more difficult.

4

Gathering Prosecution and Defense Evidence

This chapter presents an evidence-gathering guide that a merchant in any state can use in the store to identify and gather prosecution and defense evidence. The *Sources of Evidence* set forth in Figure 4.1 are simple and logical. The figure presents a step-by- step procedure that store manager or security person can use to produce evidence in the store to rely on in court to prove the elements of the offense.

The merchant obtains a conviction in court by first producing facts in the store. Weeks later in court, these facts are presented as evidence to prove the elements of the offense. All the evidence a merchant must rely on later in court is available in the store the day the suspect is detained. The value of the chart (Figure 4.1) is to ensure that store managers and security people do not overlook any facts in the store that will be needed in court. By incorporating this chart or some form of it into training programs, a merchant is reducing the chance of making an evidence-gathering mistake in the store. Evidence-gathering mistakes result in the filing of weak or nonprosecutable shoplifting cases, ones that merchants lose.

As the chart shows, a merchant must make two decisions in the store: (1) to detain the suspect for investigation of the facts and (2) to prosecute the case or release the suspect. Both decisions must be supported by evidence found in the store. The key to effective prosecution of shoplifting cases with minimal civil liability exposure is the ability to make decisions supported by evidence rather than ones based on suspicion or opinion.

There are two types of evidence presented by merchants in court to obtain convictions in a shoplifting case.

	Sources of Evidence: Two sources of store prosecution evidence needed to convict a suspect in any case involving
FIGURE 4.1	concealment

Source 1   Personal Observations Made by a Retail Employee on the Sales Floor before Detaining the Suspect for Investigation

A retail employee testifies in court that he saw the suspect do the following:

1. The suspect removed merchandise from a rack, counter, or shelf with his hands.
2. The suspect concealed the merchandise—most commonly in a pocket, purse, or shopping bag or underneath clothing.
3. The suspect continued the concealment past the last station for receiving payment for merchandise.
4. The suspect was given an opportunity to pay for the merchandise but failed to pay at the last cash register.
5. The suspect was detained after passing the last cash register.
6. The retail employee's observations were constant and unbroken.

Decision to Detain on Probable Cause

After making these observations, a store employee has established probable cause and may detain for investigation of the facts. The employee has not made a citizen's arrest but rather is detaining under the merchant's privilege as incorporated into detention statutes in each state.

Source 2   Investigated Facts Produced in a Manager's or Security Office after Detaining and before Deciding to Prosecute

The store manager or security person must testify in court about the procedure he followed in conducting this investigation of the facts.

7. The suspect was given an opportunity to explain the situation.
8. The suspect's explanation was translated into one of the two formal defenses.
   a. A suspect denies intent to shoplift by making explanations such as "I forgot to pay for the merchandise."
   b. A suspect claims ownership of the merchandise by saying, "I bought it earlier at your store" or "I bought it at another store." Sometimes suspects claim ownership by gift.
9. The concealed merchandise is recovered and examined.
10. The merchandise is identified as belonging to the store by a price tag, garment label, or other inventory-control document.
11. The employee reviewed the evidence, both prosecution and defense evidence, before making the decision to file the charge.

Decision to File the Charge or Release the Suspect

(1) Call the police and authorize them to make the warrantless arrest or (2) release the suspect because the evidence later in court will not prove the elements of the offense of shoplifting.

TESTIMONIAL EVIDENCE	Observations of a suspect on the sales floor removing merchandise from its place of display, concealing it, and leaving without paying for the goods.
REAL OR PHYSICAL EVIDENCE	The merchandise and price tag recovered by the retail employee after detaining the suspect for investigation of the facts.

When a retail employee takes the witness stand and relates the observations he made and the investigative activities he conducted, this witness is presenting testimonial evidence. In most cases, the witness is describing a person who was seen concealing merchandise. In other cases, the witness describes price tag switching, container stuffing, fitting room shoplifting, or a situation where more than one person was involved in the shoplifting effort. Shoplifting cases in all states start out with a store witness presenting testimonial evidence. The witness is testifying about what he observed and did weeks earlier in the store the day the suspect was detained.

In all shoplifting cases, the real or physical evidence consists of the recovered merchandise and the price tag. In court the store witness describes his investigative activities conducted after the suspect was detained on probable cause. The witness will tell about recovering the merchandise and examining it to determine that it was not purchased. Next, the prosecutor will ask the witness to identify the merchandise he brought to court that day and to tell if it is the same merchandise recovered on the day of the detention. Then, both the merchandise and price tag are offered into evidence by the district attorney as a store prosecution exhibit.

The third type of evidence used by merchants is *defense evidence*: the statement made by the suspect that day in the store. This statement will take one of two forms: an admission of guilt or a denial of guilt. In some cases, such as the Slacks in the Car Trunk Case in Chapter 3, the suspects elected not to make an explanation. In most cases, the explanation made by the suspect to the retail employee in the store will not be an admission of guilt. Instead the suspect will either claim ownership of the merchandise ("I bought it at another store") or will deny intent to shoplift ("I forgot to pay"). If the explanation takes either form of denial, then in court, it cannot be used as store prosecution evidence to prove the elements of the offense. There is nothing to prohibit the store witness from saying the suspect said "I forgot to pay" or "I bought it at another store," but those statements are not evidence of guilt. A denial is defense evidence. It will not prove any element of the store's prosecution case. Much of this chapter will be devoted to teaching merchants the importance of obtaining a suspect's explanation in the store as part of the evidence-gathering process.

Consider the following outline of courtroom testimony showing these three types of evidence in a hypothetical case.

Testimonial evidence in a case involving concealment: The store witness will testify as follows: "I saw the defendant standing near the rack of panty hose. She had been in the store about ten minutes. She was carrying her purse and a shopping basket. Before reaching the panty hose display rack, she had placed some other merchandise in the basket. I saw her remove the panty hose from the rack, examine them for a moment, look around, then drop them in her purse. She walked around for about five minutes, examining other merchandise. She then went through the checkout counter, paying for the items in the basket. She did not remove the panty hose from her purse and pay for them. I detained her right at the exit."[1]

Suspect's Explanation: The store witness continues: "When I detained her, I asked her if she had a receipt for the panty hose in her purse. She looked startled and said, 'Oh. I must have forgotten to pay for them.' She reached inside her purse and produced the panty hose, handing them to me. She said, 'I intended to pay for them all along but had my mind on other things. You see, I am going through a divorce [or my mother is sick in the hospital or I just lost my job].' She then said she had both cash and two valid credit cards in her purse which could be used to pay for the $1.49 pair of panty hose. She offered to pay for them, saying she had never done anything like this before. I told her she would have to come with me to the office for a few minutes. We walked to the security office."

Real or physical evidence: The store witness continues to testify: "As mentioned, she handed me the panty hose out on the sales floor when I detained her. At that instant I could see they had our price tag on it. In the security office, I examined the panty hose and price tag. It was our merchandise with out price tag on it. After listening to her explanation, I decided to have her formally arrested and prosecuted for shoplifting. I then marked the price tag with my initials and the date. The merchandise was put into a sack, dated with the case number and kept for evidence at trial." The prosecutor now asks the

---

[1]Based on these observations, the store witness has established probable cause to detain the woman and investigate the facts. Since this is not a civil action but a criminal trial, these observations must also establish the first two elements of the offense of shoplifting: the suspect's wrongful possession of the panty hose and her intention to steal (rather than pay for) them.

witness to open the sack: "Yes, this is the pair of panty hose I recovered from this defendant. Here are my initials and the date." Witness now hands merchandise to prosecutor who offers it to the judge as a prosecution exhibit.

The testimonial evidence showed the woman obtained wrongful possession of the panty hose by concealing them in her purse. It established intent to shoplift by showing she went through the checkout counter without paying or attempting to pay for them. The physical evidence established the two remaining elements of the offense—store ownership of the panty hose and their value. The witness testified about the explanation he received, not because it proved an element of the offense but for another reason. If her testimony in court was different than the explanation given in the store, the prosecutor could impeach her credibility by making reference to prior inconsistent statements. In shoplifting cases, the store witness will present testimonial physical evidence, and the defendent's statement as part of the store's prosecution case. Some prosecutors may not want the store witness to put the defendant's explanation into evidence and wait to see if the defendant makes an inconsistent statement before impeaching. This is a matter of strategy, so check with local prosecutors on the point.

Figure 4.1 (the *Sources of Evidence* chart) is an evidence-gathering chart—one merchants can use in their stores to produce evidence needed to establish a prosecutable case. The chart shows that merchants must make two decisions, both supported by evidence. It is important for merchants to understand that evidence gathering is a logical process. By using this chart to gather evidence, the retailer is better equipped to make the decision to detain and the decision to prosecute or release.

PRODUCING EVIDENCE TO ESTABLISH PROBABLE CAUSE

Probable cause to detain is established by watching a suspect on the selling floor as demonstrated by steps 1–6 on the *Sources of Evidence* chart. The term "probable cause" is not found in any shoplifting prosecution statute. It comes from the law of warrantless arrest. It is also found in the merchant's privilege statutes. Retailers sometimes think of probable cause only as the evidential test they must meet to detain a suspect without incurring false-imprisonment type liability. Probable cause has another meaning, one in criminal law. When a retail employee makes an observation on the sales floor, one that establishes probable cause, this observation will become testimonial evidence to prove two elements of the offense. By establishing probable cause, a retail employee is accom-

TABLE 4.1	Shoplifting prosecution evidence—probable cause
In the store	Later in court to establish the elements of the offense
Sales floor—Probable cause established here.	
Observations made here establish two elements of the offense, as shown in the next column.	1. Wrongful possession of the merchandise. 2. The suspect intended to shoplift it.

plishing a dual legal goal: (1) the detention is justified under the merchant's privilege so no civil liability for false imprisonment will automatically result, and (2) the employee has produced evidence to establish two elements of the offense, namely wrongful possession and that the suspect intended to shoplift.

Table 4.1 shows how the observations made on the sales floor establish two elements of the offense.

In criminal law, probable cause means the evidence shows that an offense has been committed and it is reasonable to believe that a specific person committed it. In shoplifting cases, there is usually no problem with identification of the suspect, because the merchant has the person under observation from the time of concealment to the time of detention. The more tricky question is whether the observations furnish enough evidence to form a reasonable belief the suspect is committing a crime. Just by watching a suspect the merchant produces evidence that later in court will establish wrongful possession of merchandise and that the suspect intended to shoplift it. From what has been said, it is obvious that more evidence must be produced to determine if a prosecutable case exists. Probable cause to detain and investigate the facts means just that in both the criminal law and under the merchant's privilege.

To establish the two remaining elements of the offense, store ownership of merchandise and its value, a merchant must conduct an investigation *after* detaining on probable cause. Probable cause is really a legal form of shorthand that describes the minimum amount of evidence the courts require a merchant to produce before a detention is justified. As pointed out in Chapter 3, there are five basic shoplifting situations a merchant will encounter. In each one, the suspect will have obtained wrongful possession of merchandise and be in the process of leaving without paying the full retail value when detained. The diagram (Figure 4.2) shows that merchants must meet the probable cause evidence test

FIGURE 4.2	Direct and circumstantial evidence situations

PROBABLE CAUSE TO DETAIN—must be established in all shoplifting situations encountered by retail employees in their stores

Percent of cases

Direct evidence situations

70   1. Concealment involved

30   2. No concealment involved
        3. Aiding and abetting involved
          a. Lookout situations
          b. Diversion situations
          c. Joint participation in concealment

        4. False representation involved
          a. Price tag switching
          b. Container stuffing
          c. Case refund schemes

Circumstantial evidence situations

        1. Fitting room situations
        2. Suspect not seen removing goods from their place of display

each time they detain a suspect, no matter which shoplifting situation is encountered.

How people obtain wrongful possession is not what counts from a legal point of view. All shoplifting cases have one thing in common: the suspect obtains wrongful possession of the merchandise and walks out without paying. In most cases, the suspect does not pay at all. In price tag switching cases, the suspect pays the lower or switched price, thus making his possession legally wrongful. Training programs must hammer home this point about wrongful possession. A suspect obtains possession in just one way: with his hands. After obtaining possession (with the hands), the suspect may conceal the item, switch a price tag, pass the item off to a companion who conceals it, or carry the merchandise out of the store without any attempt whatsoever to conceal it. In each situation, the suspect is in wrongful possession of the merchandise and may be detained because the probable cause evidence test has been met.

The *Sources of Evidence* chart (Figure 4.1) sets forth steps to follow in a shoplifting situation involving concealment. Probable cause to detain a suspect is established by completing steps 1–6. By now the retail employee has made sufficient observations to justify detaining the suspect for further investigation. At this point, the merchant cannot make a decision to prosecute or release the suspect, because an investigation and review of the facts has not yet taken place. The investigate phase of the encounter with a shoplifting suspect is accomplished by completing steps 7–11 on the chart. The investigation includes giving the suspect an opportunity to explain and translating that explanation into its legal meaning. Only after completing steps 7–11 is the detaining merchant in possession of enough evidence to decide whether to prosecute the case or to release the suspect. By using some form of this chart, a merchant in any state will avoid making evidence-gathering mistakes, ones which cause stores to file nonprosecutable shoplifting cases and lose them.

Establishing a prosecutable case is much like following a recipe in a cookbook. The cook may wish to prepare a cake, for example. The recipe calls for certain ingredients. If the cook fails to include one or more of those ingredients in the recipe, the cake will fall. It is the same with producing evidence to establish a prosecutable shoplifting case. If the merchant has failed to produce evidence in the store to prove one of the elements of the offense in court, the judge will say the case falls—meaning falls short legally because of insufficient evidence. The judge will dismiss the case if the store's evidence does not prove *all* the elements of the offense as found in the legal cookbook, the shoplifting prosecution statute. The first part of any legal recipe is to establish probable cause, regardless of the type of shoplifting situation. The next part is to investigate the facts and make a decision about how to handle the case.

ESTABLISHING THE SUSPECT'S DEFENSE AFTER DETAINING ON PROBABLE CAUSE

Merchants often overlook the fact there are two sides to the trial of a shoplifting case. Evidence gathering is a process by which the merchant produces facts in the store which will be used by *both* sides later at trial if the decision is to prosecute. Steps 7 and 8 require that the merchant, as part of the evidence-gathering process, produce the facts which the suspect will use at trial as the formal courtroom defense to the charge. At the time the merchant is obtaining a suspect's explanation, that merchant does not yet know if the case will be prosecuted. Consider the simple diagram which follows, for it shows how a judge or jury at trial listens to both the prosecution and defense evidence before making a decision. (See Figure 4.3).

A merchant who fails to establish and evaluate the suspect's defense is at a distinct disadvantage in deciding whether to file the shoplifting charge. The reason is obvious—the merchant has only half the evidence. In court, a judge or jury will not make a decision until hearing both the

| FIGURE 4.3 | Prosecution and defense evidence at trial |

Jury hears both sides
before making a decision

The store's prosecution case	The suspect's defense to the charge
Evidence presented by store witness to establish each element of the offense	Evidence presented to establish one defense or the other
1. Suspect obtained wrongful possession of unpurchased merchandise 2. Suspect intended to shoplift the merchandise in question 3. Store owned merchandise in question 4. Value of merchandise was a specific dollar amount	1. Suspect denies intent to shplift 2. Suspect claims ownership

Decision

1. Guilty of shoplifting
2. Not guilty of shoplifting

prosecution and defense evidence. Merchants must learn to do the same thing—listen to both sides—in the store.

There are two courtroom defenses to a shoplifting case having to do with the evidence: a defendant will either deny intent to shoplift or claim ownership. When detained in the store, the suspect will not make his explanation in formal legal terms. He will not say, "I am denying intent to shoplift," but rather "I forgot to pay" or "I intended to pay." In other situations, the suspect will not say, "I am claiming ownership by prior purchase," but "I bought it earlier at your store" or "I bought it at another store."

The merchant's first job is to recognize these explanations for what they really are: defense evidence. Consider the two defenses in the way a store manager or security person hears them expressed by a suspect in the store after detaining that suspect on probable cause:

Suspect denies intent to shoplift: By saying he forgot to pay or intended to pay, the suspect is denying the existence of criminal intent to shoplift. The suspect is admitting the removal of the item from its place of display, its concealment, the fact the concealment continued past the last cash register, that no payment was made, and that the store is the owner. The suspect is saying the reason he failed to pay was because of an accident or good faith mistake rather than because of criminal intent. In the Scarf Case in chapter 3, for example, the woman put the scarf through the loop on her purse and walked out without paying for it. When detained, she told the security person she forgot to pay. She was not claiming ownership of the scarf but simply denying intent to shoplift it.

Suspect claims ownership of merchandise by prior purchase: Most commonly, the suspect will claim ownership by saying "I bought the merchandise at another store" or "I wore the garment in the store" or "I was returning the merchandise for a refund or an exchange" or "I bought the goods last week at your store." In the Two Flair Pens Case in chapter 3, for example, the young man who had been seen taking the pens out of the blister pack and putting them in his pocket claimed ownership by prior purchase. When detained after passing through the checkout counter with the pens in his shirt pocket, he said he had them in his pocket when he entered the store.

The trial of a shoplifting case is a contest based on evidence. The side with the stronger evidence wins the contest. To convict at trial, the merchant must prove the suspect intended to shoplift and did not just forget to pay, as the suspect will be claiming in court. In other cases, the merchant must prove the store was actually the owner of the goods in question and the suspect did not previously purchase them, as the suspect will be claiming. In a contest, there is always a dispute. At the trial of a shoplifting case, the defendant will always dispute the sufficiency of the store's evidence to prove either intent to shoplift or store ownership. Store managers and security people who do not establish the suspect's defense in the store and then evaluate the merits of the defense increase the chance of filing weak or nonprosecutable shoplifting cases.

Denial of Intent to Shoplift

CASE	Razor blades case

This case involves prosecution where a single inexpensive item was involved. The problem was that the security people were not realistic about how the man's defense would be received in court. This case also shows how security people sometimes make no effort to verify a suspect's explanation after obtaining it. In this case, he was not claiming ownership. He was saying he intended to pay for the razor blades later when his wife completed her shopping. The store made no effort to find the wife and check out the man's explanation before calling the police and having him prosecuted. This man was not a professional shoplifter. He had no criminal record. He appeared to be an average citizen shoplifter, such as merchants encounter every day. In these single inexpensive item cases, these average citizen shoplifters have a good chance of being acquitted using the "I forgot to pay" defense.

In this case, a man was seen picking up a package of razor blades from the counter in a discount store. He moved toward the checkout counter area with them in his hand. When standing adjacent to the door, he folded the package of blades, placed them in his pants pocket, and began to roll a cigarette. Finally, he walked just outside the door, lit the cigarette, and was standing there smoking it when detained by a store security person. He had made no effort to move away from the door after lighting the cigarette. The security person had been watching him since he picked the blades up a few minutes earlier.

He voluntarily accompanied the security person back to the office. He said he intended to pay for them when his wife, who was still shopping in the store, came through the checkout line. He was required to empty his pockets, patted down by one of the officers to see if he was carrying a weapon (none was found), photographed, and asked to sign a document. It was a combination waiver of rights and confession of guilt form. He signed the document, explaining at trial that he did not understand what he was signing.

His testimony was that he tried, unsuccessfully, to get the guards to locate his wife. He told them she could not pay for her merchandise because she did not have check cashing authority with the store, but he did. He said it was his intention to pay for the razor blades when she finished shopping. The officers refused to try to locate her or otherwise verify his explanation. He was held for forty-five minutes and not allowed to contact anyone. When the police arrived, he was formally charged with shoplifting the razor blades. In the meantime, the store had closed. Because no effort had been made to contact her, the wife became concerned about her husband's absence. She waited in the car.

In court the only issue was whether he intended to shoplift or forgot to pay. Store ownership of the razor blades was never in dispute, either in the store or at the trial. The man was acquitted.

After winning the shoplifting case, he filed a civil action against the store. In affirming the jury award in his favor, the appellate court made the following statement about the decision to detain and the failure of security people to investigate the merits of his explanation before having him arrested and prosecuted.

> We concede [that] from what they had observed the store employees were justified in forming an initial opinion that the plaintiff [the suspect] was about to leave the premises without paying for the razor blades. However, their arbitrary refusal to investigate his explanation was unreasonable. Had this been done, it would have revealed [that] he intended to go through the checkout line with his wife to enable her to use his driver's license as identification to cash a check and pay for purchases.

> It would be improper to indulge in the presumption that he would not
> have paid for this .99¢ item at that time.

The court is saying that the decision to detain for investigation of the facts was
properly made; it was supported by observations the security people made on
the sales floor. The crucial point is that the court found the "arbitrary refusal
to investigate his explanation was unreasonable." Said another way, the court
found that the store failed to establish the suspect's defense and take it into
consideration before calling the police and having him prosecuted.

Consider another quote from this case:

> To refuse to verify information easily obtainable and within the
> confines of the store showed a complete disregard for the exercise of
> reasonable care in ascertaining all facts before making a serious
> accusation against a customer. Had this been done prior to calling the
> police it is unlikely the plaintiff would have been the victim of a
> criminal charge by the police officer.

The court is saying that failure to investigate the defense before calling the
police shows the security people did not "exercise reasonable care in
ascertaining all the facts." Simply stated, the court is saying the store must
investigate the merits of the defense before prosecuting the case. Had the
security people bothered to check with the wife, she would have verified his
explanation. They would have known she would be a defense witness in
court. They would have known from experience that convicting this man for
shoplifting a $.99 package of razor blades with his wife as a defense witness
would be next to impossible. This man was denying he intended to shoplift
razor blades, which he admitted were owned by the discount store. By
establishing his defense as part of the evidence-gathering process and
investigating it, the store could easily have decided not to prosecute.

Brasher v. Gibsons Discount Stores, 306 S.2d 843 (Louisiana, 1975)

Store managers and security people must learn to evaluate these "I
forgot to pay" cases on the basis of the surrounding circumstances and the
suspect's credibility. Compare two situations from opposite ends of the
spectrum. A nineteen-year-old male has just grabbed six pairs of designer
jeans from a counter top and bolted out the door. When detained in the
mall parking lot by two security staff members, he says, "I forgot to pay."
Clearly no judge or jury would accept this explanation as the truth in court
when offered as the formal courtroom defense. Now consider the same "I
forgot to pay" explanation when made by a sixty-six-year-old woman who
put a $.79 greeting card in her purse and left without paying. The security
staff member or store manager who files this case without giving it some
serious consideration is about to lose it. The woman has a defense, the
same one offered by the young man in the designer jeans case. The difference is that the woman's defense has an excellent chance of being

accepted later in court. Her defense will most likely produce an acquittal.

| CASE | $1.97 bra case: |

This is another example where a security person violated the last cash register rule, thereby not producing evidence to prove the suspect intended to shoplift. Two evidence-gathering mistakes were made: (1) the bra was not completely concealed and (2) the woman was detained before even starting to go through the checkout line. These two facts, coupled with her explanation denying intent to shoplift, should have told the security person not to file the case. Consider the facts as set forth by the court. Pay particular attention to the comment that she was detained before trying to leave the store:

> Appellant [the suspect] was completing some Christmas shopping in the K-Mart store when a security guard saw her place a packaged bra in her purse. She then placed the open purse in the seat part of the shopping cart which contained other merchandise she had selected. She continued her shopping. A short time later the security guard approached her. *She had not yet gone through the check-out line or attempted to leave the store.* He requested she accompany him to the security office where she denied any intent to take the bra without paying for it.
>
> At the hearing appellant testified she was preoccupied and upset while shopping. Her mind was on her mother, dying of cancer in a local hospital, and she did not realize what she was doing when she put the bra in her purse. She testified she had no intention of taking the bra but had taken out her wallet to get a shopping list and her money. The package with the bra was in her hand, and without realizing what she was doing, she put the package in her purse when she put the wallet back. [Emphasis supplied]

Commonwealth v. Bonn (Pennsylvania, 1976)

The evidence-gathering mistake in the $1.97 Bra Case was detaining before the woman passed through the checkout counter. The security officer had not yet observed the woman demonstrate that she intended to shoplift. When detained, she denied any intention to shoplift, saying she intended to pay. He had not given her enough time to demonstrate objectively whether she was going to pay or fail to pay. By contrast, the man with the razor blades had passed around (not through) the checkout counter, so the evidence to demonstrate he intended to pay was stronger. The problem was that he had a defense witness—his wife. Both cases involved single inexpensive items. Both cases demonstrate situations where a selective prosecution approach would have been effective. Under the merchant's privilege statutes, neither case had to be prosecuted. As a practical matter, neither case should have been prosecuted.

By now, the retailer knows that facts he produces in the store must be relied on later in court to establish the elements of the offense. The suspect does the same thing: relies on what happens in the store as his defense later in court. To defend the charge, a person will point out evidence-gathering mistakes made by a retail employee. If a security person detains a suspect before that suspect has passed the last cash register (in a department store) or before the suspect has gone through the checkout counter (in a discount, drug, or food store), it is a sure bet that the security person will hear the following argument later in court. Suppose the case involved the $1.49 pair of panty hose:

> *Defense lawyer*: I move this case be dismissed and my client found not guilty because the store's evidence fails to establish the element of intent to shoplift. The security officer testified he stopped her right after she dropped the panty hose in her purse. He did not wait until she passed through the checkout line and failed to pay for those panty hose. In other words, he did not give her an opportunity pay for the merchandise before detaining and charging her with shoplifting. She told him she "intended to pay" for the $1.49 item, that she had two valid credit cards as well as $33 in cash to use in making the purchase. The store has failed to produce evidence that shows my client intended to shoplift. The case should be dismissed because the store has failed to prove the element of intent to shoplift as required by the shoplifting prosecution statute.

Security people with experience in court have heard this defense argument made, and with success. For this reason, they wait until the suspect has passed the last cash register before detaining. They know the defense lawyer will rely on this type of evidence-gathering mistake in court.

A Claim of Ownership

The second defense to a shoplifting charge is a claim of ownership. In the two cases which follow, the persons detained told the retail employee they had previously purchased the items in question, thereby setting up the courtroom defense of ownership. If the store files a charge, the store is claiming to be the owner. If the suspect has claimed ownership in his explanation in the store, this means both parties are saying they own the merchandise in question. In court guilt will be decided on the basis of whether the store can prove its ownership.

One reason merchants make no effort to establish a suspect's defense is they mistakenly believe that "concealment equals guilt." The fact that a retail employee sees a person conceal merchandise *does not* relieve that employee of the duty to establish the suspect's defense by giving that person an opportunity to explain the circumstances surrounding his possession. An investigation of the facts begins by giving the person an opportunity to explain. Merchants produce evidence with both their *eyes* *and ears*. The Socket Wrench and Toothpaste Cases which follow are excellent examples of stores ignoring a suspect's explanation (a claim of ownership in both cases), then filing and losing the shoplifting case. After losing the shoplifting cases, both stores (one in Virginia and one in Oregon) were sued civilly for malicious prosecution. It all happened because the security people handling the cases had not been taught to establish the suspect's defense after detaining on probable cause.

CASE	Socket wrench case

In the Socket Wrench Case, two security employees of a national department store in Portland, Oregon, saw a man place some socket wrenches in his hip pocket while in the hardware department. He was detained just as he went through the double doors leading to the street. The testimony of the two employees shows they believed that concealment equals guilt. One said that because he saw the man put the sockets in his pocket that he never considered the possibility that he was telling the truth about having previously purchased them. The other officer said he made the decision to file the shoplifting charge when the man went through the doors and before talking with him. He further testified that the purpose of the "interrogation," as he called it, was twofold: to hold the man for the arrival of the police and to obtain a confession-type statement. Neither security man testified that it was store procedure to detain and investigate the facts before making the decision to call the police.

The suspect testified that following his detention, he was taken to a security office, searched for weapons, photographed,* and asked to sign a confession-type statement. He refused to sign the statement and tried to tell the security people that the sockets had been previously purchased. He had no sales receipt but said he had shown them to the service manager at a garage who told them they did not properly fit and to take them back, which he was doing. The security people ignored his explanation, failing to translate it into the courtroom defense of a claim of ownership. They also failed to recognize that the service manager could become a defense witness at trial, verifying the suspect's claim of ownership.

Neither employee mistreated the suspect. There was no use of force, no accusations of shoplifting made, no forcing of a search or threats of prosecution made to obtain the confession or civil liability release. The mistake made here was an evidence-gathering one, pure and simple. These security people made no effort to establish and investigate the merits of the man's defense before making their decision to prosecute the case.

At trial, the shoplifting case was lost because the store's prosecution evidence failed to establish an element of the offense—ownership of the socket wrenches. Both the defendant and the service manager testified the sockets had been previously purchased. This was exactly what the defendant had told the two security men that day in the store. He was telling them the evidence reason they would lose the shoplifting case if one was filed. This national department store apparently had no policy requiring security people to establish a suspect's defense and then investigate the merits of it *before* deciding to have suspects arrested and prosecuted. The defense evidence—a claim of ownership—was there and available to the security men that day in the store, but they failed to recognize its legal meaning or value. This store policy was not based on using an evidence- gathering chart, one which required employees to consider the merits of the defense before making the decision to prosecute.

As Figure 4.4 shows, probable cause to detain was established. The security employees could answer "yes" to steps 1–6 (from Figure 4.1). Their answers to steps 8–11 were "no" because all they did was recover the wrenches (step 7). Remember that the suspect will also be relying on facts in court to establish his defense. Here the man relied on what he told the security people: that he had a witness who would verify his claim of ownership. He also relied on the fact that the store employees did not produce a price tag, which admittedly would have been difficult considering the merchandise was a hardware item. They should have realized it was harder to prove store ownership without a price tag, especially when their suspect was claiming ownership and had a witness to back up his claim.

Lambert v. Sears, Roebuck and Co., 570 P.2d 537 (Oregon, 1977).

*This is a highly questionable practice. No detention statute authorizes a detaining merchant to take photographs of shoplifting suspect.

CASE	Toothpaste case

In the Toothpaste Case, the store had an opportunity to establish and investigate the woman's explanation (a claim of ownership), but failed to do so. The result was the filing of a nonprosecutable shoplifting case followed by an acquittal and a civil action for malicious prosecution. A woman had previously purchased some items from a grocery store. An hour later she returned to make additional purchases. The toothpaste, shampoo, and hair conditioner she had previously purchased were in her purse. A checker noticed the items when she went through and informed store security. The woman was detained just outside the store, in the parking lot. She went back inside the store with the security man.

She explained about buying the three items an hour earlier and that her husband, sitting in their car in the parking lot, had the sales receipt. The

FIGURE 4.4	Socket wrench case analysis

Analysis of case: The decision to prosecute was made based only on sales floor evidence. This store made no attempt to establish the defense. There was no recovery for false imprisonment because this store did have sales floor evidence that justified the initial detention. Hence they were not civilly liable for false imprisonment.

	Prosecution evidence	Defense evidence
Sales floor evidence 1. Take: yes 2. Conceal: yes 3. Wrench: yes 4. Leave store: yes 5. Without paying: yes 6. Surveillance: yes	Probable cause to detain for investigation was established	
Security office evidence Investigated evidence produced by the store		*Defense evidence* a. Statement of ownership b. Store had no tags to prove that it owned the items c. A potential defense witness

7. Recover the wrench: yes
8. Obtain suspect's version of possession:
  a. no statement taken
  b. no attempt to take statement
9. Investigate suspect's version of possession:
10. Review all evidence:
11. Evaluation of case:
	No, this store did not attempt to establish the defense before calling the police.
	
	No
	No
	No	

Comment: This store failed to conduct a logical and systematic investigation of the facts (steps 7–11) after properly detaining the suspect. This caused the filing of a shoplifting case where the evidence was not sufficient to establish the elements of the offense at trial.

security man refused to walk out and talk with the husband before summoning the police. The shoplifting case was lost because the woman brought her husband and the receipt to court and proved she had previously purchased the items as she had told the security man. Following her acquittal she sued, receiving a jury award of $5,000 in actual damages and $50,000 in punitive damages. The case was reversed on a technicality. The facts clearly show that when stores do not make some effort to investigate the merits of a suspect's explanation, they are setting themselves up for a civil action.

In the malicious prosecution civil action, the judge made the following comments about the failure of the store employee to investigate the woman's explanation of ownership by prior purchase:

> It can hardly be claimed that, under the circumstances, Phlegar [the security officer] acted as a prudent and reasonable man. *His disregard of information communicated to him* constituted an aggravated circumstance which supports the finding of the jury that there was want of probable cause. [Emphasis supplied]

The court is clearly saying that ignoring the meaning of the woman's explanation is an evidence-gathering mistake. As her defense to the shoplifting charge, she testified to buying the items earlier and supported it with the testimony of her husband and the sales receipt. This information was available to the security man in the store but he had not been taught to establish a suspect's defense as part of the evidence-gathering process. It was reasonable to detain the woman because the checker had observed food store merchandise inside her purse. It was not reasonable to call the police and have her prosecuted without first checking out the merits of her explanation. If this store had been using a selective prosecution approach, the charge would never have been filed.

Failing to establish the suspect's defense and failing to investigate the merits of the explanation is an evidence-gathering mistake in any state. When a suspect claims ownership, make some effort to verify or disprove the claim in the store. In court it will be too late. Consider the argument a defense lawyer would make to a judge in the Socket Wrench and Toothpaste Cases:

Defense lawyer in Socket Wrench Case:
Your Honor, the store's evidence is that the security officers made the decision to have my client arrested before investigating the facts. They paid no attention to his explanation that he bought the sockets earlier at that store or that he had a witness who could verify the purchase. The evidence on the question of ownership is disputed. There is more evidence before the court that my client owns

the sockets than there is evidence the store is the owner. I move the charge be dismissed because the store's evidence fails to establish the element of ownership of merchandise as required in the shoplifting prosecution statute. Thank you, Your Honor.

Defense lawyer in Toothpaste Case:

Your Honor, the evidence before this court conclusively proves that my client and not the food store is the owner of the toothpaste, hair conditioner, and shampoo. My client told the officer she had purchased these items an hour earlier and that her husband, sitting a few feet away in the car, had the receipt. The security officer refused to even talk with her husband before summoning the police to have her arrested and prosecuted for shoplifting. We have introduced the receipt into evidence as defense exhibit 1, and it was received. Therefore, I move the charge be dismissed because the store's evidence utterly fails to establish the element of ownership as required by the shoplifting prosecution statute. Thank you, Your Honor.

It sounds almost absurd to tell merchants to be sure they can prove store ownership of the goods before filing the case. Yet the fact remains there are cases on the books like the Socket Wrench and Toothpaste Cases where a charge was filed without sufficient evidence to prove ownership being produced in the store. Even national and regional merchants with full-time security deparments will take cases to court where the evidence to show ownership is questionable. Ownership is a factual question, one proved with two types of physical evidence: the merchandise and its price tag. The only way to find out if a suspect is claiming ownership is to give that suspect an opportunity to explain.

As the Socket Wrench Case, showed, the fact that a person claims ownership yet does not have a sales receipt will not guarantee a conviction. In all states, the merchant has the evidence-gathering burden to prove the elements of the offense. If the suspect claims ownership and does not have a sales receipt yet the merchant does not produce a price tag, the case can be lost in court. Seeing a person conceal merchandise on the sales floor is not evidence proving store ownership of that merchandise. Evidence proving ownership is the merchandise itself and a price tag, garment label, inventory control tag, or some other type of physical evidence. The strongest case is one like the Two Flair Pens Case in Chapter 3, where the drug store security officer recovered the blister pack and the pens, introducing both as pieces of store prosecution evidence at the trial.

Consider six commonly encountered situations where the suspect is claiming ownership and may not have a sales receipt.

1. *"I bought it elsewhere"* or *"I bought it earlier at your store."* This explanation is encountered quite frequently. Here the merchandise

in question is the key to the investigation. The detaining employee must know if the store does in fact offer this type of item for sale. It is the merchant, not the suspect, who has the burden of proving ownership in court. If the store does not have a price tag or garment label and the suspect does not have a sales receipt, the case becomes what the lawyers and judges call a "swearing match" on the issue of ownership. Some investigative activity is always required when the merchant encounters this explanation.

2. *The companion defense witness*: The suspect tells the detaining retail employee that his companion will verify the merchandise was previously purchased. The merchant can rest assured that in court, this companion defense witness will testify in support of the suspect's claim of ownership by prior purchase. If the merchant has no price tag or other documentary evidence to prove ownership, the case will be lost.

3. *The absent defense witness*: This is the same situation as the previous one except the suspect's witness is not present in the store when the suspect is detained. The Socket Wrench Case was an example of an absent defense witness who later testified and corroborated the suspect's claim of ownership by prior purchase.

4. *Ownership by gift*: This explanation has credibility because, as merchants know from common experience, persons do remove price tags, garment labels, and so forth from items they purchase and give as gifts. It is also common knowledge that persons who receive gifts do not always get the sales receipt from the gift giver. A store must be careful in filing a case when the suspect says he received the item as a gift.

5. *Returning merchandise for refunds or exchanges*: Normally a person returning merchandise will have the sales receipt to verify the previous purchase. These situations are tricky because there are persons who shoplift merchandise and then return it for a cash refund. Store policy must be specific about how to investigate claims that the suspect is returning goods.

6. *The swearing match over the question of ownership*: The first five situations are ones the merchant will encounter. The swearing match is what happens in court if neither the store nor the suspect produces documentary evidence to substantiate their claim of ownership. A judge hearing the case will listen to a store detective say the goods are owned by the merchant while the defendant is also claiming ownership. Since the store does not have a price tag and the defendant does not have a sales receipt, there is no physical or documentary evidence presented by either side. Judges and lawyers call these situations swearing matches. Obviously both sides cannot own the same piece of merchandise. Since the prosecuting store has the

evidence-gathering burden of proof, a swearing match case is a weaker one, where the chances of an acquittal are higher. Store policy must be specific about whether to file the charge when no price tag or other inventory-control document is recovered in the store.

Part of the retailer's problem is that most of the merchant's privilege statutes are not specific about what to do once the suspect is detained on probable cause. Too many of them (like the Oregon detention statute in Chapter 2) tell merchants to detain and "interrogate the person in a reasonable manner and for a reasonable period of time." Only the better-drafted statutes, like the Illinois Retail Theft Act in Chapter 2, tell merchants the purpose of detaining is to "make a reasonable investigation of the ownership of such merchandise." Store policy must not be vague and confusing like many of the merchant's privilege statutes. Store policy must tell employees to detain and determine whether the store can prove the element of ownership in court as part of the evidence-gathering process.

There are six excellent cases in this book demonstrating situations where merchants failed to see that the evidence to prove store ownership was lacking. They are the Toothpaste and Socket Wrench Cases in this chapter, the Aspirin and Returned Gloves Cases in Chapter 6, the Hat Case in Chapter 9, and the Snowmobile Suit Case found in Chapter 1. In three of those cases (Snowmobile Suit, Toothpaste and Hat) the security people were aware of adult witnesses present in the store when the suspect claimed ownership. In all three, they ignored both the suspect's claim of ownership and the fact potential defense witnesses were present, ones who would come to court and corroborate the suspect's ownership defense. In all three cases, those adult witnesses did testify at the shoplifting trial on the issue of ownership. All three cases resulted in acquittals because store prosecution evidence was not sufficient to establish the element of ownership.

Stores file and lose shoplifting cases because they make evidence-gathering mistakes in the store. Study these six cases, because they demonstrate situations where the merchants could have easily decided *not* to prosecute. Said another way, these cases demonstrate situations where a selective prosecution policy would have paid off. If a suspect is detained and claims ownership, give the explanation serious consideration and investigate it before deciding to call the police and have that person prosecuted. Merchant's privilege statutes give stores a legally reasonable time in which to conduct an investigation of the facts. That reasonable time should be used to determine ownership of the merchandise in question.

Merchants must acquire the ability to look at *both* the prosecution

| TABLE 4.2 | Analyzing prosecution and defense evidence in a case |

| | Legal meaning of suspect's explanation | | |
Shoplifting situations	Deny intent to shoplift	Claim of ownership	No explanation
Concealment			
Two Flair Pens Case		X	
Razor Blades Case	X		
Socket Wrench Case		X	
Toothpaste Case		X	
No concealment			
Scarf Case	X		
Leather Jacket Case		X	
Aiding and abetting			
Slacks in the Car Trunk Case			X
Five Shirts Case		X	

and the defense evidence if they are to be effective in handling shoplifting cases. Eight cases discussed in Chapter 3 and in this Chapter are diagramed in Table 4.2. This table forces the retailer to look at the type of shoplifting situation he is handling— concealment, no concealment, or aiding and abetting. It also forces the merchant to consider the defense in each case. For example, the Two Flair Pens Case is a concealment situation with an ownership defense. In the Razor Blades Case the merchant was confronted with a concealment situation and a defense denying intent to shoplift. The Scarf Case presented a no concealment situation with a defense denying intent to shoplift. By learning to look at both sides of a case, the merchant will be more effective in deciding when strong prosecutable cases exist and when the store's prosecution evidence is weak or nonexistent.

RECOVERING THE MERCHANDISE AND PRICE TAG

Up to this point, (keeping the *Sources of Evidence* chart in mind) the merchant is dealing with observations (steps 1–6) and the suspect's explanations (steps 7 and 8). Now the emphasis switches to the physical evidence—recovering the goods themselves and a price tag (steps 9 and 10). Under detention statutes in all states, the store owner, manager, or security person is authorized to recover the merchandise—the merchandise the suspect was seen concealing minutes earlier on the selling floor. The recovered merchandise itself is evidence and so is the price tag, garment label, or other inventory control tag. To establish a prosecutable case, a merchant must recover the goods and be able to prove its value. Value is important because it determines whether the case is filed as a misdemeanor or a felony.

The Two Flair Pens Case in Chapter 2 was a good example of how the security officer recovered both the pens (in the suspect's shirt pocket) and the blister pack (which he discarded in the basement). She brought both pieces of physical evidence to court, identified them, and introduced both into evidence on behalf of the prosecuting store.[2] The Green Leather Coat Case showed how a department store had to bring the buyer to court to prove ownership and value. The woman claimed she had purchased the coat but had no sales receipt. It shows how sometimes it will take more than one store employee to prove ownership and value. Store policy should be specific about recovering the merchandise and a price tag. The detaining employee should initial and date the price tag. Then the evidence should be put in a specific place in a security office or manager's office. On the day of trial, it should be brought to court. Many stores put the merchandise in a sack with a card stapled to it with the date, case number, and other vital statistics. A case may be postponed several times before trial. After each court appearance the recovered merchandise should be returned to the office. In most jurisdictions, a person convicted of misdemeanor shoplifting is entitled to appeal. The recovered merchandise must be kept for the new trial at the appellate level.

The purpose of following this type of procedure is to establish a chain of custody for the recovered merchandise. In all criminal cases, the prosecution must show the evidence recovered at the crime scene is the same evidence introduced at trial as a prosecution exhibit. Shoplifting cases are no exception. Normally the security staff will set up the chain of custody procedures, returning the evidence to the property section of the security office after each court appearance. In stores without a security staff, the manager or owners should have a specified place in the office where recovered merchandise is kept while waiting trial. This is important, because a case may be dismissed if the prosecuting merchant cannot

---

[2]I prosecuted this case in 1981. Because the store detective recovered the blister pack and brought it to court along with the two pens, a conviction resulted. If she had not brought the blister pack to court, the case would have been in the questionable category. It would have been a swearing match because neither the prosecution nor defense would have had any physical evidence to corroborate claims of ownership.

produce the recovered goods and price tag on the day of trial and introduce them into evidence as a prosecution exhibit.

REVIEWING PROSECUTION AND DEFENSE EVIDENCE BEFORE MAKING THE DECISION TO PROSECUTE OR RELEASE A SHOPLIFTING SUSPECT

Step 11 of the *Sources of Evidence* chart (page 86) has two parts: (1)
Review the prosecution evidence which will be used at trial to establish
the elements of the offense, and (2) Evaluate the merits of the suspect's
explanation (whether it be a claim of ownership or a claim of ownership),
because that explanation becomes the courtroom defense to the shoplifting charge. In court a judge or jury will listen as intently to the defense
evidence as it listens to the prosecution evidence presented by the store.
Merchants must learn to do the same thing in their stores—listen to the
suspect's explanation. As the Razor Blades, Socket Wrench, and Toothpaste Cases demonstrated, merchants are not always good at listening to
a suspect's explanation. They ignore or disregard them, not realizing that
in court these explanations become evidence—defense evidence. A judge
or jury can decide the defendant did forget to pay for merchandise or a
suspect did purchase the merchandise at another store. When this happens, the prosecuting store loses the shoplifting case.

     In the Socket Wrench Case, the security people did not stop and
think about what evidence they would use in court to prove the element
of store ownership of the sockets. All they really had was an observation
of the man putting the sockets in his pocket. They had no supporting
physical evidence like a price tag to offer as a prosecution exhibit at trial.
They knew the man was claiming ownership by prior purchase and that
he had a witness who would (and did) come to court to testify that the man
bought the sockets. The fact that the suspect did not have a sales receipt
did not make the store's case any stronger. The merchant, not the suspect,
has the burden of proving each element. The fact he had no sales receipt
did not make up for the fact the store had no price tag or other label
proving department store ownership. The question of ownership was in
direct dispute. When this happens, the store's case is weaker. A judge or
jury could choose to believe the suspect or the store. Under these facts,
there was more evidence to support the man's claim of prior purchase than
there was to support the store's claim of ownership.

     When reviewing prosecution and defense evidence, always ask the
following question: "If this case is lost in court, what will be the evidence
reason—failure to prove intent to shoplift or failure to prove store ownership?" Merchants must learn to be objective about their cases—to keep
an open mind about what the evidence will prove in court. Do not fall into

the *concealment equals guilt* trap like the two security people in the Socket Wrench Case. They admitted they made the decision to have the man prosecuted based only on what they saw. They admitted they paid no attention to his explanation claiming ownership. Obviously this store had not taught its security personnel to obtain the suspect's explanation, then to review both the prosecution and defense evidence before making a decision about how to handle the case.

When reviewing and evaluating the case, do not discuss it by using conclusions or by expressing opinions. Avoid saying the suspect is "guilty" because that conclusion or opinion has no evidential value in court. A judge will decide guilt (or lack of it) based on evidential facts. Discuss the case by asking if the evidence will prove the elements of the offense. Discuss the case by asking what the defense evidence will show. Talk about the evidence or the lack of it. In many cases, the evidence will be in direct conflict. In the Razor Blades Case, the store's evidence showed the man intended to shoplift, because he was outside the store and had the blades in his pocket. His evidence showed just the opposite—that he had no intention of shoplifting the blades and was going to pay for them by check when his wife came through the checkout line. Either version of "what happened" is possible. In the Socket Wrench Case, both the store and the suspect claimed ownership. Learn to analyze these cases objectively based on what both versions of the evidence (the prosecution and the defense) will show to a judge or jury in court.

To assist merchants in being objective in their production and review of evidence a *prosecution evidence checklist* is presented in Figure 4.5. It should be used when reviewing the facts after they have been produced by following steps 1–10 on the *Sources of Evidence* chart presented above. By using the checklist, a merchant can learn to be more objective—to concentrate on what the evidence shows rather than fall victim to suspicion, opinion, conclusion, or circumstance which have no evidential value at a trial.

CONCLUSION

Decision making based on evidence best describes the role of a merchant in handling shoplifting cases. Gathering evidence is a systematic process. Evidence must be produced to establish each element of the offense. Evidence must be produced to establish the suspect's defense. Under the merchant's privilege statutes in all states a retailer is given a legally reasonable period of time after detaining a suspect to produce, review, and evaluate the evidence. The decision to detain for investigation is based solely on observations made on the selling floor. The decision to prosecute (or to release a suspect without prosecution) is made only after investigating the facts. The decision to prosecute is then made based on observed

FIGURE 4.5	Store prosecution evidence checklist

1. Possession of the merchandise
    A. Was it removed from place of display with the hands?   Yes____ No____

2. Concealment
    A. What was the exact place it was concealed?
        1. Pocket   ____
        2. Purse   ____
        3. Shopping bag   ____
        4. Under or inside of clothing   ____
        5. Other (describe place of concealment here) _____

    _____

2A. More than one person involved (if applicable to case)
    A. Which type of shoplifting situation was encountered?
        1. Lookout   ____
        2. Diversion   ____
        3. Joint participation in concealment   ____
        4. Cashier/customer involved in sliding   ____

3. Continuing concealment
    A. What did the suspect do after concealing the merchandise?
        1. Leave almost immediately   Yes____ No____
        2. Browse for a while   Yes____ No____
    B. Did suspect have other merchandise in his possession that
       was not concealed?   Yes____ No____
        1. Describe other merchandise: _____

    _____

4. Opportunity to pay
    A. Was the suspect given an opportunity to pay before being
       detained?   Yes____ No____
        1. If answer is "no" explain: _____

    _____

5. Place of detention
    A. Did suspect pass the last cash register without paying?   Yes____ No____
    B. (front end cash register stores) Did suspect go through or
       around the checkout counter without paying?   Yes____ No____
    C. Was place of detention outside the store?   Yes____ No____

6. Constant and unbroken observations
    A. Was the suspect out of my sight for any time?   Yes____ No____
        1. If answer is "yes," explain: _____

    _____

7. Recovery of merchandise and price tag
    A. Was merchandise recovered?   Yes____ No____
    B. Was a price tag recovered?   Yes____ No____

FIGURE 4.5	Continued

Elements of the Offense
1. Possession   Yes____ No____
2. Intent to shoplift   Yes____ No____
3. Store ownership   Yes____ No____
4. Value   misdemeanor____   Felony____

evidence, investigated evidence, and on the basis of the suspect's explanation. Forget about shifty eyes and furtive gestures, because they are not evidence to use in court to prove an element of the offense. Sure people may look around before they conceal merchandise, but it is the concealment and the leaving without paying (not the shifty eyes) that counts in court.

5

Miscellaneous Aspects of Shoplifting Prosecution

The first four chapters dealt with the fundamentals of shoplifting prosecution. This chapter discusses some of the technicalities, such as the hearsay evidence rule, admissibility of photographs as evidence, the defense of voluntary intoxication, and credit card theft. They are presented to give the merchant a broader perspective about evidence gathering and establishing the elements of the offense and defense.

HEARSAY EVIDENCE RULE

CASE	Blue leisure suit case

Consider the facts of the case as set forth by the court:

The State's first witness, Paul Adams, who on November 25, 1975, was employed as a store detective at the John A. Brown Department Store located in Penn Square Mall in Oklahoma City. While on duty that day he received a security page directing him to report to the Men's Sportswear Department. When he arrived there he had a conversation with one of the salesmen. The witness [Mr. Adams] testified that as a result of this conversation he observed and then followed the defendant around the store. After walking through the store, the defendant went out to the parking lot and got into her car. Mr. Adams testified that he watched the defendant from inside the glass doors of the entrance to the mall. He saw her reach into the back seat of the vehicle, bringing out a white pillow case, place it on the front seat, and then return it to the floorboard. The defendant then exited the car and returned to the mall through a different entrance. Mr. Adams noticed that defendant's purse appeared flat.

After the defendant returned to the mall, Mr. Adams went to the vehicle, reached inside and removed the white pillow case. Upon looking inside he discovered a man's blue leisure suit with a John A. Brown label, perforated in the middle and both sides intact. The witness testified that when merchandise is sold, half of the tag is torn off and kept by the store. The price tag on the garment showed a price of $110.00. At this point Mr. Adams returned to the store and told what he had seen to Mr. John Lundell, the store's security director. Mr. Lundell suggested they wait until the defendant returned to the car. Both men got in Mr. Lundell's car, which was parked on a raised part of the parking lot, from which they could observe defendant's car. After a 20 minute wait, the defendant returned to her vehicle, and the witnesses noticed that her purse was "bulging."

Mr. Lundell and Mr. Adams then drove up behind her car and asked her to step out. The defendant complied. She was asked to show the contents of her purse to Mr. Lundell. The defendant handed him her purse. Inside the purse were a ladies' beige pant suit and a black dress with John A. Brown labels still attached, indicating that the pant suit and dress had not been paid for. The combined price of these items was $320.00. The white pillow case was then removed from the car, opened and the blue leisure suit removed. The defendant was escorted to the security office inside the store where she was advised of her rights. The witness then stated that the defendant was held at the security office until the police arrived. Later the defendant was taken to the city jail. When the case was prosecuted, the store detective tried to testify to what he was "told" by the clerk.* The judge refused to allow the store detective to prove the woman concealed the garment by testifying to what he had been told by the clerk. The exclusion of this hearsay evidence was not fatal to the store's prosecution effort here because after having the conversation with the clerk, the store detective made his own observations and conducted his own investigation. The facts he produced independently of what he was told by the clerk established probable cause to detain. In affirming the woman's conviction, the court stated:

> Nevertheless, this Court thinks that even with the limited testimony available regarding what preceded surveillance of the defendant, it has before it sufficient evidence to determine that the security guards had probable cause to think that the defendant committed a crime, and that therefore their actions with regard to detaining and searching her were proper under provisions of 22 O.S.1971, Section 1343.

White v. Oklahoma, 572 P.2d 569 (Oklahoma, 1977)

*It is obvious the clerk saw the woman remove the leisure suit from its place of display and conceal it in her purse.

The rule of evidence demonstrated by this case is simple: a retail employee will not be able to testify in court about what he was told by a second employee. Suppose the store detective in the Blue Leisure Suit

Case knew the sales clerk was reliable and detained the woman based on what the clerk told him. He would have found concealed and unpurchased merchandise—the leisure suit. If a charge had been filed against the woman, both the clerk and the store detective would have been required to testify at the shoplifting trial to establish a prosecutable case. Probable cause to detain (steps 1–6) of the *Sources of Evidence* chart would have been established by the clerk, based on his sales floor observations. The investigation of the facts (steps 7–10) and the decision to prosecute the case (step 11) would have been made by the store detective. The evidence needed to establish a prosecutable case (all four elements of the offense) would have to be produced by two employees rather than one.

In court, a witness must testify about facts within his own personal knowledge. In shoplifting cases, this means that store witnesses must testify to what they observed. In reviewing the evidence that will be used in court, a merchant may have a case where more than one witness has to testify. Fitting room cases often involve two employees. For example, store detective A may see a woman enter a fitting room with three sweaters. Detective B may join him. They both see the woman exit with only two sweaters visible. The woman is carrying a purse. She replaces two sweaters on the counter and moves into another department. Detective B then makes a fitting room check while detective A follows the woman. If B does not find the missing sweater, he may inform A, who then detains the woman for investigation, finding the third sweater in her purse. In court, detective A will not be permitted to testify that detective B told him there was no missing sweater in the fitting room. Store detective B must come to court and testify to his own personal observations that he found no sweater when he made the fitting room check. It would be a violation of the hearsay evidence rule to let A testify to what B told him about what was or was not found in that fitting room. Security people should ask local prosecutors about the hearsay evidence rule as it applies to shoplifting cases. An otherwise prosecutable case could be lost if the merchant does not have all store witnesses present in court to establish each element of the offense.

DEFENSE OF VOLUNTARY INTOXICATION OR A DRUGGED CONDITION

By claiming this defense, a person is saying he was not capable of forming the requisite state of mind to intend to shoplift. Rather than saying, "I forgot to pay" or "I intended to pay," this defendant is saying, "I was too drunk and did not know what I was doing." In other situations, the defendant may say he was too "stoned" to know what he was doing, meaning under the influence of some type of drug. If a suspect appears to be intoxicated or on some type of drug this fact should be noted on the report form.

CASE	Blanket case

A man entered a Pennsylvania department store, going directly to the domestics department, where he browsed for five to eight minutes. During this time, he picked up a blanket and put it under his arm. He then walked into the furniture department, staying there only about thirty seconds. From the furniture department he went directly out, the blanket under his arm at all times. He made no effort to contact a store employee or pay for the blanket. He was detained about thirty feet outside the store. The case contains no record of what explanation, if any, he made when detained. At trial, he testified that he was daydreaming and inadvertently left the store without paying for the blanket. He was convicted. On appeal the evidence was found to be sufficient to sustain the trial court's finding of guilty.

During the trial, the defendant testified he had been drinking before being detained and arrested. He was trying to set up the defense of voluntary intoxication. When asked if he was intoxicated, he specifically said that he was not drunk at the time he was detained. The trial court would not let the jury consider his defense of intoxication, citing section 18-308 of Pennsylvania Statutes Annotated: "Neither voluntary intoxication nor voluntary drugged condition is a defense to a criminal charge, nor may evidence of such conditions be introduced to negate the element of intent of the offense."

In affirming the conviction, the court held that this statute is not unconstitutional and the trial court was correct in refusing to let the jury consider this man's defense of voluntary intoxication.

Commonwealth v. McConnell, 436 A.2d 1201 (Pennsylvania, 1981)

If merchants file cases where the suspect has been drinking heavily or appears to be under the influence of drugs, they should alert the prosecutor to this fact before trial. The person could raise this defense, as was done in this case.

ADMISSIBILITY OF PHOTOGRAPHS OF RECOVERED MERCHANDISE

A universal complaint by retailers is that they must bring the recovered merchandise to court and introduce it as prosecution evidence. There are three types or categories of evidence:

1. *Testimonial evidence*: oral testimony given by a store employee based on the observations of a store detective or store manager on the sales floor.
2   *Documentary evidence*: includes the price tag or other identifying labels and inventory control devices and the merchant's offense report and the police report.
3. *Real or physical evidence*: the merchandise.

Before real or physical evidence can be admitted at trial, the prosecution must show some connection between the item and the defendant. In shoplifting cases, the store witness must explain that the merchandise about to be introduced into evidence was the merchandise that the suspect concealed on the sales floor and was then recovered when the person was detained. The witness must be able to identify the merchandise as belonging to the store and that it was not paid for at the time of recovery. In short, the store employee must identify the merchandise as that which was concealed by the suspect and then recovered that day in the store. The merchandise itself is an element of the offense and, like all other elements, it must be proved at trial by competent, relevant, and admissible evidence.

Some states, either by statute or case law, permit retailers to use photographs of recovered merchandise as prosecution exhibits at trial. This means the prosecuting store can photograph the goods then return them to stock after the case is filed. For stores that file a large number of shoplifting cases each year this rule means substantial savings.

| CASE | Nine leisure suits case |

The defendants appeared to be professional shoplifters or "boosters." The amount of merchandise stolen led to the conclusion they were shoplifting for resale of the goods to a fence rather than for personal use. Professional shoplifters travel from city to city and from mall to mall within a city to shoplift. Based on their observations, the store employees possessed facts sufficient to conclude shoplifting had taken place, although they could not positively identify the three suspects. They knew that three people had left the store with their trench coats bulging, thus establishing the element of possession. They knew none of the trio had paid or offered to pay for the goods, thus establishing intent to shoplift. By their investigative efforts they established that a large quantity of merchandise was missing, thereby establishing ownership and value. Armed with these facts, they called the police and reported theft of merchandise. It was reasonable to conclude that if the police stopped the car they described, the merchandise would be found in it.

Consider the facts of this case as recited by the court:

On December 16, 1974, one woman and two men were observed

leaving the P. N. Hirsh store in Jackson, Missouri, wearing long, dark topcoats that bulged in the back. They entered a dark brown Oldsmobile whose license number was noted by an employee of the store. A check of the department from which direction the trio had come revealed nine men's leisure suits of the value of $33.00 each were missing. The police were notified, and a description of the automobile and its occupants was sent over the radio. Although the defendant (in this case) could not be identified by employees of the P. N. Hirsch store as personally present, he was identified as one of the trio in other stores from which merchandise had been taken in the same area on the same day.

Later the same day, the automobile was seen by a special officer of the Cape Girardeau, Missouri police department [a city not far from Jackson, Missouri]. The officer followed the car and prevented its occupants, the defendant and his companions, from leaving after it was parked in front of a restaurant. A regular officer was called to take the trio into custody. In the automobile the officers later discovered a cache of merchandise stolen from several stores in the vicinity, including the suits from the P. N. Hirsh store.

From the facts it was obvious these three people had been driving from city to city shoplifting as they went. The law enforcement officers wisely photographed the merchandise recovered from the several stores, realizing there would most likely be three trials, one for each person charged. At the trial of this defendant, no merchandise was offered into evidence. Instead the retail employees testified using the photographs taken by the police. The photographs sufficiently identified the goods as coming from the store. The man was convicted of felony shoplifting.

He appealed, and his conviction was affirmed as being supported by the evidence presented at trial. One of the grounds he raised on appeal was that the trial court made a mistake by using the photographs as evidence rather than requiring the police and merchant to produce the leisure suits themselves. To support his contention, the defendant said that the photographs were not properly identified nor was a proper foundation laid for their introduction as evidence at trial. Finally, he claimed that the photographs were not the best evidence and the actual garments should have been used.

The court rejected this argument saying the following about the use of the photographs as store prosecution evidence:

> It is obvious that the best evidence rule does not apply here because the rule pertains only to documents and not to objects [citing a case to support the rule]. Testimony revealed that the photographs were a fair and accurate representation of the objects shown therein. Testimony of the arresting officer traced the objects from the automobile in which defendant was riding to their removal, identification and photographing in his presence at police headquarters. Sufficient identification was made, and proper foundation for admision was laid [citing a case to support the rule].

State v. Savu, 560 S.W.2d 244 (Missouri, 1977)

This case shows how merchants and law enforcement officers can work together to photograph and identify merchandise so that only the photographs need be presented at trial. This shoplifting situation involved three defendants, each with the right to have a separate trial. This means that the merchant would have to come to court three separate times, bringing the merchandise on each occasion unless it was photographed. By the end of the trial, the merchandise could have been damaged or out of season, and the merchant would have to take a markdown or a total loss.

In this Nine Leisure Suits Case, the court talked about the officers showing a chain of custody of the photographs as part of a proper foundation for their being admitted as prosecution evidence. A chain of custody means proving who took the photographs, when they were taken, and where they were kept until trial. The photographs should be marked with the case number and kept in a specific place until trial. Police departments have a property room for this purpose. Merchants should establish similar procedures in their stores so they can prove this chain of custody, either of merchandise or of photographs.

If the merchandise is photographed, it is wise to use an instamatic polaroid-type camera. The retail employee who will testify in court should take the photographs then mark them with his initials and the date. They should be kept in the manager's or security office, in a specific place, until trial. At trial the employee can testify that the photographs are a fair and accurate representation of the merchandise because he took them. The witness can also testify as to the chain of custody. If a retail employee other than the one who took the photographs tries to testify in court, the photographs may not be admitted into evidence.

THEFT BY CREDIT CARD[1]

Some shoplifting situations involve removal of merchandise from stores by making a false representation. In a price tag switching case, the suspect represents that the altered or switched price tag is the actual selling price and pays for the goods at the lower price. In a container stuffing case, the suspect offers to pay only for a container, such as a clothes hamper, failing to mention there is additional unpurchased merchandise inside. In other situations, a person will present merchandise that has actually been shoplifted and ask for a cash refund. In a credit card case, a person is also making a false representation to the merchant in order to obtain possession of goods. The false representation is that the person is authorized to use the credit card when in fact the person knows he does not have such

---

[1]For a case involving a civil action arising out of detention of persons using credit cards, see the Plaza Alert Case in Chapter 10.

authority. As with price tag switching, container stuffing, and cash refund cases, these credit card cases require the merchant to rely on the false representation as being true before the offense is committed.

Most states have passed a specific theft by credit card statute. It is normally found in the theft or larceny section of the penal code. These statutes vary in title and specific language. Consider the Missouri statute, which is simple and concise.

| STATUTE | Missouri penal code |

570.130. Fraudulent use of a credit device

1. A person commits the crime of fraudulent use of a credit device if he uses a credit device for the purpose of obtaining services or property, knowing that:
   (1) The device is stolen, fictitious or forged; or
   (2) The device has been revoked or cancelled; or
   (3) For any other reason his use of the device is unauthorized. 2. Fraudulent use of a credit device is a class A misdemeanor unless the value of the property or services obtained or sought to be obtained within any thirty-day period is one hundred fifty dollars or more, in which case fraudulent use of a credit device is a class D felony.

(L.1977, S.B.No.60, p. 662, § 1, eff. Jan. 1, 1979.)

This Missouri statute prohibits unauthorized use of a credit card when the person knows he has no right or authority to do so. The definition of a credit card is broadened by calling it a *credit device*. The statute applies to situations where a person obtains both property and services. The statute lists five instances where a person obtains both property and services. The statute lists five instances where a person has no authority to use the credit device: when the device is stolen, fictitious, forged, revoked, or cancelled. Subsection 3 says that the offense is committed if for any other reason the use of the credit device is unauthorized. The statute says the use of the device must be "fraudulent," meaning a false representation is made to the merchant and the store must rely on this representation is parting with the goods. For a prosecution to be successful, the store's evidence must establish that the card was stolen, forged, revoked, cancelled when presented, or fictitious. The key to prosecution in these cases is showing the suspect did not have lawful authority to use the credit device.

| CASE | Gloves and credit card case |

A saleswoman in the glove department of a department store testified she sold the defendant a pair of gloves. He handed her a credit card, she prepared the sales slip, and he signed the name printed on the card. She notified special services about this transaction, and a store detective responded. The detective testified that upon approaching the glove counter, he saw the defendant running down a main aisle in the store. After talking with the saleswoman, he followed the man, detaining him outside the store. The man was prosecuted and convicted, and, on appeal of the case, his conviction was affirmed.

To prove he was using the card without consent or authority, the man named on the credit card was called as a witness. He testified he made application for the card, received it through the mail, his name was printed on it, he had never used the card, had never signed the card, did not know the defendant, and had never given the defendant permission to use it. His wife testified that she lost the credit card bearing her husband's name some months before the day the defendant attempted to purchase the gloves at the department store.*

The prosecutor introduced the recovered credit card into evidence.† The saleswoman identified it as the one she had been handed the day in question. The husband and wife identified it as the one they had received in the mail and that the wife had lost. To establish lack of consent, it was necessary to recover the card and have the person to whom it was issued testify that the defendant had not been given consent or permission to use it. The false representation was established by the testimony of the saleswoman.

On appeal, the defendant did not attack the sufficiency of the evidence to prove lack of authority to use the card, but he did contend the store had not proved he intended to defraud by using it to purchase the gloves. The court rejected this argument:

> It is well established that intent is a state of mind, which if not admitted, can be shown by surrounding circumstances. In the instant case the evidence reveals that defendant sought to purchase a pair of gloves by using a credit card bearing the name of Robert R. Brinkman, that he signed Brinkman's name to the sales slip, that Brinkman had not consented to his use of the card and that he [defendant] ran from the scene while the sales clerk was awaiting the arrival of a store detective. These circumstances sufficiently establish defendant's fraudulent intent.

People v. Enright, 275 N.E.2d 294 (Illinois, 1971)

*The card was issued by the department store. It was not a bank card or one issued by a private credit card company.

†The case does not mention whether the gloves were introduced into evidence as a prosecution exhibit along with the credit card. Since the transaction slip will have a description of the merchandise, the prosecutor may not need the items themselves as evidence. In many cases where the suspect is not detained at the time of using the credit card, the merchandise will never be recovered. Generally the sales transaction document is sufficient to prove the suspect received the merchandise. It may be wise to check with local DAs and prosecutors on this point when filing credit card theft cases.

This case was easy to prove because both the sales clerk and store detective could identify the defendant. He was detained minutes after presenting the credit card, which he had most likely found. In other credit card cases, the fact that the person using the card had no authority to do so may not be discovered for weeks or months after the date of the fraudulent use of the card. The salesperson may not be able to remember the person who presented the card, so some other method of identification of the defendant may be required before a prosecutable case exists.

Documentary evidence becomes more important in credit card cases than in a routine shoplifting case. The merchant will always have the sales transaction slip with a signature, but it will never be the suspect's actual signature because the name of the cardholder is signed. In the case presented here, the merchant also recovered the credit card. In many credit card cases, the card itself is not recovered. It is important to analyze the facts closely in these cases to see how the elements of the offense can be proved in court. In many such cases, it is easy to prove the loss of merchandise and that the person did not have consent or authority from the cardholder to use the card. The problem is finding and identifying a suspect. Often extensive investigative work is required in cases where it is not determined until after the use of the credit card that the person using the card had no authority to do so. Most private credit card companies have investigators who can assist merchants in deciding if a prosecutable case exists. Stores with a full-time security staff often have several of their own employees assigned to credit card cases. Merchants should check with local prosecutors about the evidence they need to present in court to establish the elements of the offense and build those requirements into store policy.

CASE	$10,000 in merchandise credit card case

In some situations, the merchant may have the option of filing under the credit card statute or under the general theft-stealing statute. In this case, a woman took over $10,000 in merchandise from a fashionable Dallas, Texas store over a period of three months by using a credit card she obtained by making a false application. She was ultimately charged under the Texas theft statute, convicted, and her conviction affirmed on appeal. She argued on appeal that the theft statute was not broad enough to cover unlawful taking of property by use of a fraudulently obtained credit card. The court said there was some overlap between the two statutes, but the unlawful conduct set out in the credit card statute could also be prosecuted under the general theft statute.

The woman had been divorced for over two years when she applied to the department store for one of its credit cards. She used only her husband's credit references in making application for the card. He testified she had no authority to use his lines of credit since the divorce, thus establishing that the application was fraudulent. The woman used the credit account numerous times in the Dallas store, always making the purchases from the same salesperson. During 1975 and 1976, she charged $1,338 in merchandise, making only a $55 payment. During the first three months of 1976, she charged over $10,000 in merchandise and made no payments on the account. In July 1976 she met with the credit manager, promising to return that day with a $5,000 cash payment. She did not return and made no payment. In regard to these facts, the court said, "The taking of merchandise with no intention of ever paying the charge would be theft [under one statute] in addition to credit card abuse [under another statute].

Turcola v. State, 643 S.W.2d 164 (Texas, 1982).

This case would most likely be followed in other states. It demonstrates that when contemplating the filing of charges in credit card situations, the merchant may elect to prosecute under either the general theft by deceit or false representation statute or under the credit card abuse section.

As demonstrated with shoplifting cases in Chapter 2, the merchant must prove the elements of the offense. The same is true for credit card abuse cases. As a general rule, credit card abuse is proved by establishing the following elements:

1. A person
2. with intent to obtain property or service fraudulently
3. presents or uses a credit card
4. with knowledge that the card was not issued to him and
5. with knowledge that it is not used with the effective consent of the cardholder.

Since many credit card fraud cases are not discovered until after the person has left the store and since the merchandise is often never recovered, the merchant may want to devise a *Sources of Evidence* chart specifically for credit card prosecutions.

Another point to consider is that recent credit card abuse statutes often contain definitions of terms used only in prosecution of credit card cases. These defined terms may vary from state to state, so close reading of the statute is necessary when setting policy. The definition sections of the Wisconsin and California credit card statutes are presented here. Notice that Wisconsin calls a credit card a "financial transaction card" in an attempt to broaden the definition. California approaches the subject by defining a "cardholder" and a credit card as any "card, plate, coupon book or other credit device." It is always wise to check with local prosecutors to see what evidence they feel is necessary to prove these specially defined terms at trial.

| STATUTE | Wisconsin Credit Card Statute |

943.41 Financial transaction card crimes

(1) Definitions. In this section:

(a) "Alter" means add information to, change information on or delete information from.

(am) "Automated financial service facility" means a machine activated by a financial transaction card, personal identification code or both.

(b) "Cardholder" means the person * * * to whom or from whose benefit * * * a *financial transaction* card is issued * * *.

(c) "Counterfeit" means to manufacture, produce or create by any means a * * * *financial transaction* card or purported * * * *financial transaction* card without the issuer's consent or authorization.

(d) Repealed by L.1981, c. 288, § 5, eff. May 1, 1982.

(e) "Expired credit card" means a * * * *financial transaction* card which is no longer valid because the term shown thereon has elapsed.

(em) "Financial transaction card" means an instrument or device issued by an issuer for the use of the cardholder in any of the following:

1. Obtaining anything on credit.

2. Certifying or guaranteeing the availability of funds sufficient to honor a draft or check.

3. Gaining access to any account.

(f) "Issuer" means the business organization or financial institution which issues a * * * *financial transaction* card or its duly authorized use of a financial transaction card.

(h) "Revoked * * * *financial transaction* card" means a *** *financial transaction* card which is no longer valid because permission to use it has been suspended or terminated by the issuer.

(2) **False statements.** No person shall make or cause to be made, whether directly or indirectly, any false statements in writing, knowing it to be false and with intent that it be relied upon, respecting his identity or that of any other person or his financial condition or that of any other person or other entity for the purpose of procuring the issuance of a ** *financial transaction* card.

| STATUTE | California credit card statute |

§ 484d. Definitions

As used in this section and Sections 484e to * * * 484j, inclusive:

(1) "Cardholder" means * * * any person * * * to whom * * * a credit card is issued * * * or any person who has agreed with the card issuer to pay obligations arising from the issuance of a credit card to another person.

(2) "Credit card" means any * * * card, * * * plate, * * * *coupon book, or other credit device existing for the purpose of being used from time to time upon presentation to obtain* money, * * * *property, labor, or* services * * * *on credit.*

(3) "Expired credit card" means a credit card which shows on its face it has elapsed.

(4) "Card issuer" means * * * *any person who* issues a credit card * * * or * * * *the* agent *of such person with respect to such card.*

(5) * * * "Retailer" means every person who is authorized by an issuer * * * to furnish money, goods, services or anything else of value upon presentation of a credit card by a cardholder.

* * * (6) A credit card is "incomplete" if part of the matter other than the signature of the cardholder which an issuer requires to appear on the credit card before it can be used by a cardholder has not been stamped, embossed, imprinted, or written on it.

* * * (7) "Revoked credit card" means a credit card which is no longer authorized for use by the issuer, such authorization having been suspended or terminated and *written* notice thereof having been given to the cardholder.

(Amended by Stats. 1971, c. 1019, p. 1963, § 5.)

All credit card cases involve fraudulent representation. Merchants should be sure to produce evidence to show that the suspect lacked the consent of the cardholder and knew he did not have permission to use the card on the day in question. This is best accomplished by deciding whether the card was stolen, forged, revoked, or cancelled on the day of its use. In other situations, use of the card may have been fictitious, such as when the woman made the false application using her husband's credit references. There is generally no problem in proving the store relied on the false representation because the suspect has charged the goods and taken them from the store. The best way to approach these cases is to analyze the facts. Then the investigative effort can be channeled in the proper direction. It may be simple to prove the card was stolen but not quite so easy to establish its use was fictitious.

STATUTES PERMITTING MERCHANTS TO SUE FOR DAMAGES

The state of Washington has passed a civil recovery statute that permits merchants to sue persons detained for shoplifting for money damages. This statute does not require that the person detained be convicted under the theft/shoplifting prosecution statute in order to file the civil action for damages. The merchant may sue an adult, an emancipated minor, or the parent and/or legal guardian of a minor. To prevail in this civil action, the merchant must prove the following:

1. The person detained took possession of goods, wares, or merchandise displayed for sale without consent of the seller or owner.
2. The person did so with the intention of converting such goods, wares, or merchandise to his own use without paying the purchase price.

If the merchant establishes liability, it is possible to recover actual damages in the amount of the retail value of the shoplifted merchandise. If the merchandise is damaged, the retailer can get the difference in value between the actual price and the salvage value. The court may also award a penalty in the amount of the retail value, not to exceed $1,000 if the defendant is an adult or an emancipated minor. The statute also provides for an additional penalty of not less than $100 or more than $200. If the defendant is the parent or guardian of a minor, the penalty is limited to $500 plus the additional penalty of $100 to $200. The statute also permits a civil action against a customer of a retaurant or eating establishment who orders a meal and leaves without paying for it after consuming a portion of it. Consider the language of this Washington statute.

| STATUTE | Washington |

4.24.230. Liability for conversion of goods or merchandise from store or mercantile establishment, leaving restaurant without paying—Adults, minors—Parents, guardians

(1) An adult or emancipated minor who takes possession of any goods, wares, or merchandise displayed or offered for sale by any wholesale or retail store or other mercantile establishment without the consent of the owner or seller, and with the intention of converting such goods, wares, or merchandise to his own use without having paid the purchase price thereof shall be liable in addition to actual damages, for a penalty to the owner or seller in the amount of the retail value thereof not to exceed one thousand dollars, plus an additional penalty of not less than one hundred dollars nor more than two hundred dollars. A customer who orders a meal in a restaurant or other eating establishment, receives at least a portion thereof, and then leaves without paying, is subject to liability under this section.

(2) The parent or legal guardian having the custody of an unemancipated minor who takes possession of any goods, wares, or merchandise displayed or offered for sale by any wholesale or retail store or other mercantile establishment without the consent of the owner or seller and with the intention of converting such goods, wares, or merchandise to his own use without having paid the purchase price thereof, shall be liable as a penalty to the owner or seller for the retail value of such goods, wares, or merchandise not to exceed five hundred dollars plus an additional penalty of not less than one hundred dollars nor more than two hundred dollars. The parent or legal guardian having the custody of an unemancipated minor, who orders a meal in a restaurant or other eating establishment, receives at least a portion

thereof, and then leaves without paying, is subject to liability under this section. For the purposes of this subsection, liability shall not be imposed upon any governmental entity or private agency which has been assigned responsibility for the minor child pursuant to court order or action of the department of social and health services.

(3) Judgments, but not claims, arising under this section may be assigned.

(4) A conviction for violation of chapter 9A.56 RCW shall not be a condition precedent to maintenance of a civil action authorized by this section.

Added by Laws 1975, 1st Ex.Sess., ch. 59, § 1. Amended by Laws 1977, Ex.Sess., ch: 134, § 1; Laws 1981, ch. 126, § 1.

The April 1983 issue of *Peter Berlin Report on Shrinkage Control* contains an excellent article on this Washington statute. In it, a security director for a Washington retailer is quoted as saying that 95 percent of the claims filed under this statute result in judgments favorable to merchants. Merchants are always looking for a more cost-effective way to deter shoplifters. These civil damage statutes may be an excellent vehicle.

California has recently passed a similar statute. It does not contain a provision saying whether the person detained must be prosecuted and convicted before filing the civil action. Subsection b only says that should an unemancipated minor's "willful conduct would constitute petty theft . . . any merchant or library facility who has been injured by such conduct" may file a civil action. Subsection c says only that "when an adult or emancipated minor has unlawfully taken merchandise from a merchant's premises" may civil action be filed. California merchants should have their legal departments research this language to see if it is possible to file a civil action when the suspect has not been prosecuted. Consider the language of this statute:

STATUTE	California

§ 490.5. Petty theft of retail merchandise or library materials; punishment; civil liability; detention

(b) When an unemancipated minor's willful conduct would constitute petty theft involving merchandise taken from a merchant's premises or a book or other library materials taken from a library facility, any merchant or library facility who has been injured by such conduct may bring a civil action against the parent or legal guardian having control and custody of the minor. For the purposes of such actions the misconduct of the unemancipated minor shall be imputed to the parent or legal guardian having control and custody of the minor. The parent or legal guardian having control or custody of an unemancipated minor whose conduct violates this subdivision shall be jointly and severally liable with the minor to a merchant for the retail value of his merchandise, if not recovered in merchantable condition or to a library facility for the fair market value of its book or other library materials, plus damages of not less than fifty dollars ($50) nor more than five hundred dollars ($500) plus costs. Recovery of such damages may be had in addition to, and is not limited by, any other provision of law which limits the liability of a parent or legal guardian for the tortious conduct of a minor. An action for recovery of damages, pursuant to this subdivision, may be brought in small claims court if the total damages do not exceed the jurisdictional limit of such court, or in any other appropriate court; however, total damages, including the value of the merchandise or book or other library materials, shall not exceed five hundred dollars ($500) for each action brought under this section.

The provisions of this subdivision are in addition to other civil remedies and do not limit merchants or other persons to elect to pursue other civil remedies, except that the provisions of Section 1714.1 of the Civil Code shall not apply herein.

(c) When an adult or emancipated minor has unlawfully taken merchandise from a merchant's premises, or a book or other library materials from a library facility, the adult or emancipated minor shall be liable to the merchant or library facility for damages of not less than fifty dollars ($50) nor more than five hundred dollars ($500), in addition to the retail value of the merchandise, if not recovered in merchantable condition, or the fair market value of the book or other library materials, if not recovered in undamaged condition, plus costs. An action for recovery of damages, pursuant to this subdivision, may be brought in small claims court if the total damages do not exceed the jurisdictional limit of such court, or in any other appropriate court. The provisions of this subdivision are in addition to other civil remedies and do not limit merchants or other persons to elect to pursue other civil remedies.

6

Statutes Granting Merchants Immunity from False Imprisonment Actions

On Christmas Eve in the basement of an Oakland department store, a twenty-seven-year-old former process server placed a string of electric light sockets inside his overcoat. Three store employees, two of them members of the security staff, saw him. The security director stopped the man, taking him to a room on the second floor to investigate the matter. The account of what happened in that room varies greatly depending on whether one reads the store's or the suspect's version. The young man said he had paid for the lights and refused to sign a statement to the effect he had failed to pay for them. After a twenty-minute detention, the police arrived and took him to the station. Two days later the security director signed the complaint charging him with misdemeanor shoplifting. Several weeks later, he was acquitted and then filed a two-count civil action, alleging false imprisonment and malicious prosecution.

The jury found for the department store on the malicious prosecution count but held the store liable on the count for false imprisonment, awarding $3,500 in damages. The California Supreme Court reversed the jury verdict in 1936. In so doing the merchant's privilege to detain on probable cause was born. The court found that probable cause is a defense to a false imprisonment action, provided the detention and subsequent investigation of the facts are legally reasonable. The court commented:

> We are here concerned only with the right of the defendant store to detain the plaintiff [the suspect] for the purpose of investigation to secure a confession after three persons had seen him pilfer articles from among those displayed . . . there seems to exist considerable confusion in the cases as to

whether probable cause is a defense in a false imprisonment cases involving misdemeanors.[1]

In this case for the first time, a state supreme court said a merchant can detain on probable cause, investigate the facts, and if later sued for false imprisonment can plead compliance with the privilege as a defense. The merchant's privilege was available even though the shoplifting case involved a misdemeanor.

State legislatures have recognized this privilege first announced in 1936, by incorporating it into the detention statute.[2] In 1965, the American Law Institute codified the privilege in the Restatement of the Law of Torts. Before considering the detention statutes themselves, read closely the codification of the merchant's privilege as set forth by the American Law Institute.[3]

> Restatement of the Law of Torts Temporary detention for
> Investigation (section 120A)
> One who reasonably believes that another has tortiously taken chattel upon his premises, or has failed to make due cash payment for a chattel purchased or services rendered there, is privileged, without arresting the other to detain him on the premises for the time necessary for a reasonable investigation of the facts.[3]

Today the law recognizes the concept of a temporary detention without declaring the stopping of a shoplifting suspect to be a warrantless citizen's arrest. The detention must be justified by observations which establish probable-cause type evidence. Following the detention for probable cause, the investigation of the facts must be legally reasonable in three respects—manner, method, and time. State legislatures have gone further than the actual privilege, saying that if the retail employee's conduct while handling the shoplifting situation falls within the scope of the privilege, the store shall not be found liable for false imprisonment.

The following list of detention statute titles was selected at random. It is clear from just the titles that the state legislatures did not intend to give merchants the authority to make warrantless citizen's arrest in shoplifting cases. As the titles clearly show, the subject of these statutes is detention on probable cause, an investigation of the facts, and a defense to use if the store is sued civilly as a result of the encounter with the shoplifting suspect.

---

[1]Collyer v. Kress, 54 P.2d 20 (California, 1936)

[2]The terms "merchant's privilege statutes" and "detention statutes" mean the same thing in this book.

[3]Restatement of the Law of Torts, Second Edition, Chapter 5, page 202 (1965), The American Law Institute, St. Paul, Minnesota.

State	Title of Merchant's Detention Statute
Alaska	Reasonable Detention as a Defense
Arizona	Shoplifting—Detaining Suspect—Defense to Wrongful Detention
Colorado	Questioning of Person Suspected of Theft without Liability
California	Petty Theft—Civil Liability—Detention
Illinois	Detention
Indiana	Immunity from Civil or Criminal Action for Detention
Michigan	Suspected Shoplifting—Probable Case as a Defense in Civil Action
Mississippi	Shoplifting—Detention of Suspects for Questioning without Incurring Civil Liability
Nebraska	Shoplifting—Detention—No Criminal or Civil Liability
Oregon	Detention and Interrogation of Persons Suspected of Theft in a Store—Probable Case
Washington	Reasonable Grounds as a Defense

As a general rule, the language of these detention statutes is vague and even confusing. Regardless of the wording, the common denominator of these statutes is this: they authorize retailers to detain a shoplifting suspect on probable cause. This stopping is legally known as a detention for investigation of the facts rather than a citizen's arrest. Once the suspect is detained, the retail employee can conduct an investigation of the facts which is legally reasonable in manner, method, and time. During the investigation, the merchant is authorized to ask the suspect questions about ownership of the merchandise, to ask the suspect to produce concealed merchandise for examination relative to ownership, to recover unpurchased merchandise, and to hold the suspect until the arrival of a peace officer if the detaining merchant elects to have the person formally arrested and prosecuted.

If the retail employee handling the shoplifting situation does not violate any provision of the detention statute during the encounter with the suspect, the statute gives the store a defense to use if the suspect later sues that store for false imprisonment. As a defense, the store can show the employee's compliance with all provisions of the detention statute. If the jury finds that the employee's conduct while handling the case was within the scope of the statutory privilege, the store wins the false imprisonment case. On the other hand, if the jury finds a store owner, manager, or security person violated any of the provisions of the statutory privilege, then liability for false imprisonment is established against the store. The jury can then award actual and punitive damages to the plaintiff.

Sometimes merchants mistakenly believe the only value of these statutes is for their lawyers to use in preparing a defense *after* a civil action has been filed. Nothing is further from the truth. Store owners, managers, and security personnel should learn to comply with the provisions of these merchant's privilege statutes as part of shoplifting loss-prevention training programs. The best defense against a civil action in any state is to *prevent that civil action from being filed in the first place.* This loss-prevention goal is accomplished in just one way—by teaching employees how to comply with the tests found in the detention statute. Later in this chapter, there are five tests for retailers to meet when handling shoplifting situations so that their conduct will fall within the scope of the statutory privilege. It is absolutely necessary that persons authorized to handle shoplifting cases in the store understand how to meet these tests.

Before examining some of these statutes and the tests that must be met to comply with them, merchants in all states must remember one thing—*these detention statutes are 100 percent neutral about prosecution of the shoplifting case.* Said another way, they do not require that any person detained on probable cause be prosecuted. The privilege is one to detain and investigate the facts without automatically incurring false imprisonment liability. As pointed out in Chapter 1, these statutes are the legal basis for a selective prosecution policy. The decision to prosecute the case or to release the suspect is left entirely up to the detaining merchant. Under these statutes, a merchant may prosecute as many or as few cases as that merchant determines will be a sufficient deterrent to future shoplifting attempts. Simply stated, the legal beauty of detention statutes is that they authorize selective prosecution with minimum civil liability risk.

DETENTION STATUTES DISCUSSED AND DISTINGUISHED

Regardless of the name given to the statute by the legislature, all detention statutes cover the same subject. They all incorporate the concept of a temporary detention and investigation of the facts into their provisions. They all permit the merchant to detain and investigate without declaring the stopping a citizen's arrest. They do not grant police power to the otherwise private citizen merchant. They all give the store a statutory defense to plead compliance with if later sued civilly for false imprisonment. Even though they vary in title and wording, these detention statutes all grant conditional and limited immunity to a merchant who complies with their provisions.

The Missouri detention statute[4] is confusing and rambles in its wording.

STATUTE	Missouri

2. Detention (§ 537.125, Mo. Stats. Ann.)

Any merchant, his agent or employee, who has reasonable grounds or probable cause to believe that a person has committed or is committing a wrongful taking of merchandise or money from a mercantile establishment, may detain such person in a reasonable manner and for a reasonable length of time for the purpose of investigating whether there has been a wrongful taking of such merchandise or money. Any such reasonable detention shall not constitute an unlawful arrest or detention, nor shall it render the merchant, his agent or employee, criminally or civilly liable to the person so detained.

Any person willfully concealing unpurchased merchandise of any mercantile establishment, either on the premises or outside the premises of such establishment, shall be presumed to have so concealed such merchandise with the intention of committing a wrongful taking of such merchandise . . . , and the finding of such unpurchased merchandise concealed upon the person or among the belongings of such person shall be evidence of reasonable grounds and probable cause for the detention in a reasonable manner and for a reasonable length of time, of such person by a merchant, his agent or employee, in order that recovery of such merchandise may be effected, and any such reasonable detention shall not be deemed to be unlawful, nor render such merchant, his agent or employee criminally or civilly liable.

The main shortcoming of this statute is its failure to tell the merchant to investigate the question of ownership after detaining the suspect on probable cause. The Missouri Legislature tells merchants to detain and investigate to see if a "wrongful taking" of either money or merchandise has occurred. A store manager or security person reading this statute would have no idea that he is supposed to investigate the factual question of ownership of merchandise after detaining a suspect on probable cause. A retail or security executive charged with the job of writing a training program would also be completely in the dark about what facts should be investigated to determine if a prosecutable case exists. With a high-sounding purpose, the statute says that any reasonable detention shall not

---

[4]Statutes like this one exist largely because retail trade associations do not devote time and effort to lobbying. Retailers leave the job of drafting legislation to legislators who are not familiar with the dual legal aspects of handling shoplifting cases. The result too often is a wordy, confusing, rambling detention statute of no practical benefit to store managers and security people.

constitute an unlawful arrest or detention, which is to say nothing helpful to a retail employee who is about to detain a shoplifting suspect in his store.

The Florida detention statute is clearly drafted regarding the purpose for detaining on probable cause:

| STATUTE | FLORIDA—Retail Theft |

Section 812.015

(3) A peace officer, merchant, or a merchant's employee who has probable cause to believe that merchandise has been unlawfully taken by a person and that he can recover it by taking the person into custody, may for the *purpose of attempting to effect such recovery or for prosecution,* take the person into custody and detain him in a reasonable manner for a reasonable length of time. Such taking into custody and detention by a peace officer, merchant or merchant's employee, if done *in compliance with all the requirements of this subsection,* shall not render such police officer, merchant or merchant's employee criminally or civilly liable for false arrest, false imprisonment or unlawful detention. [Emphasis supplied]

This statute minces no words. It comes out and says that the purpose of detaining on probable cause is to recover the merchandise or to prosecute the suspect. All detention statutes are neutral, as this one demonstrates. The merchant may effect the recovery of unpurchased goods and release the suspect without formal prosecution, or the suspect may be charged with shoplifting and the case put through the court system. This statute also contains a clear statement that retail employees must comply with all the provisions in order to use it successfully as a defense if later sued for false imprisonment, false arrest, or unlawful detention. It is very important to notice that this statute (typical of almost all other detention statutes) *does not* provide the store with a statutory defense to use if later sued for malicious prosecution. See the Flower Seeds Case in chapter 8 where the Florida court clearly said the detention statute provided the store with a defense to a false imprisonment action but not to one for malicious prosecution.

The New Jersey detention statute emphasizes recovery of unpurchased merchandise.

| STATUTE | New Jersey Statute |

2. Detention (2C:20-11e)

A law enforcement officer, or a special officer, or a merchant, who has probable cause for *believing* that a person has wilfully concealed unpurchased merchandise and that he can *recover* the merchandise by taking the person into custody may, for the purpose of attempting to effect recovery thereof, take the person into custody and detain him in a reasonable manner for not more than a reasonable time, and the taking into custody by a law enforcement officer or special officer or merchant shall not render such person criminally or civilly liable in any manner or to any extent whatsoever. [Emphasis supplied]

This statute is of more help to merchants than the Missouri type but not as well drafted as the Florida statute. Here the emphasis is on recovering merchandise after detaining on probable cause. Of course, a New Jersey merchant, like one in any other state, can also decide to prosecute the person detained in addition to recovering the goods.

The Kansas detention statute is another poorly worded detention statute.

STATUTE	Kansas

2. Detention (§21-3424(3), Kans. Gen. Stats.)

Any merchant, his agent or employee, who has probable cause to believe that a person has actual possession of and (a) has wrongfully taken, or (b) is about to wrongfully take merchandise from a mercantile establishment, may detain such person (a) on the premises or (b) in the immediate vicinity thereof, in a reasonable manner and for a reasonable period of time for the purpose of investigating the circumstances of such possession. Such reasonable detention shall not constitute an arrest nor an unlawful restraint.

This statute tells merchants to detain and investigate the "circumstances of such possession," which is to say nothing of value to a retail employee about stopping a shoplifting suspect on the sales floor of a store. Store managers and security people need to know to investigate the question of ownership after detaining on probable cause.

Most retailers who conduct any training at all on handling shoplifting cases understand the probable cause to detain requirement of these statutes. They understand an employee must see the suspect obtain wrongful possession of goods and leave the store without paying before detaining that suspect. They understand that people obtain wrongful possession by concealing goods, by switching price tags, by stuffing containers, by shoplifting in fitting rooms, by passing merchandise off to companions, and sometimes by walking out of the store with merchandise in plain view. Cases where stores have been successfully sued civilly demonstrate many merchants are confused about how to conduct an investigation of the facts once a shoplifting suspect has been detained on probable cause. Part of the reason this confusion exists is because detention statutes in many states are so poorly drafted. The retail community must accept the responsibility for part of its civil liability dilemma because they do not lobby for better detention statutes. Retailers and their trade associations should lobby for Retail Theft Act type detention statutes, such as found in Illinois, Pennsylvania, and Florida.

In Chapter 2, the Kentucky detention statute (also a better drafted one) was cited to show the legislature authorized merchants to detain and then investigate the factual question of ownership. This statute comes out and tells merchants what to do once the suspect has been detained on probable cause. It is specific, so merchants can learn from it. The statute says a merchant can detain for any or all of the following purposes:

STATUTE	Kentucky

(c) To make reasonable inquiry as to whether such person has in his possession unpurchased merchandise, and to make reasonable investigation of the ownership of such merchandise;

(d) To recover or attempt to recover goods taken from the mercantile establishment by such person, or by others accompanying him;

(e) To inform a peace officer or law enforcement agency of the detention of the person and to surrender the person to the custody of a peace officer, and in the case of a minor, to inform the parents, guardian or other person having custody of that minor of his detention, in addition to surrendering the minor to the custody of a peace officer.

(Enact. Act 1958, ch. 11, § 2; 1968, ch. 49, § 2; 1978, ch. 75 § 1, effective June 17, 1978.)

Training programs must be specific about the *purpose* of the investigation following a detention for probable cause. Store owners, managers, and security people must understand that they must obtain the suspect's explanation because it has legal meaning. Most of the time the explanation is *not* a confession but just the opposite—a denial of guilt. They must understand that examination of the merchandise is essential in determining whether the store or the suspect owns it. One suggestion is to base the investigation procedures along the lines of the purposes set forth in this Kentucky statute. In this way, the detaining employee knows what to do once the suspect has been detained on probable cause. Guidelines will get merchants in trouble because the employee can make

FIGURE 6.1	Tests to meet in complying with the merchant's privilege

Detention Phase

1 Detain on probable cause

Investigation of Fact Phase

2 Treat suspect in a legally reasonable manner

3 Investigate facts in a legally reasonable method

4 Complete investigation in a legally reasonable time

Decision-making Phase

5 Justify decision to prosecute the case by reviewing the facts that will be used later in court to establish the elements of the offense.

Reason for review: So that store manager or security person handling case will possess a "reasonable belief" that a prosecutable case exists before filing it.

Note: The merchant may decide not to prosecute the case because a review of the facts shows that in court, the facts will not establish that the suspect intended to shoplift merchandise owned by the store. In this situation the suspect is released.

a mistake, thereby violating the privilege. When the privilege is violated, the store loses the civil liability immunity granted by the detention statute.

FIVE TESTS RETAILERS MUST MEET TO COMPLY WITH THE MERCHANT'S PRIVILEGE STATUTES

As shown, the names and wording of these statutes vary from state to state. The point to remember is that they are all based on the same privilege. The five tests in Figure 6.1 were designed to help merchants reduce the risk of having the store sued for false imprisonment, false arrest, slander, assault and battery, and malicious prosecution. Merchants in any state can incorporate these tests into training programs because they are based on the privilege. The tests cover the three phases of the encounter with a shoplifting suspect.

Now consider each test with some comments and examples.

Detention Phase

Test 1: Detain on probable cause

Example of Violation: Detaining on suspicion or on the basis of a conclusion rather than actually seeing the suspect obtain possession of merchandise and conceal it will violate this test. To comply with it, a retail employee should see the suspect remove the item from its place of display (with his hands) then conceal it, and continue in possession of the concealed merchandise past the last station for receiving payment. Detain only after the suspect has been given an opportunity to pay and has failed to pay.

Investigation of Fact Phase

Test 2: Treat the suspect in a legally reasonable manner
Examples of Violations: Detaining and then doing any of the following violate this test:
1. Using excessive force, either to detain or while investigating the facts
2. Making an accusation that the suspect was shoplifting or stole something
3. Forcing a search to obtain concealed merchandise without first obtaining the suspect's consent to search
4. Making threats of prosecution for any reason, but specifically to obtain either a confession or a civil liability release

Test 3: Investigate the facts in a legally reasonable method
Comment: To avoid violating this test, the investigation should be conducted in a logical and systematic method as suggested in the *Sources of Evidence* chart in Chapter 4. A summary of the investigation part of the chart is as follows:
1. Always give the suspect an opportunity to explain so as to establish the defense.
2. Translate the explanation into its legal meaning.
3. Recover the merchandise and examine it to be sure that later in court, store ownership can be established.
5. Review the evidence to be sure it will establish the elements of the offense.
6. Make the decision—to prosecute or to release—based on facts.

Test 4: Complete the investigation in a legally reasonable time
Comment: Most detention statutes do not set forth a specific time period in which the investigation must be completed. Where no time is stated, one hour is generally safe. If retail employees have the skills to investigate the facts, it should not take sixty minutes to complete it, especially in cases where the suspect is detained and says, "I forgot to pay." It will take longer to investigate the facts where the suspect is detained and then claims ownership of the merchandise in question.

Decision-Making Phase

Test 5: Justify the decision to prosecute by reviewing the facts
Comment: The facts produced must be used in court to establish the elements of the store's case. The facts produced by giving the suspect an opportunity to explain will be used by the suspect in court as the formal defense to the charge filed by the store. Both sets of facts must be reviewed. A retail employee must possess a reasonable belief that a prosecutable case exists before calling the police and authorizing prosecution. For this reason, the facts, both prosecution and defense facts, must be reviewed before making the decision to prosecute. In some situations, a review of the facts will reject the decision to file the charge and support the decision to release the suspect without formal prosecution.

The fact that detention statutes are on the books does not prohibit a person from filing a civil action against a store. They do make it more difficult for a person to establish liability. The store can defend the civil action by showing its employees did comply with the tests found in those statutes. In a civil action, the plaintiff will always allege that the conduct of a store employee violated the civil tort law duty to use reasonable care. The store defends by saying that the conduct of its employee in handling the case was within the scope of the merchant's privilege so no liability exists. The jury then decides whether the employee met the tests in the merchant's privilege. In the cases that follow, retail employees were found to have violated one or more of the tests so liability against their stores was determined to exist. By seeing how these retail employees acted outside the statutory privilege, a merchant can identify these liability-creating mistakes and avoid making them.

CASES WHERE STORES WERE SUED FOR FALSE IMPRISONMENT AND COULD NOT SHOW AS A DEFENSE THAT THEIR EMPLOYEES DETAINED ON PROBABLE CAUSE

It is extremely important to realize a store can be successfully sued whether or not a shoplifting charge is filed. In the two cases which follow, neither suspect was formally arrested and prosecuted. In both cases, the employees violated test 1 because the decision to detain for investigation was not supported by probable cause evidence. They detained on suspicion, opinion, or hunch rather than on the basis of observations that established probable cause or reasonable grounds. When later sued, these stores could not show that their employees complied with the merchant's privilege.

CASE	Jar of deodorant case

The manager of this outlet of a national department store in Mississippi was authorized to detain suspects based on his personal observations or on information supplied to him by employees. Under all merchant's privilege statutes, this is lawful because they permit detention by a merchant, his agent, or his employee.*

In this case, a lone female entered the store, carrying a purse with a paper bag in it containing a pair of shoes. First, she looked at some beads and then at cosmetics. Before detaining the woman, the manager received sources of information from two different employees. One sales employee told him she became "suspicious" because the shopper said she did not want any salesperson assistance. The other employee told the manager she "thought" the woman put a jar of deodorant inside her purse. Neither employee told the manager she saw the woman remove the deodorant from its place of display with her hands and place it in her purse.

The manager approached the woman and grabbed her by the arm, demanding she pay for the deodorant (an obvious violation of test 1). He asked her to empty the contents of her purse and the bag on the floor, in front of both customers and store employees. After he was satisfied she did not have the deodorant or any other store merchandise in her possession, he admitted he made a mistake.

The jury found the manager violated test 1 because he did not possess probable cause type evidence to justify his decision to detain her for investigation. This act of restraining her freedom of movement without a legal reason—called *probable cause type evidence*—created liability for false imprisonment. In defending the manager's conduct, the detention statute was of no value because test 1 had been violated. The court properly affirmed the jury finding of liability and awarding of damages. Most stores instruct employees to conduct the investigation of the facts off the sales floor in an effort to comply with the reasonable investigation provisions. Apparently the manager's grabbing of her arm was not aggravated because the civil action contained no count for assault and battery type liability, but obviously this manager made a mistake by touching her when the evidence was that she made no effort to resist or leave.

J.C. Penney v. Cox, 148 S.2d 679 (Mississippi, 1967)

*See the following cases in Chapter 8 where merchants were sued only for false imprisonment because they did not file shoplifting charges: New Blue Purse, Pocket Comb, Wrong Woman, Store Greeter, and Vest Cases. In all those cases, the courts found the store employee's decision to detain was not supported by probable cause, thereby violating the merchant's privilege.

The real problem here was that the manager did not understand the probable cause to detain requirement of detention statutes. No store in any state could successfully plead employee compliance with the merchant's privilege in a shoplifting situation demonstrated by the Jar of Deodorant Case.

CASE	Random stopping case

This case is a classic example of not understanding that probable cause to detain means the suspect must be seen obtaining wrongful possession of merchandise in some way. This food store was experiencing constant losses of cigarettes. Its solution was to detain persons seen standing near the cigarette display for any period of time. There was no requirement that an employee see a person remove cigarettes from the display. One customer who was detained "at random" filed a false imprisonment action after being detained and released. No cigarettes were found on the person.

There was no allegation that the plaintiff was mistreated in any way, only that the store lacked probable cause to detain for investigation. The court found false imprisonment liability to exist, so the store had to pay damages. A random stopping type approach will not meet the probable cause to detain test in any state. Merchants should always train employees to ask the following question—"Did I see the suspect remove the merchandise from its place of display with his hands?" In both the Jar of Deodorant and Random Stopping Cases, no store employee witnessed a suspect obtaining possession of merchandise with the hands. Accordingly, both stores violated the probable cause to detain requirement of the merchant's privilege. Because they acted outside the scope of the privilege, neither store had a defense to use when later sued for false imprisonment. Both stores made evidence-gathering mistakes on the sales floor, mistakes which permitted their suspects to sue civilly.

Isiah v. Great Atlantic & Pacific Tea Co, 174 N.E.2d 128 (Ohio, 1959)

In the Infant Seat Case, a security person detained a person on information supplied to him by a sales employee. All detention statutes say a suspect may be detained by a *merchant, his agent, or his employee* if the probable cause test is met. Most stores with full-time security staffs (like department and discount stores) do not permit detentions to be made unless the security staff member observes the suspect obtaining wrongful possession of merchandise and leaving without paying for it. If a sales employee witnesses a person concealing unpurchased merchandise, the sales employee is instructed not to detain for investigation, although detention statutes authorize it. The sales employee is told to summon a security person to the department. The security employee must witness that suspect conceal additional merchandise before detaining to investigate the facts. The net effect of such a policy is that many people who have been seen concealing merchandise by sales employees are not detained unless they shoplift again in the presence of the security staff member. Department and discount stores justify this approach by saying it would be too easy for a sales employee to make a mistake that would permit a civil action to be filed.

| CASE | Infant seat case |

The Wisconsin court in this case said the store was not liable for false imprisonment when a security employee detained on information given to him by a sales employee. Here a woman went to a store to buy some diapers and cans of motor oil. She took her small child along, carrying the infant seat she had purchased at the discount store two or three weeks earlier. A large discount store price tag was still attached to the seat. She picked out the diapers, motor oil, and some children's clothing and then went through the checkout line paying for all the merchandise. She was then detained by a man who said, "You're under arrest" or "I'm putting you under arrest." She testified that she was scared but knew she had done nothing wrong. She went to the office with the man, a security employee of the store.

She denied shoplifting the baby seat and told the security officer about having bought it earlier. She demanded to see the person who had accused her of stealing the merchandise. In a few minutes, a sales employee came to the office and said she saw the woman take it off the table and put the baby in it. The suspect then showed the employees that the seat had cat hairs, food crumbs, and milk stains on it as evidence she had previously purchased the infant seat. The security office recognized she had demonstrated ownership and said, "I'm really sorry, there's been a terrible mistake. You can go." She had been detained twenty minutes.

Based on this evidence, the court found as a matter of law that the discount store had probable cause to detain the woman and investigate the facts. The trial judge did not submit the question to the jury, and the appellate court approved. Consider what the appellate court had to say:

> Because defendant is a corporation it must transact business through its officers and employees. Section 943.50(3) [the detention statute] permits a merchant to detain a shopper if certain conditions are met, one of which is that the merchant have probable cause for believing that the shopper stole the merchant's goods. Plaintiff's deposition shows that the defendant's security officer believed that she stole the infant seat because another K-Mart employee told him that she saw plaintiff steal it. . . . The merchant received word through one of its employees that plaintiff removed an infant seat from the shelf, put her child in it and left

the store without paying for the seat. *We hold as a matter of law that the merchant, through its security guard, had probable cause based on this report to believe that plaintiff had shoplifted.* [Emphasis supplied]

This case is solid authority that a security person may detain a suspect and investigate the facts where the probable cause evidence is supplied by a sales employee. The same was found in the Slacks in the Car Trunk Case in Chapter 3, where the probable cause to detain evidence was supplied by the store tailor who saw the man and woman roll up the slacks and conceal them in the woman's purse.

Merchants with security staffs (like department and discount stores) generally do not permit security personnel to detain on information provided to them by department heads or sales employees. A suggestion to these stores is to train sales floor personnel in high-incident shoplifting departments to comply with the probable cause and reasonable investigation requirements of the merchant's privilege. The sales floor employee could then notify security who would respond and obtain the facts from the sales floor employee. Presumably the security employee is better trained to understand if the probable cause to detain for investigation requirement has been met. The security employee could then decide if the sales floor employee's observations demonstrated wrongful possession of merchandise and intent to shoplift by leaving without paying. If the security employee was satisfied that the probable cause test had been met, that security person could handle the detention and investigation of the facts. Such an approach would avoid the absurd situations where a sales employee witnesses a person conceal merchandise but no detention is made because that person does not shoplift a second time when being watched by a security staff member.

Johnson v. K-Mart, 279 N.W.2d 74 (Wisconsin, 1980)

The Infant Seat Case is an excellent example of how the courts recognize that three or four security people in a department or discount store cannot possibly witness every shoplifting attempt. The court clearly said the security person had probable cause to justify the detention based on the information reported to him by a sales employee. It is not suggested that sales employees be given authority to detain. It is suggested that retailers could make better use of the authority given to them under detention statutes. If merchants train selected sales floor people in high-incident shoplifting departments to recognize probable cause and then report this evidence to a security staff member, that store is making better use of sales floor employees in preventing shoplifting losses.

Retailers all know they detain only one in fifteen or twenty persons who are actually shoplifting. As they also know, shoplifting losses in some departments will run 6 percent or more. Since both the legislatures and courts permit detentions as found in the Infant Seat Case, a department or discount store should at least be aware of this fact when reviewing shoplifting detention policies and procedures. Specialty stores without full-time security people on their selling floors have no choice but to authorize the manager to detain on information supplied by sales employees. The store manager can review the information supplied by a sales employee and decide if the probable cause test had been met. The store manager can then effect the detention and conduct a legally reasonable investigation of the facts as authorized by the merchant's privilege statute.

A final point about the Infant Seat Case must be made. The private citizen store detective who actually "stopped" the woman used the word "arrest" to describe what he did. According to the testimony he said, "You are under arrest" or "I am putting you under arrest." The Wisconsin detention statute (like other detention statutes) does not authorize private citizen retail employees to make citizen's arrests.

In the civil action which followed, the store pleaded compliance with the detention statute as its defense, yet the security person told the lady she was under arrest. The court did not comment on this point, but of course it is inconsistent. A court could find that by telling a suspect he is under arrest, the stopping is not a detention under the merchant's privilege but a citizen's arrest. Vocabulary is important. Store owners, managers, and security personnel should avoid using the word "arrest" to describe the stopping of suspects. This statement could be used as evidence that the store did not ever intend to comply with the provisions of the detention statutes because the statute does not authorize arrests. Many security people have law enforcement backgrounds. They must remember there is a big difference in the authority of a public law enforcement officer's job (which is to fight crime) and that of a security officer (which is to protect private assets). It sounds macho to say, "I arrested two shoplifting suspects," but it makes more loss-prevention sense to say, "I detained a shoplifting suspect for investigation of the facts."

SITUATIONS WHERE A MERCHANT FILED A NONPROSECUTABLE SHOPLIFTING CASE, LOST THAT CASE, AND WAS SUCCESSFULLY SUED FOR MALICIOUS PROSECUTION

Each time a shoplifting suspect is detained, the possibility of formal arrest and prosecution exists just as the possibility of releasing the suspect exists. The store owner, manager, or security person handling the situation has, under the detention statute, a reasonable time to conduct an investigation of the facts and make a decision—prosecute or release. In the three cases that follow, the stores decided to prosecute, but their decisions were not supported by evidence that would establish the elements of the offense. The Discarded Sweater Case was lost because the store's evidence failed to prove the woman intended to shoplift the sweater. In the Aspirin and Returned Gloves Cases, the prosecution failed to prove the food store owned the aspirin and the department store owned the gloves. These stores filed nonprosecutable cases, lost them, and were then sued for malicious prosecution. It is more difficult to defend a malicious prosecution action because the store cannot plead compliance with the detention statute as a defense. The merchant's privilege is one to detain and investigate the facts, not one to prosecute. Stores that file nonprosecutable cases lose them and typically wind up paying out money on malicious prosecution cases.

False imprisonment and malicious prosecution are two separate and distinct civil actions. A person suing for false imprisonment claims he was detained without probable cause or that after being properly detained he was legally mistreated in some way. No shoplifting charge need be filed and lost before a person is entitled to sue a store for false imprisonment. The store defends the action by saying its employee detained on probable cause then conducted a legally reasonable investigation. In other words the store defends by pleading compliance with the detention statute.

A person suing for malicious prosecution is less concerned with the detention aspect of the situation. The thrust of the action is wrongful initiation of a shoplifting charge. Said another way, the malicious prosecution plaintiff alleges that the store did not investigate the facts properly and this failure to investigate resulted in a shoplifting charge being filed without evidence to justify it. Stores cannot plead compliance with a detention statute when sued for malicious prosecution because they do not apply to actions for malicious prosecution.

Consider the sample petition which shows the allegations and the defenses in false imprisonment and malicious prosecution actions.

Plaintiff's petition

1. False imprisonment
Plaintiff says his freedom of movement was restrained in the store by a store employee without a legal reason or excuse. [The plaintiff is really saying the decision to detain was not supported by observations made by the store employee on the sales floor.]

Store's defense

1. Defense of merchant's privilege
Merchant defends by saying its employee detained on probable cause and conducted an investigation of the facts that was legally reasonable in manner, method, and time.

As part of the defense, the merchant says its employee did not mistreat the suspect by using excessive force, by making allegations of shoplifting, by forcing a search without first obtaining consent of the suspect, or making any threats of prosecution to obtain a confession or a civil liability release.

2. Malicious prosecution
Plaintiff says the store caused the case to be prosecuted without probable cause and such prosecution was legally malicious. [The plaintiff is really saying the decision to prosecute was not supported by a thorough investigation and review of the facts after he was detained.]

2. Defense of merchant's privilege is not available on this count because detention statutes do not provide the store with a defense to a malicious prosecution.

The store defends by showing its employee complied with test 3 (investigation of the facts) and test 5 (review of facts before deciding to file the charge). Compliance with these tests is evidence that the employee possessed a reasonable belief a prosecutable case existed before authorizing it to be filed.

In the three cases which follow, the stores could not plead compliance with the detention statute as a defense. Instead, they had to rely on store policy. The problem was that all three stores had not adequately trained employees to investigate and review the facts *before* authorizing shoplifting cases to be prosecuted. It is easy to see in the Discarded Sweater Case that the Washington, D.C. department store had no training program—the security person did not even try to investigate the facts. He simply detained the woman and called the police to come out and formally arrest her. In the Aspirin Case the food store manager and contract security guard did go through the motions of an investigation before calling the police. In the Returned Gloves Case the department store security people were more thorough. They obtained her explanation, then examined the gloves and her receipt before having her prosecuted. The common factor in all three cases is this: store training did not adequately teach security employees to determine if a prosecutable case existed before filing it. When the suspect was acquitted and sued for malicious prosecution these stores had no defense. The merchant's privilege did not give them one nor did store policy.

These cases demonstrate that merchants need to develop the skills to investigate and review the facts *after* the suspect has been detained on probable cause. The reason these cases resulted in acquittals followed by civil actions was violations of tests 3 and 5. These stores did not conduct an independent investigation of the facts before deciding to have their suspects formally arrested and prosecuted. None of the three cases had to be filed. The lady discarding the sweater, the man with the aspirin bottle in his pocket, and the woman with the gloves could all have been released without formal prosecution. Had this been done, the only civil action any of them could have filed was for false imprisonment—a civil action to which the merchant always has a statutory defense. These cases are examples of stores not realizing the value of a selective prosecution policy as authorized by the merchant's privilege statutes. When there is any doubt about whether the evidence will establish the elements of the offense, the better approach is not to prosecute.

Always remember that by filing a case the store's civil liability exposure *increases* from false imprisonment alone to false imprisonment, false arrest, and malicious prosecution. If a security person or store manager does not conduct a thorough investigation and review of the facts before deciding to prosecute the case, that merchant will file nonprosecutable cases. The reason to detain and investigate the facts is to see if the evidence supports or rejects the decision to prosecute. The facts in the three cases which follow are not complicated. They demonstrate situations encountered by merchants in free standing stores and in shopping malls every day. The problem found in each case was the same—the stores did not understand the civil liability consequence of filing a nonprosecutable case. These stores did not understand that by following a selective prosecution policy (as authorized by the detention statute) they were also minimizing exposure to malicious prosecution liability.

CASE	Discarded sweater case

This store's policy was to detain people and hold them for the arrival of the police without conducting an investigation of the facts. This procedure did not require the security officer to obtain a suspect's explanation or to consider the legal meaning of it as defense evidence. There was no requirement for the security person to review the facts before calling the police. Succinctly stated, this store's policy was not based on any understanding of the merchant's privilege.

A security officer saw a young woman remove a man's sweater from a counter on the second floor in the men's department, although she did not conceal the item. She next went to the basement. On the way, she stopped and purchased a woman's raincoat. In the basement, she met a female companion and handed the sweater to her. The companion handed it back. Up to this point, the sweater had never been concealed. The guard testified that at this point, the woman partially concealed the sweater under her coat. When she saw he was watching her, she discarded it on the floor under a bra counter. She took the escalator to the first floor, where she was detained just as she was about to go out the door.

Nichols v. Woodward & Lothrop, 322 A.2d 383 (D.C., 1974)

The woman was charged with shoplifting the sweater and acquitted. At trial she testified about having a conversation with a female sales clerk in the basement, asking the clerk if the sweater could be returned there or had to be taken back to the second floor men's department. Because store policy did not require security employees to obtain a suspect's explanation before having them charged with shoplifting, the security man knew nothing about the conversation with the sales clerk. At trial the sales clerk did testify, corroborating the woman's explanation. Had the security man investigated the facts he would have realized that at best he had an attempted shoplifting case. Because she did not continue the concealment of the sweater past the cash register and to the door, there was not sufficient evidence produced to establish the element of intent to shoplift.

This shoplifting case should never have been filed. Under both the store's evidence and under the woman's evidence the sweater was discarded in the basement.[5] She was not in wrongful possession of unpurchased merchandise. Many security professionals would question the decision to detain her in the first place—and rightly so. Why detain her at all? The store had the sweater and she had purchased a raincoat. There was neither a legal nor a practical reason to detain this woman. There was no reason whatsoever to have her prosecuted.

This Washington, D.C. store was lucky. The jury found malicious prosecution liability to exist and awarded damages. This finding would be the result in all jurisdictions where a store does not instruct its security employees to investigate the facts before having shoplifting suspects arrested and prosecuted. The appellate court bailed the store out by reversing the jury finding of malicious prosecution liability. Technically then, this store "won" the civil case because it did not have to pay out actual and punitive damages. As a practical matter, the store lost because of its policy. The store had to spend time and money defending a civil action in a situation where a shoplifting charge should never have been filed in the first place. The real problem here was the absence of any store policy requiring employees to investigate the facts after detaining shoplifting suspects. Even though the jury award was reversed the judge in this case realized the problem was with the store policy and commented:

> The record indicates that all persons arrested at the store on suspicion of larceny were turned over to the Metropolitan Police Department to be charged formally, and there *was no policy providing for an internal review by the store's security personnel of the merits of particular cases.* Woodward & Lothrop's security director testified that he had no knowledge of any

---

[5]This department store violated the continuous concealment rule by not waiting until she passed the last cash register before detaining for investigation of the facts. It is particularly important in department stores that security people let suspects pass several cash registers before detaining.

conversation between appellant [the young woman] and the store saleswoman. [Emphasis supplied]

The author of a law review article has commented on the civil liability danger of using a *no investigation before filing charges* type of policy as found in this Discarded Sweater Case.

> Many retailers feel that if they simply hold the suspect without questioning him until the police arrive, or if they simply direct the police to arrest the suspect without personally detaining him, there is no danger of civil liability. *They are mistaken.* [Emphasis supplied][6]

No store in any state should use a policy like the one found in this Discarded Sweater Case. By failing to investigate the facts, the merchant is increasing the chances of filing a nonprosecutable case, losing that case, and having the store sued for malicious prosecution—a civil action to which there is no defense available under the merchant's privilege statutes in most states.

CASE	Aspirin case

A Georgia food store manager and a contract security guard did not want to believe what they heard: the suspect claimed ownership by prior purchase. They wanted only to believe what they saw: the man put a bottle of aspirin in his sweater pocket and left. They apparently believed a conviction would result because of their observations and did not investigate the factual question of ownership before calling the police to have him arrested and prosecuted. These two retail employees did not produce any evidence in their store to rely on in court to prove the element of ownership of the aspirin, although the suspect was claiming ownership. The case was dismissed, and the man sued the food store for malicious prosecution.

In this case, a contract security guard saw the man place a bottle of aspirin in his sweater pocket. The man was detained and taken to a stock room at the rear of the store. The manager was called because he had to authorize the filing of all shoplifting charges. The security guard told the manager about witnessing the concealment and also that he saw the man "ditch" the box. The man did not have a sales receipt. He told them he bought the aspirin earlier that afternoon at a nearby drugstore. He said he put the box and probably the receipt in a trash can just outside the drugstore. He further said he had taken two of the aspirin before entering the food store and asked them to count the remaining tablets. He denied shoplifting, saying he was comparing prices between the two stores. He repeated the explanation in front of the police when they arrived to arrest him.

---

[6]"The Law of Shoplifting," 55 Minnesota Law Review, 825, 854 (1971).

Without requiring the security guard to look for the missing box, the manager authorized prosecution. This was an evidence-gathering mistake that came back to haunt the store in the civil action. The manager did not understand about having to establish the suspect's defense. Rather than taking the explanation of ownership seriously, he ignored it. He testified in the civil action that he thought it was the job of the police to check out a person's explanation. This testimony shows that store policy had not taught employees to be sure they had made an effort to verify or disprove the suspect's explanation. Finally, the man was handcuffed to a large metal container in the stockroom pending arrival of the police. This procedure is questionable at best and was completely unnecessary here. The suspect had made no threats of violence and had not tried to leave. He was only explaining the circumstances.

The shoplifting charge was dismissed, apparently because no food store employee appeared to testify at the trial. The man successfully sued the food store for malicious prosecution of the shoplifting case. He received $400 in actual and $175,000 in punitive damages from a jury. The store appealed, claiming, among other things, the punitive damages award was excessive. The appellate court affirmed the jury award of punitive damages saying it was entirely reasonable based on the employee's failure to investigate and review the facts before authorizing his formal arrest and prosecution.

Colonial Stores v. Fishel, 288 S.E.2d 21 (Georgia, 1982)

Analysis of this case is easy. The decision to detain was proper, based on the observations made by the contract security guard. The problem was much like the one in the Discarded Sweater Case: no investigation of the facts. There was no effort made to look for the box (a valuable piece of store prosecution evidence to prove ownership), and neither employee took the suspect's explanation seriously. The manager testified that the investigation was just a "formality" before calling the police to have the man prosecuted. Consider the comments of the appellate court on this point:

The store manager testified that the normal procedure followed when a suspected shoplifter was spotted by the security guard was to take the person to the stock room in the rear of the store. The manager would be told what happened by the security guard as a *formality*, then the person would be prosecuted for shoplifting.

Evidence presented indicated that the store manager was aware of a reliable source of information which was readily available by telephoning or by sending someone to the nearby drug store in an attempt to verify Mr. Fishel's story. Also the store manager had the ability to look *in his own store for the box which Mr. Fishel supposedly "ditched" but he failed to do this before placing him in police custody.* [Emphasis supplied]

After hearing this testimony from the store manager about the investigative procedures used, one thing was abundantly clear to the jury: neither the manager nor security guard had made any effort to determine who owned the bottle of aspirin. They simply went through the motions of an investigation and had the man prosecuted for shoplifting. These employees made no effort to determine if a prosecutable case existed before filing it, they made no effort to review the facts and see if this evidence would establish the elements of the offense at a shoplifting trial. It was relatively easy for the jury to decide liability for malicious prosecution existed and that $175,000 in punitive damages was appropriate.

This court is saying that merchants must learn to use their ears as well as their eyes when producing evidence. Detention statutes say that a merchant must investigate the facts in a legally reasonable method. This means to investigate and review both the store's prosecution evidence and the suspect's defense evidence. In the Aspirin Case, both the store and the suspect were claiming ownership of the same bottle of aspirin, a fact the store manager and security guard knew before calling the police. The suspect told them he had bought the aspirin at a nearby drugstore, clearly claiming ownership by prior purchase. By failing to look for the missing box, the employees went to court without any physical evidence to corroborate their claim the store owned the aspirin. Because they did not listen to their suspect, these employees filed a shoplifting case that should never have gone to court.

As the Aspirin Case demonstrates so well, evidence to prove ownership is not produced just by watching a man place a bottle of aspirin in his pocket. Observations made on the sales floor do not conclusively establish store ownership in court. The detaining retail employee must examine the merchandise and listen to what the suspect has to say about who owns it. In some cases, like the Razor Blades Case in chapter 4, the suspect will not claim ownership but will deny intent to shoplift by saying, "I forgot to pay." When suspects say they intended to pay or they forgot to pay they are saying more legally. They are admitting the store owns the merchandise and denying they intended to shoplift that store merchandise. Later in court both sides agree the store owns it. The only dispute is whether the defendant "forgot to pay" or "intended to shoplift."

By contrast, in cases like the Aspirin Case, the dispute is totally about ownership. Both sides are claiming they own the aspirin. Detention statutes authorize merchants to detain on probable cause for a specific purpose—to investigate the factual question of ownership. If a store owner, manager, or security person did not believe (based on observations) that the store owned the merchandise, that retailer would not detain the suspect in the first place. The reason to investigate is to confirm the fact the store does own it and that fact can be proven later in court if the case is prosecuted. In the Aspirin Case, the food store manager thought it was the job of the police to determine ownership. It is not the job of the responding peace officer to determine ownership. The evidence-gathering burden is on the merchant. Detention statutes give retail employees a legally reasonable time in which to conduct that investigation concerning ownership. Merchants should avoid the mistake made in this case and always require employees to detain and investigate the facts—starting with the fact of who owns the merchandise in question.

An Example of A Store Violating Test 5

The Discarded Sweater and Aspirin Cases demonstrate situations where the detaining merchant really conducted no investigation at all after detaining a shoplifting suspect. The Returned Gloves Case shows department store security people conducting an investigation of the facts after detaining their suspect. The real problem here was failing to review the facts after completing the investigation. These security people failed to see that a prosecutable case did not exist. The evidence they produced showed that the woman rather than the store was the owner of the gloves, yet the shoplifting charge was filed anyway. They filed a nonprosecutable case, lost it, and then the store was sued civilly—not for false imprisonment but for malicious prosecution. The woman was properly detained but the decision to prosecute her was not supported by the evidence produced during the investigation. This case shows that stores may properly decide to detain then improperly decide to prosecute.

CASE	Returned gloves case

In this case the woman was seen standing by the glove cart with a pair of gloves in her hand. Neither security officer actually saw her pick the gloves up from the cart. They watched her with them in her hand then saw her bend down and place them in a shopping bag. She left the department and was heading toward the escalator when detained. In the security office, she explained the gloves had been purchased a month earlier at that store on her father's charge account, which she was authorized to use. She said she had been returning the gloves for an exchange but had seen none she liked better than hers and decided to keep them. She gave the security officers the charge account receipt, showing the purchase of one pair of gloves about thirty days before at the price of the gloves in question. At no time did any store employee ever see her with more than this one pair of gloves.

After obtaining her explanation and examining the gloves and receipt, the security people decided to file the charge—the wrong decision based on the facts known to them at that time. The woman had demonstrated ownership by the charge account receipt, a fact that security people did not appreciate. A prosecutable case did not exist because she could corroborate her claim of ownership and the store could not.

In the civil action that followed, the woman did not challenge the store's decision to detain as being improper. The case centered around the decision to prosecute. The jury concluded that the facts known to the security people rejected a decision to prosecute and supported a decision to release her. Because these facts were known yet disregarded by the security people, the jury concluded the decision to prosecute was not reasonable. In legal terms, they found this department store maliciously prosecuted the shoplifting case. This does not mean the jury felt the store decided to prosecute her for reasons of spite, ill will, or hatred or that any of the security people acted with an evil motive or any type of animosity—not at all. It means the jury decided the security people acted in a reckless manner by disregarding the legal meaning of the explanation, supported by the sales receipt. As the judge's comments show, there was an apparent rush to call the police and have the woman prosecuted. The security people did not review the facts after examining the gloves and the receipt, and listening to her explanation.

Consider the comments of the judge about the method in which these department store security people investigated the facts after the woman was detained. Notice that he is not talking about the sufficiency of the evidence to justify her detention in the first place. He is talking about the events after the detention.

> We also consider the events after the detention. . . . *the production of her sales ticket* showing a regular account of her father at the store and listing specifically the purchase of a pair of gloves at the price in question . . . *the complete denial* by the woman of taking the gloves from the counter . . . *the utter disregard* of this disclosure, *the total failure to investigate* her status and reputation . . . the fact it was *never shown she had two pairs of gloves in her possession* when apprehended . . . *the apparent rush to call the police* . . . the fact she had a little paper sack *with the store name on it* in her shopping bag in which she said *she brought the gloves back.* [Emphasis supplied]

The judge is summarizing the evidence the jury heard at trial about the investigation conducted by these department store security people. There is no claim that the initial detention was wrongful or that she was mistreated after being detained. The whole case revolves around the facts these security people knew before deciding to prosecute the case. The time factor was not unreasonably long but just the opposite; the security people seemed to be in a hurry to call the police and have her removed from the store. From this evidence, it is clear these security people violated test 5. They did not review both store prosecution and suspect defense evidence before authorizing prosecution. Based on the facts known to them, a prosecutable case did not exist, yet they filed the charge anyway.

Hoene v. Associated Dry Goods (Stix, Bear and Fuller Division), 487 S.W.2d 479 (Missouri, 1972)

The stores in the Discarded Sweater, Aspirin, and Returned Gloves Cases were all sued for malicious prosecution and for the same reason: store policy had not taught them how to conduct an investigation of the facts and then to review those facts, even though to do so was permitted by the merchant's privilege. The following list isolates the investigative effort of the store employees in these three cases.

Case	Investigative effort
Discarded Sweater Case (Location of store: Washington D.C.) Suspect's Defense: Denial of intent to shoplift sweater	No independent investigation and review of the facts was required by store policy. The department store security officer detained the woman and immediately called the police.
Aspirin Case (Location of store: Georgia) Suspect's defense: Ownership of aspirin by prior purchase	No independent investigation and review of the facts was required by store policy. The food store manager said his investigation was just a formality as he listened only to a recitation of the facts by the contract security guard. He further testified that he thought it was the responsibility of the police to investigate a shoplifitng suspect's explanation rather than to conduct any investigation himself.
Returned Gloves Case (Location of store: Missouri) Suspect's defense: Ownership of gloves by prior purchase	An independent investigation of the facts was conducted here. The security people listened to the suspect's explanation, examined both the gloves and receipt, but did not then review the merits of the evidence they possessed. She had given them both testimonial and physical evidence to show she had previously purchased the gloves, yet they ignored this evidence and had her prosecuted.

The bottom line is simply this: none of these three stores, in three different jurisdictions, had taught their employees the skills needed to conduct an independent investigation of the facts before authorizing prosecution of the case. Their employees glossed over the investigation of the facts phase, filed nonprosecutable shoplifting cases, and lost them. The stores then had to defend a civil action for malicious prosecution. These stores could not use the detention statute because it does not provide stores with a defense when sued for malicious prosecution. The defense to malicious prosecution actions must be provided by store policy, one that requires employees to comply with tests 3 and 5.

LIMITATIONS OF THE MERCHANT'S PRIVILEGE TO DETAIN AND INVESTIGATE THE FACTS

Almost everybody has a drivers license. A state grants its residents the privilege (not the right) to operate a motor vehicle. This privilege can be suspended or revoked it the driver accumulates too many tickets. The same is true with the merchant's privilege to detain shoplifting suspects and investigate the facts without incurring civil liability. The privilege is not absolute but is a conditional one. If the merchant mistreats a shop-lifting suspect when detaining or while investigating the facts, the privi-lege is lost and the store can be successfully sued civilly.

The problem is that the detention statutes do not specifically set forth the limitations imposed on a merchant who attempts to detain on probable cause and then conduct an investigation of the facts which is legally reasonable. The limitations are imposed by silence. The state legislatures did not set forth a list of limitations on a merchant's conduct which will violate the privilege. There are six of these limitations of silence in detention statutes.

1. They do not grant authority to search a suspect unless that suspect consents or agrees to be searched.
2. They do not grant authority to use force, either to detain or while conducting an investigation of the facts.
3. Most statutes do not give the store a defense to use if sued for malicious prosecution, slander, or assault and battery.
4. Most statutes do not tell merchants how long is a "reasonable time" in which an investigation of the facts must be completed.
5. Statutes do not grant immunity when the detention is based on information provided by a nonemployee or agent such as a customer.
6. None of the detention statutes tell the merchant to conduct the investigation off the selling floor.

No Authority Granted To Search A Shoplifting Suspect

Because detention statutes do not grant merchants the authority to make warrantless citizen's arrests, they do not grant merchants the right to search a shoplifting suspect after detaining on probable cause. There are both prosecution and civil liability problems presented by the fact that detention statutes withold the authority to search. The prosecution evidence-gathering problem is that most people have concealed merchandise before being detained. A store owner, manager, or security person needs to examine that merchandise in determining if a prosecutable case exists. The civil liability problem is that by forcing a search, the merchant risks violating the detention statute and incurring civil liability exposure. The general rule is that retail employees are not authorized to search shoplifting suspects unless that suspect agrees or consents to be searched. The Iowa statute sets forth a good statement of this basic rule:

| STATUTE | Iowa detention statute |

Detention and search in theft of library materials and shoplifting (Section 808.12)

2. No search of the person under this section shall be conducted by any person other than someone acting under the direction of a peace officer except where permission of the one to be searched has first been obtained.

The Ohio detention statute also sets forth the rule, adding that the merchant may not use "undue restraint" while investigating the facts. Consider the pertinent section of this statute:

| STATUTE | Ohio detention statute |

(Section 2935.041 Ohio Rev. Code)

(D) The officer, agent, or employee of the merchant or his employee or agent acting under division (A) or (B) of this section shall not search the person, search or seize any property belonging to the person detained without the person's consent, or use undue restraint upon the person detained.

The California detention statute applies to detentions made by merchants and employees of a library. It is of more help than some others because it deals with situations where the merchandise is both in plain view and concealed. Section 3 permits the merchant to examine items that are in plain view for the purpose of ascertaining ownership. Section 4 authorizes the detaining retail employee to ask the suspect voluntarily to surrender concealed merchandise. If the person refuses, the merchant is permitted to conduct a limited and reasonable search of packages, shopping bags, handbags, or other property in the immediate possession of the suspect. The statute wisely says that no search of clothing worn by the person detained is permitted. Although the California statute does not answer the crucial question of how to obtain consent, it does provide some help to merchants in setting policy. As a practical matter, none of these statutes will tell the merchants how to set policy but will only provide the framework within which the merchant can operate in obtaining consent to search.

STATUTE	California detention statute

Items in plain view (Section 490.5(3))

(3) During the period of detention any items which a merchant or any items which a person employed by a library facility has probable cause to believe are unlawfully taken from the premises of the merchant or library facility and which are in plain view may be examined by the merchant or person employed by a library facility for the purposes of ascertaining the ownership thereof.

Items that are concealed (section 490.5(4))

(4) A merchant, a person employed by a library facility, or an agent thereof, having probable cause to believe the person detained was attempting to unlawfully take or has taken any item from the premises, may request the person detained to voluntarily surrender the item. Should the person detained refuse to surrender the item of which there is probable cause to believe has been unlawfully taken from the premises, a limited and reasonable search may be conducted by those authorized to make the detention in order to recover the item. Only packages, shopping bags, handbags or other property in the immediate possession of the person detained, but not including any clothing worn by the person, may be searched pursuant to this subdivision. Upon surrender or discovery of the item, the person detained may also be requested, but may not be required, to provide adequate proof of his or her true identity.

No Authority Granted To Use Force

Almost all detention statutes omit any reference to use of force, either to detain the suspect or while conducting an investigation of the facts. The merchant may want to infer that the right to use reasonable force exists from the fact the statutes authorize detention and investigation. After all, the right to detain is meaningless unless the suspect can be compelled to remain in the store after being stopped. Since the detention statutes are silent on this use of force question, the merchant must consult decisional law. The problem is that the case law decides only if the retail employee used too much force under the circumstances found in each case. The courts do not set forth a list of rules on the point. This means that in setting policy and conducting training programs, merchants must decide on two things: (1) the circumstances in which force can be used, and (2) what amount of force is legally permissible.

Use of force by a retail employee can be found to be justified in three situations.

1. The suspect attempts to leave the store after being detained. (It is better to block the person's exit or try to convince him orally to stay in the store than to grab an arm.)
2. The suspect initiates violence. The merchant, like any other citizen, has the right of self-defense.
3. The suspect tries to destroy or otherwise get rid of the merchandise.

The amount or degree of force is an equally difficult subject to consider. The Wisconsin statute is helpful. It says that the merchant cannot use deadly force or force that may cause great bodily harm when a merchant is protecting only property.

STATUTE	Wisconsin annotated statutes

Detention (939.49, Section 2)

A person is privileged to threaten or to intentionally use force against another for the purpose of preventing or terminating what he reasonably believes to be an unlawful interference with his property. Only such degree of force or threat thereof may be intentionally used as the actor reasonably believes is necessary to prevent or terminate the interference. It is not reasonable to intentionally use force intended or likely to cause death or great bodily harm for the sole purpose of defense of one's property.

This statute talks about using force or threatening to use it. Telling a suspect the store has the right to require him to remain in the store is preferable to grabbing the person. Techniques are very important. Speaking in a firm but polite voice while subtly blocking a suspect's exit route should always be the first approach. Avoid touching the suspect if at all possible. Technically, touching the suspect constitutes a battery and could be found to violate the "reasonable manner" provision of a detention statute. However, in the law of assault and battery there is a distinction between offensive and harmful touching. If it becomes necessary to touch a suspect, the touching of an elbow or arm, accompanied by nonaccusatory words indicating the suspect is not free to leave, will most likely qualify as offensive rather than harmful touching. By contrast, grabbing, wrestling with, or dragging a suspect is likely to be considered harmful touching.

The Vermont statute has a good definition of minimum force in shoplifting detention situations.

STATUTE	Vermont annotated statutes

Definitions (Section 2572)

(e) Reasonable Force—that minimum amount of force necessary to detain the person who the merchant has probable cause to believe has committed retail theft.

The emphasis here is on the word *minimum*. Store policy should take the same approach. If the merchant cannot talk the suspect into cooperating or if blocking the person's exit route does not work, then a firm but gentle touching of an elbow or arm is most likely to qualify as "minimum" force. If sued, the merchant is in a good position to defend by saying the amount of force was reasonable under the circumstances.

The California statute dealing with both merchants and employees of libraries reads as follows on the "use of force" point:

STATUTE	California

(Section 490.5)

(2) In making the detention a merchant or a person employed by a library facility may use a reasonable amount of nondeadly force necessary to protect himself or herself and to prevent escape of the person detained or the loss of property.

This California statute is helpful. It says that only nondeadly force may be used to protect the employee, to prevent the suspect from escaping, or to prevent loss of the property in question. The Wisconsin, Vermont, and California statutes are unique in that they mention the difficult question of using force following a detention on probable cause. A good fundamental rule for merchants to consider is this: *never be the aggressor; always be a neutral and objective investigator.* This means to avoid initiating the use of force if possible. Always remember, many shoplifting cases involve single inexpensive items concealed by the average citizen type shoplifter. Most of these people will respond to the firm request to accompany the merchant to the office.

Use of excessive force can result in two separate civil tort actions being filed by the suspect. Use of unreasonable force can violate the reasonable manner provision of the detention statute, subjecting the store to a false imprisonment action. It can also give rise to an action for assault and battery, particularly if the force is of the harmful rather than the offensive variety. By always defining the circumstances in which force can be used, the retailer will best avoid civil actions based on use of excessive force.

A final point must be well understood. Detaining on probable cause does not automatically permit a retail employee to use force. Probable cause to detain is the legal reason a merchant has for restraining a suspect's freedom of movement. Detaining is justified because the merchant just saw the suspect conceal merchandise, switch a price tag, stuff a container, pass merchandise off to a companion, or walk out with goods in plain view. Because a merchant has established the legal right to detain a suspect, this does not mean the suspect can be tackled. The probable cause to detain and the legally reasonable investigation of the facts are separate requirements of the merchant's privilege. Both tests must be met for the store to say its employee complied with the detention statute. Said another way, the merchant may comply with the probable cause test yet still violate the privilege by using legally unreasonable force once the suspect is stopped.

Scope of Immunity Granted In Statute Will Differ From State to State

All detention statutes say the store can plead compliance with it as a defense if the civil action is for false imprisonment. Some statutes will say the store has a defense if sued for both false imprisonment (sometimes called unlawful detention) and false arrest. Almost none of the detention statutes provide stores with a defense if the shoplifting case if filed, lost, and the suspect then sues for malicious prosecution. Some detention statutes do say the store has a defense if sued for slander or assault and battery, but this group is in the minority.

The Georgia detention statute covers only actions for false imprisonment and false arrest.

STATUTE	Georgia

2. Detention
(Sections 105–1005, 105-1006, Ga. Code Ann.)

Whenever the owner or operator of a mercantile establishment or any agent or employee of such owner or operator shall detain or arrest, or cause to be detained or arrested, any person reasonably thought to be engaged in shoplifting and, as a result of such detention or arrest, the person so detained or arrested shall institute suit for false arrest or false imprisonment against such owner, operator, agent or employee, no recovery shall be had by the plaintiff in such action where it is established by competent evidence that the plaintiff had so conducted himself, or behaved in such manner, as to cause a man of reasonable prudence to believe that such plaintiff was committing the offense of shoplifting, as defined by the statute of this State, at or immediately prior to the time of such detention or arrest, or provided that the manner of such detention or arrest and the length of time during which such plaintiff was detained was under all of the circumstances reasonable.

Most companies are doing business in states with a detention statute like the one found in Georgia. Compliance with this statute can be successfully pleaded as a defense only if the store is sued for false imprisonment or false arrest. The Aspirin Case above in this chapter came from Georgia. The food store was sued for malicious prosecution, so the store did not have the statutory defense available.

By contrast, the Virginia detention statute is comprehensive. It says the statute may be used as a defense when the store is sued for any six civil tort actions: (1) unlawful detention, (2) slander, (3) malicious prosecution, (4) false imprisonment, (5) false arrest, and (6) assault and battery.

STATUTE	Virginia

Detention (Section 18.2-105.1)

A merchant, agent or employee of the merchant who has probable cause to believe that a person shoplifted . . . may detain such person for a period not to exceed one hour pending arrival of a law enforcement officer.

A merchant, agent or employee of the merchant, who causes the arrest or detention of any such person . . . shall not be held civilly liable for unlawful detention, if such detention does not exceed one hour, slander, malicious prosecution, false imprisonment, false arrest, or assault & battery of the person so arrested or detained. Whether such arrest or detention takes place on the premises of the merchant or after close pursuit from such premises.

Retail and security executives need to know the exact scope of immunity granted by the detention statute in each state where the company is doing business. To assist merchants in this respect, it is suggested that a checklist similar to that in Figure 6.2 be used.

FIGURE 6.2	Scope of immunity checklist, State _____

Civil tort mentioned in detention statute	Yes	No
False imprisonment	X	
False arrest	X	
Malicious prosecution		X
Slander		X
Assault and battery		X

Most Detention Statutes Do Not Define a Length of Time Which Is Legally Reasonable

In the Returned Gloves Case above the judge commented that the department store security people seemed to be in a hurry to call the police and have the woman prosecuted. No doubt this happens more often than is realized. Part of the reason is that only a few detention statutes tell merchants how long they have to complete the investigation of the facts after detaining suspects on probable cause. Most detention statutes say only that the merchant is given a "reasonable time" to investigate the facts and decide whether to prosecute the case or release the suspect. Where the statute makes no reference to a specific time period, one hour can be used as a general rule.

Some statutes do set forth a time period. For example, West Virginia says thirty minutes is a legally reasonable time. Others, such as Louisiana, say the investigation shall be completed in one hour.[7] The New York statute discussed in Chapter 2 does not specifically define the time factor. It does say a reasonable time means the time necessary for the suspect to make or refuse to make a statement and the time necessary for the detaining merchant to investigate the question of ownership. The Indiana detention statute sheds some light on the reasonable time problem and what happens if a suspect refuses to produce concealed merchandise for examination concerning ownership:

STATUTE	Indiana revised statutes

(35-3-2.1-2)

Such a detention must be reasonable and may last only for a reasonable time, not

---

[7]West Virginia Code, Sec. 61.3A-4; Louisiana Code for Criminal Procedure, Art. 215.

to extend beyond the arrival of a law enforcement officer, or one (1) hour, whichever first occurs.

The Indiana approach is one to consider in setting reasonable time policies and procedures. It recognizes that the suspect may rightly refuse to produce the concealed merchandise for examination, and the detention may have to be continued for a peace officer assisted investigation.

As a practical matter, merchants should be able to investigate the facts and decide whether to prosecute the case or release the suspect within one hour. Any investigation lasting more than sixty minutes runs the chance of violating these reasonable time provisions in detention statutes. The case law indicates the problem is not taking too long to investigate the facts but rushing the situation. When merchants just "go through the motions" (as in the Aspirin Case) they end up making mistakes and file nonprosecutable shoplifting cases. Training programs must stress a systematic and logical approach to investigating the facts following a detention on probable cause. The first thing to do is to avoid making accusatory statements to the suspect. Next, give the suspect an opportunity to explain. Many will, as part of their explanation, produce the concealed goods for examination. This gets the detaining employee around the tricky problem of obtaining consent to search parcels or belongings. The purpose is to produce the evidence without mistreating the suspect. By using a step-by-step evidence-gathering guide as presented in Chapter 4, a store manager, owner, or security person will know what to look for and what it means legally.

As all with experience in handling shoplifting cases know, many suspects will hand the merchandise back and say nothing more startling than, "I forgot to pay" or "I intended to pay." In these situations, the suspect is not claiming ownership but actually saying the store owns it. If the merchandise still has the store's price tag or garment label affixed to it, the investigation is complete. The merchant knows that if a charge is filed, the formal courtroom defense will not be a claim of ownership but a denial of intent to shoplift. These "I forgot to pay" cases are much easier to review and evaluate than ones where the suspect claims ownership. There is always more investigative work (and time) required in a situation where the suspect says he bought the merchandise earlier, received it as a gift, was returning merchandise, or other such statements claiming ownership.

Detaining on Information Supplied by Nonemployees

Only the merchant, his agent (a contract security guard, for example), or his employee (any employee) has the authority to detain a shoplifting suspect. If a security staff member, for example, detains on information provided to him by a customer, this detention would not be privileged under the detention statute. Employees of contract guard service companies are typically found to be "agents" of the retailer who employs them for the purpose of immunity under detention statutes.

Suppose the manager of a record shop takes a break and walks down the mall to visit with his friend, the manager of a specialty apparel store. Both men have known each other for about two years. The apparel store manager leaves the selling floor for a moment. When he returns his friend, the manager of the record and tape store, tells him a lady put a beige purse inside a shopping bag she is carrying. The apparel store manager watches her for a few minutes. She makes no attempt to pay for the beige purse when leaving and is detained on the mall in front of the specialty store. She refuses to produce anything from inside her shopping bag, and an argument ensues. She starts to leave and the apparel store manager grabs her arm. She pulls away. He yells, "Stop thief! You just stole a purse from my store." By this time, a half dozen people on the mall are watching. When things settle down it is determined she has no apparel store merchandise in the shopping bag. The beige purse was purchased at another store and she was just comparing it with accessories in the apparel store. If she sues the apparel store, the manager cannot defend by using the merchant's privilege statute because the source of his information about possible shoplifting did not come from an agent or employee but from his friend, the manager of the record and tape store.

Conducting the Investigation off the Sales Floor

All detention statutes require the investigation of the facts to be legally reasonable in manner, method, and time, but none tells the merchant where it should be conducted. Common sense tells the detaining merchant to conduct the investigation off the selling floor. Most companies conduct it in a security office or a manager's office, to minimize attention to the situation. Another reason is so the employee can investigate the facts in a logical and systematic method. Recall the Jar of Deodorant Case earlier in this chapter where the store manager required the woman to empty the contents of her purse on the sales floor—in front of both employees and customers. It will be very easy for a jury in a civil case to find this type of investigation was legally unreasonable in "manner" because it was conducted in public in front of witnesses.

CONCLUSION

There is no substitute for understanding the detention statute. It is the key to more effective prosecution and to reducing a store's civil liability exposure. Since many of these statutes are poorly worded, merchants should consult the Illinois Retail Theft Act as a place to begin. Even if the company is not doing business in Illinois, reading this well-drafted statute will help to better understand the detention statute where they are doing business. Remember, the basic merchant's privilege is the same in all states, it is just the language of the statutes (as in Missouri) that causes confusion. The retailer can also incorporate the five tests found in this chapter into training programs. Set up a detention-investigation decision-making approach that is logical and systematic, one which requires employees to make the decision to detain and the decision to prosecute or release on the basis of evidence. In this way, the merchant can learn to use these statutes and to make them a valuable tool in the shoplifting loss-prevention training program.

7

Shoplifting and the Law of Warrantless Arrest

The U.S. Constitution and all state constitutions have provisions dealing with arrest, search, and seizure. The Fourth Amendment to the U.S. Constitution reads as follows:

> The right of the people to be secure in their persons, houses, papers, and effects, against unreasonable searches and seizures shall not be violated, and no warrants shall issue but upon probable cause, supported by oath or affirmation, and particularly describing the place to be searched and the persons or things to be seized.

Most people think of the Fourth Amendment in connection with the law of search and seizure of evidence. It also protects individuals from seizures of their person—an unlawful arrest or detention. An arrest, whether by a peace officer or a private citizen, is a seizure of one's person. The U.S. Supreme Court has said several times, "The simple language of the amendment applies equally to seizures of persons and to seizures of property."[1]

An arrest by a peace officer has been defined many times. A standard definition is found in the Missouri statutes.

---

[1] Payton v. New York,—332 US 463, 100 5Ct 1371, 63 L.Ed 2d 639 (1980).

STATUTE	Missouri

Arrest (Section 544180)

An arrest is made by an actual restraint of the person of the defendant, or by his submission to the custody of the officer, under authority of a warrant or otherwise. The officer must inform the defendant by what authority he acts, and must also show the warrant if required.

As commonly understood, an arrest by a peace officer means that the person arrested is taken into the control and custody of the officer for the purpose of being charged with violation of a public criminal law. In determining whether a peace officer made a lawful arrest, the courts will look at four essential factors:

1.　actual or assumed legal authority by which the arrest is made
2.　intention of the officer to arrest
3.　seizure or restraint of the person's physical movements
4.　understanding by the person being seized that he is under arrest

In addition to the authority to restrain physically the person of the arrestee, an officer has other authority in connection with arresting. Incident to a lawful warrantless arrest, the officer may search the person without obtaining consent. Also the officer may use force, even deadly force in appropriate circumstances, to effect the arrest. In 1968, the U.S. Supreme Court held[2] that a peace officer can make investigative stops without the court's declaring the stopping a formal arrest. A police officer who encounters a suspicious set of circumstances or unusual conduct on the street now has four additional investigative rights: (1) stop suspects on suspicion, (2) frisk them for weapons, (3) detain them temporarily, and (4) ask questions. There is no violation of the Fourth Amendment in these stop-and-frisk situations, as they are popularly called.

ARREST UNDER WARRANT AND WARRANTLESS ARRESTS BY PEACE OFFICERS

There are two ways in which peace officers make arrests. The first and most basic one is under authority of an arrest warrant issued by a judge. The only authority expressly permitted by the U.S. Constitution is arrest under a warrant. The Fourth Amendment sets forth the evidentiary stan-

---

[2] Terry v. Ohio, 392 U.S. 1, 20 L.ED.2d 889, 88 S.Ct. 1868 (1968).

dards under which a warrant may be issued by saying that "no warrant shall issue but upon probable cause, supported by Oath of affirmation and particularly describing . . . the thing to be seized." Codes in all states permit a peace officer to make an arrest after a judge has issued a warrant for the person.

In the typical shoplifting situation, however, the peace officer responding to the store does not have an arrest warrant issued by a judge. The officer makes a *warrantless arrest* on probable cause or reasonable grounds. In the law of warrantless arrests, these two terms mean the same thing. The Illinois statute is typical of many. In section 1, the officer is granted authority to make arrests under a warrant. In section 3, the legislature authorizes the officer to make an arrest on reasonable grounds.[3]

| STATUTE | Illinois |

Arrest by peace officer (Section 38-107(2))

1. He has a warrant commanding that such person be arrested; or
2. He has reasonable grounds to believe that a warrant for the person's arrest has been issued in this State or in another jurisdiction; or
3. He has reasonable grounds to believe that the person is committing or has committed an offense.

Ill. Rev. Stat. 38-107(2).

A peace officer does not have to witness an offense being committed to possess probable cause to make a warrantless arrest. Probable cause in the law of warrantless arrest means that the officer has knowledge of facts and their surrounding circumstances that would lead a reasonably prudent person to believe two things:

1. A crime has been committed, a crime the officer did not witness being committed.
2. In all probability, the person he is about to arrest committed that crime.

When a peace officer responds to a store, that officer possesses no facts about the case that can be used in court to prove the elements of the offense. All the facts an officer receives will come from the store owner,

---

[3] This book uses the term *probable cause*, although some arrest statutes and some detention statutes use the term *reasonable grounds*, as found in the Illinois code.

manager, or security person handling the case. The officer may hear a retail employee describe a concealment or a no concealment situation. The retailer may relate facts concerning price tag switching, container stuffing, fitting room shoplifting, a lookout situation, a diversion set of facts, or a case where one person passed merchandise off to another. In other words, the officer makes a warrantless arrest based on facts supplied to him by the merchant. For this reason the merchant actually causes the formal arrest to be made by a peace officer who did not witness the offense being committed.

In the typical shoplifting situation, the merchant will detain and investigate the facts under authority of the merchant's privilege.[4] After completing steps 1–11, the decision may be to summon a peace officer to the store and cause a warrantless arrest to be made. The Two Flair Pens Case in Chapter 3 is a good example. The store detective saw the man take the pens from a rack and remove them from the blister pack, discarding the blister pack on the floor. He put the pens in his shirt pocket and then went through the drugstore checkout line, paying for other merchandise but failing to pay for the two pens in his pocket. When she detained the man, the detective gave him the opportunity to explain, thereby establishing his defense, which happened to be a claim of ownership. She reviewed the evidence and saw it would establish the elements of the offense, even though he was claiming ownership. She then had the police respond to the store and recited facts to them that established probable cause. The officer, knowing only what he was told by the store detective, has the legal authority to make the warrantless arrest in a misdemeanor shoplifting case. This case was filed as a violation of the city ordinance prohibiting shoplifting. By detaining under the merchant's privilege, this store detective (without incurring civil liability) produced facts to justify the officer's decision to make a warrantless arrest for an offense the officer did not witness being committed.

The Slacks in the Car Trunk Case in Chapter 3 is another example of how merchants produce evidence and then supply it to a peace officer, one who did not witness the offense being committed. The store tailor saw a woman hand her purse to her male companion. He held it open as she removed the slacks from the rack, rolled them up, and stuffed them in the purse. He handed the purse back to her, and they left the department store, going directly to a car parked in the mall lot. The tailor continued to watch as the couple put the slacks in the car trunk. The police were then notified. When the officer arrived, the store tailor supplied facts that established probable cause. The officer could then make the warrantless arrest of both

---

[4] This is what happened in the cases in Chapter 3. The retail employee detained and investigated the facts under the privilege and then decided to cause the warrantless arrest to be made by calling a peace officer to the store.

the man and woman. Incident to the warrantless arrest, the officer had authority to search the trunk without consent of the couple—which he did. The recovered slacks were properly admitted into evidence as a store prosecution exhibit in the felony shoplifting case.

As both these cases demonstrate so well, the peace officer knows nothing about the specific facts of the case until those facts are recited to him by the retail employee. In both cases, the facts showed the offense of shoplifting had been committed. It was reasonable to believe the man with the pens in his pocket and the couple who put the slacks in the car trunk had committed shoplifting. Most states will have a statute like the one in Illinois authorizing peace officers to make warrantless arrests on probable cause evidence supplied to them by private citizen merchants.

Because the responding officer is relying totally on facts produced by the merchant, it is crucial that merchants do not detain on suspicion, opinion, or hunch. They must produce, investigate, and review evidence according to a logical system such as the sources of evidence chart in Chapter 4. The duty to investigate the facts after detaining a suspect under the merchant's privilege is on the retailer—not on the police.

Suppose a store security person detains, investigates the facts, and concludes there is sufficient evidence to justify formal arrest and prosecution. The police are notified and take thirty minutes to arrive. Many detention statutes do not specifically say that one purpose of detaining and investigating the facts is to continue the detention for the arrival of the police to make a formal warrantless arrest. Merchants can validly ask whether they are violating the reasonable time provision of a detention statute by continuing the detention for the arrival of a peace officer. This question was dealt with in a New York case. Here, following the detention and investigation of the facts, the store decided to prosecute. It took the police twenty minutes to arrive. They made the warrantless arrest, then took the suspect to the station for formal booking on the shoplifting charge. The court held the store was not civilly liable for continuing the detention until the police arrived to make the formal warrantless arrest. Consider the well-thought-out comments of the court:

> Though not spelled out in Section 218 [the detention statute], the merchant's defense for reasonable detention extends, as a matter of implementing the policy of the statute if not as a matter of logical necessity, to the turning over of the suspect to the police under reasonable circumstances and the execution of an information or complaint necessary for his initial arraignment.[5]

This court said that immunity from false imprisonment liability does not end once the merchant recovers the unpurchased merchandise and decides to prosecute. The statutory immunity continues for the reasonable

---

[5] Jacques v. Sears, Roebuck & Co., 285 N.E.2d 871 (New York, 1972).

time it takes for an officer to arrive at the store and make the warrantless arrest. As the court said so well, it is a matter of logical necessity to permit a merchant to continue the detention after deciding to prosecute. Otherwise the policy of the detention statute would be defeated. This exact point may not have been decided in each state where a merchant operates a store or stores. Since the merchant's privilege in each state is fundamentally the same, this New York case could be advanced as authority that continuing the detention is part of the merchant's privilege.

STATUTES AUTHORIZING POLICE TO ISSUE A SHOPLIFTING CITATION

In the typical shoplifting arrest, the suspect is removed from the store by the responding peace officer, then taken to the station and formally charged—or booked as it is called. In most states booking involves fingerprinting, photographing, and posting of bond to secure release. The person is released to appear in court some weeks later to answer the charge. A speeding motorist is normally given a traffic citation at the location of the violation and released. If the driver fails to appear in court a few weeks later, the judge issues a warrant for his arrest. Some states permit peace officers to respond to retail stores and handle shoplifting cases like traffic tickets—by issuing a citation. Under a citation system, the shoplifting suspect is not taken to a police station and formally booked but is cited in the store and released to appear in court several weeks later. The police generally like the citation approach to handling shoplifting cases for this obvious reason—it is less time consuming for them. In some jurisdictions, a peace officer may issue a citation or book a shoplifting suspect. The retailer should know which system is used in all jurisdictions where the company has a store. It may vary from city to city within the same state, so always check. Kentucky has authorized the citation system by passing the following statute:

STATUTE	Kentucky

Citation for misdemeanor or violation—Citation in lieu of arrest—Failure to appear.—(Section 431.015(1))

A peace officer may issue a citation instead of making an arrest for a misdemeanor committed in his presence, if there are reasonable grounds to believe that the person being cited will appear to answer the charge. The citation shall provide that the defendant shall appear within a designated time.

OBTAINING AN ARREST WARRANT

The authority for a peace officer to make a warrantless arrest on probable cause in a misdemeanor case is purely a creature of statute. Some states may not permit the officer to make the warrantless arrest where the misdemeanor was not committed in the officer's presence. Merchants should never assume the peace officer has the authority to make these warrantless arrests; they should always research the point. Where the authority is not granted by statute, the store manager or security person must obtain an arrest warrant from a judge.

The procedure for obtaining an arrest warrant will vary from place to place. Generally the merchant will release the suspect, take the case file to the police, and sign a complaint. The case will be sent to a prosecutor, who reviews it for sufficiency of the evidence. The prosecutor will send it to a judge, who will review it for sufficiency of evidence before issuing the arrest warrant. The warrant will name a specific person on complaint of the prosecuting merchant. In some jurisdictions, the merchant may be able to take the case file directly to an assistant prosecutor or district attorney for review. This assistant prosecutor is often known as the warrant desk officer and is a good person for merchants to get to know. He may also handle bad check and other cases of interest to the merchant.

If the merchant needs to obtain the arrest warrant, it is a good idea to design some forms specifically for this purpose. A visit to the warrant desk will save time and ensure that all information is obtained and placed in the case file. The procedure may vary from jurisdiction to jurisdiction, so guideline-type material coming out of the merchant's corporate office will be of little value. Obtaining an arrest warrant is a technical process. Time spent preparing will be rewarded on down the line.

ARRESTS MADE BY OFF-DUTY PEACE OFFICERS WORKING FOR THE STORE AND THE CIVIL LIABILITY CONSEQUENCES OF THESE ARRESTS AND PROSECUTIONS

There are two basic rules merchants must understand when deciding whether to employ peace officers part time in their security departments:

1. A shoplifting arrest is not automatically valid just because it was made by a peace officer working part time for the store.
2. A store will not automatically be immune from civil liability because the arrest and filing of the shoplifting charge was handled by a peace officer who works part time for the store.

An off-duty police officer must meet the probable cause tests (steps 1–6) of the *Sources of Evidence* chart just as store managers and security personnel must. Otherwise the officer's arrest may not be valid. After arresting the suspect, the officer must investigate the facts (steps 7–10) and then review the facts (step 11) before making the decision to prosecute. A store can be sued successfully where the shoplifting case is handled by an off-duty peace officer. A private employer is not immune from civil liability just because the employee has the status of a peace officer.

There are two sources of authority by which an off-duty officer may stop a shoplifting suspect. Since the officer is a part-time employee of the store, it could be argued that the officer detains suspects under the merchant's privilege. The other legal argument is that the officer must arrest shoplifting suspects because he is an agent of the state by virtue of holding the commission. The general rule is that an officer makes an arrest rather than detains on probable cause under a detention statute. Most jurisdictions say their officers are on duty twenty-four hours a day. Officers have a duty to make arrests when offenses are committed in their presence. Officers, when they arrest, must give suspects a *Miranda* warning, while private citizens do not. Retailers should assume that off-duty peace officers working for their stores have to arrest shoplifting suspects and do not detain them for probable cause under a detention statute. If there is any question, the courts will most likely find that the stopping by the off-duty officer is an arrest.

Off-duty peace officers who staff security departments must be given training about how to comply with the merchant's privilege. The officer will be found to be an employee of the store if a civil action is filed. The courts will say the purpose of employment is to protect store property. The store cannot successfully defend a civil action just by showing the employee had a commission. If a civil action is filed, the store will defend by showing that the conduct of the officer was within the scope of the merchant's privilege. The fact that the decision to stop a shoplifting suspect or the decision to prosecute the case was made by an off-duty peace officer is no guarantee in avoiding liability. It will not ensure that a valid arrest was made, nor will it ensure a conviction later in court. It will not be an absolute defense to a false arrest or malicious prosecution action. Training programs should not exempt off-duty peace officers. Even though they are commissioned peace officers, they too must comply with the merchant's privilege while gathering evidence to prove the elements of the offense.

CASE	Swim trunks case

A department store was defending itself in a false arrest action. The jury had found that the off-duty police officer did not support his decision to arrest the

man with sufficient facts and held against the store. The officer testified he saw
the man conceal swim trunks under the left side of his coat and then walk
from the men's department to the adjoining camera department, where he was
arrested.* He asked the man if he was going to pay for the swimsuit.
According to the officer's testimony, the man said "What swimsuit?" and the
question was repeated. The officer said the man then took out the blue swim
trunks from under his coat.

The plaintiff's testimony was in direct dispute on the point of concealment. He
said he never put the trunks under his coat but at all times had them over his
left arm. He said they were always visible and that he intended to pay for
them when he finished looking at film in the camera department. (Notice that
his explanation was a denial of intent to shoplift and not a claim of
ownership.) The man was taken to the office. After nearly an hour the store
manager authorized the filing of a shoplifting charge. An on-duty police officer
responded to the store, took the man to the station, and booked him under
city ordinance violation for shoplifting.

The store argued the arrest was valid because the officer witnessed conduct of
the suspect in the store so the jury finding should have been reversed. The
court disagreed, saying the fact the employee was an off-duty police officer
did not justify the arrest. The jury could have found that no offense took place
because the plaintiff said the swim trunks were never concealed and that he
intended to pay for them. The jury had a clear choice, and it chose to believe
the plaintiff rather than the officer.

Nelson v. Macys, 437 S.W.2d 767 (Missouri, 1968)

*Right off the bat, it is obvious the officer violated the last cash register rule by not giv-
ing the suspect an opportunity to pass several cash registers and fail to pay.

The point to learn from this case is that off-duty peace officers also
must comply with steps 1–6 on the *Sources of Evidence* chart when they
arrest shoplifting suspects. The observations they make on the sales floor
determine if the arrest was valid, not the fact that the officer has a peace
officer's commission.

CASE	Plastic bag case

An off-duty detective for the Little Rock, Arkansas, police department arrested
a school teacher and accused her of shoplifting. He was in uniform and had
worked two years for the store handling security matters, including shoplifting.
In the unlawful detention action, he testified that the woman took a scarf and
put it in a plastic bag. Right after the arrest, he questioned her in a back room.
He then took her to the station, made out an offense report describing the
violation as shoplifting and listed the department store as the

complainant-victim. She was then searched; no store merchandise was found. No formal charges were filed because no merchandise was recovered.* She then sued the store for unlawful arrest.

The store tried to defend by saying the officer had a duty to make arrests when an offense was committed in his presence, as did the store in the Swim Trunks Case. This argument was to avoid the general rule that the store is liable for its employees' tortious conduct when the acts were committed in the scope of employment and for the benefit of the employer. The court held that the store could not immunize itself from unlawful arrest liability by hiring an off-duty police officer and then saying the officer was acting as a public law enforcement official rather than as an agent or employee of the store.

The evidence showed the police officer had worked for the last two years in the security department, one of his duties being to handle shoplifting cases. The jury found he was an agent of the store even though he did hold a peace officer's commission and had a public duty to make arrests. Under this evidence, the officer was found to be an employee of the store, acting in the scope of his employment when he made the arrest. The store was liable to the teacher by virtue of the unlawful arrest made by the officer. The jury found that his decision to arrest was not supported by evidence produced in the store.

Dillard Department Stores v. Stuckey, 511 S.W.2d 154 (Arkansas, 1974)

*This store did not seem to have a policy requiring investigation of the facts in the store as permitted by the detention statute. Even though the employee handling the case was an off-duty peace officer, he could have investigated the facts in the store rather than taking the teacher to the station. Such an approach would have been easier to defend in the subsequent civil action.

| CASE | Blue car coat case |

A man and woman were shopping in a national department store two weeks before Christmas. They had just come from a shoe store less than a block away from the department store because they were looking for galoshes. Finding the department store did not carry galoshes, they separated and shopped for twenty or thirty minutes. She bought a tie. He bought nothing. The fifty-seven-year-old man was an employee of a local utility company, with no criminal record whatsoever—not even the proverbial parking ticket. Two weeks earlier, he had purchased the blue car coat he was wearing from that outlet of the national department store. When the couple left, they were stopped outside by an off-duty city police officer, one working part time in the security department.

Both were taken to the security office.* The coat was confiscated. The man denied shoplifting the coat, telling the officer he had purchased it two weeks earlier and had the sales receipt at home. To substantiate his claim of ownership, he offered two other pieces of evidence. First, his companion told the officer he wore the coat into the store. Second, the suspect told the officer a red-headed shoe salesman down the block had commented on the unusual color and texture of the coat when they were there a few minutes earlier. The officer ignored the explanation, the offer to produce the sales receipt, and the existence of two defense witnesses. He overlooked the fact that no price tag had been found on the suspect or in the men's department. He produced no physical evidence to corroborate the store's claim of ownership. He filed the charge despite the fact the suspect had two defense witnesses who would testify in court the man had purchased the coat earlier.

In court, the officer could not justify his decision to arrest the man. He testified to a conclusion rather than relating specific facts that showed an offense had been committed in his presence. He testified that he saw the man "right after he had taken the coat off the rack." In direct opposition to the officer's testimony, the man said he wore the coat in the store and never took it off at any time. He also offered the sales receipt into evidence and called the shoe salesman and his companion as defense witnesses. He was acquitted because the store failed to prove the element of ownership. Then he sued the store. He received a jury award of $10,000 in actual and $46,000 in punitive damages in his claim for malicious prosecution. The fact that the arrest, investigation of the facts, and decision to prosecute were made by an off-duty peace officer was not found to be a valid defense.

Bouquist v. Montgomery Ward & Co., 516 S.W.2d 769 (Missouri, 1974)

*There is no evidence in the case explaining why the woman was taken to the office. She had never been seen in the men's department near the car coats. There was not even a hint that this was an aiding and abetting shoplifting situation.

This case demonstrates that off-duty peace officers can also make evidence-gathering mistakes, ones that create civil liability for stores. It shows the necessity of including peace officers in training programs conducted by the store for its full-time employees. Unsophisticated retailers can easily fall into the trap of thinking "everything will be OK because we use police officers in our security department." Too often retail executives feel that security is only a police function, implying there is just one dimension to the problem: arresting shoplifting suspects. This book has gone to great lengths to point out that handling of shoplifting cases has a dual legal consequence. All employees, including part-time peace officers, need to understand the merchant's privilege and how to comply with it.

In the Blue Car Coat Case, the court discussed the statute under which peace officers make warrantless arrests. The statute provided that an officer can make an arrest and cause a complaint to be filed whenever "any person may have committed an offense within view of a member of such police force." The court said that if the officer had observed the commission of a crime, he would have been entitled to make an arrest and instigate criminal proceedings. The problem was that this officer did not observe any facts that supported a decision that the offense of shoplifting had been committed in his presence. Consider the comments of the court:

> The real question on this phase of the matter is whether anything actually occurred within view of Weir [the off-duty police officer] which constituted the commission of a crime by plaintiff or which could give Weir reasonable ground to believe that this had occurred.
>
> Weir testified that he observed plaintiff right after he had taken the coat off the rack and that he saw plaintiff put it on. In opposition, plaintiff testified he had the coat on when he came into the store and at all times thereafter until the coat was ultimately taken away from him by Weir after the arrest. That testimony was strongly supported by the testimony of Jones [his companion] and McQueen [the shoe salesman]. Plaintiff's version of the facts is also powerfully supported by his cash register receipt showing he had purchased this coat on October 31, 1970. All this evidence produced by plaintiff was in squaretoed contradiction to Weir's testimony that he had actually viewed the plaintiff stealing the coat on December 12, 1970. The jury had a choice to make and it chose to disbelieve Weir. Accordingly, it is no longer open for defendant [the store] to argue that a criminal offense occurred "within view" of Weir.

As this case shows, retail employees must observe facts justifying the reasonable belief that a suspect obtained wrongful possession of merchandise. Otherwise they will subject the store to civil liability. This is true if the stopping is a detention on probable cause made by a private citizen employee under the merchant's privilege statute or an arrest made by an off-duty peace officer working in the store security department.

AUTHORITY OF SPECIAL OFFICERS

A special officer is not a member of a police or sheriff's department, although special officers have the same powers of arrest as a regularly sworn or commissioned member of a law enforcement agency. A merchant could have one of its store detectives apply for a special officer commission with the appropriate county, city, or state agency. Normally that agency is the municipal or state police. In some states, a county sheriff may issue a special officer commission. Special officers are employed by private companies like retail concerns or contract guard services. Their authority to make arrests is limited to the premises of the employer. They can make warrantless arrests, search incident to an arrest without obtaining the arrestee's consent, use force to effect an arrest, carry weapons, and wear uniforms. Like a peace officer, the special officer is an agent of the state so *Miranda* warnings must be given to persons arrested. The only practical difference between authority of regular and special officers is that the latter's powers of arrest are limited to the employer's premises.

As a general rule, merchants do not employ special officers in their security departments, because they do not want uniformed security personnel on the selling floor. By contrast, the mall where the store is located may desire to have uniformed, commissioned, and armed officers on the payroll to handle security matters. Malls sometimes employ uniformed off-duty peace officers. Merchants should understand that not all uniformed security personnel working in the mall security department are special or regular officers. Many malls hire contract security guards, ones without special commissions. Shopping centers will use any combination of off-duty peace officers, specially commissioned officers, or noncommissioned contract security guards. The regular and special officer can make a warrantless arrest while contract security guards are private citizens like the store manager, owner, or store security staff member.

CASE	Sewing machine case

Since special officers have the same authority as regularly sworn or commissioned peace officers, they have the same requirement placed on them to give a *Miranda* warning. A conviction for stealing a $170 sewing machine from a national department store was reversed in this case. The court held it was improper to admit the suspect's statement made to a special officer in Maryland who had not first given the *Miranda* warnings. When asked what qualifications he had to arrest the suspect, the special officer replied as follows: "I have been sworn as a state officer by the State of Maryland, by the governor of Maryland as a police officer to protect the property of Montgomery Wards at 6200 Annapolis Road in Prince George's County." This testimony established without dispute that the security person was a special officer and not a private citizen. The court found the incriminating statement of the defendant was given to the special officer after being taken into custody by him. There was no dispute about the observations that supported his arrest: the suspect was on the loading dock in possession of the sewing machine and had no receipt for it. The court held the statement was not voluntary so the prosecution could not use it because the officer failed to give a *Miranda* warning first.

Pratt v. State, 263 A.2d 247 (Maryland, 1970)

Merchants use various approaches to staffing the security department. Some hire only noncommissioned store detectives who are always private citizens. Others use a combination of store detectives and off-duty police who work only part time. Still others use store detectives and specially commissioned officers who work full time for the store. A final approach is to hire a contract guard service. Generally a contract guard service employee will not hold a special officer's commission. Some guard services will send out specially commissioned officers if the merchant wants a person on the premises who is authorized to make arrests. The Special Officer Case and the Mall Security Case demonstrate both prosecution and civil liability problems actually encountered. They will assist merchants in making decisions about the best way to staff the security department.

| CASE | Special officer case |

This merchant had a special officer on the payroll who possessed statutory authority to make warrantless arrests and conduct full searches under authority of the New York special officer's statute. This meant the special officer had to make an arrest of a suspect (rather than detain the suspect under the merchant's privilege) and give a *Miranda* warning before asking questions and obtaining answers. A store detective, one not holding any type of commission, properly detained two suspects, following them into the elevator. Neither suspect could produce a sales receipt for merchandise in his possession. They were taken to the security office. During an investigation of the facts, both signed statements admitting they intended to shoplift unpurchased goods belonging to the store.*

After the store detectives obtained the signed admissions, the special officer was called in to give *Miranda* warnings. Store detectives were not permitted to give *Miranda* warnings under this merchant's procedure. The store detective testified that only after the suspects made the incriminating statements and signed them did he make the decision to prosecute. In considering this store's approach, the court commented on the testimony of the store detective and special officer:

> Both detective Reid and Special Patrolman Flannigan in effect testified there was a "procedure" and "store policy" which they followed. That "store policy" was in effect that the store detective did not give Miranda warnings and the store supervisor made the decision whether or not to prosecute only after the questioning of suspects and then only after a statement had been taken. After that time the special patrolman was called in and he finally gave the Miranda warnings.

This court found that having a special officer on the payroll and "hovering in the wings" while noncommissioned store detectives detained and investigated (under the detention statute) without giving *Miranda* warnings was the same as having the special officer present. The signed statements were not permitted to be used as store prosecution evidence.

People v. Glynn, 435 N.Y.S.2d 516 (New York, 1978)

*The record was clear that the special officer did not even know about this detention and investigation of the facts nor was he present when the statements were signed. He did know the store's procedure was to detain and investigate, then summon him if the decision made by the store detectives was to prosecute.

If stores are using this approach, they could encounter the same prosecution problem as found in the Special Officer Case.

Many stores prefer to use only noncommissioned private citizen store detectives to staff the security department. In this way, it is clear that no store employee has the authority to make a warrantless arrest but rather all detain for investigation of the facts under the merchant's privilege. In these stores, the security people detain and conduct an investigation of the facts independently of any commissioned officer, regular or special. These stores can point to the fact that the investigation was conducted and the decision to prosecute made before contacting any law enforcement agency. They can also demonstrate that if the decision was to release a suspect, a peace officer was never involved. Stores using this approach want their security people to remain private citizen's at all stages of the encounter with a shoplifting suspect. They prefer to rely totally on the authority of the merchant's privilege statute when handling shoplifting cases.

One advantage to this approach is that private citizen store detectives acting under authority of a detention statute are not required to give *Miranda* warnings before obtaining a shoplifting suspect's explanation. Detention statutes do not grant any police powers of arrest to private citizen merchants. These stores do not feel it is any advantage to have either a special or regular officer with powers of arrest handling shoplifting situations. Since many stores use a selective prosecution policy, there is merit to the idea of employing only private citizen store detectives not holding any type of commission. The retail security function is to protect assets and prevent loss   not to fight crime. Store detectives can always elect to cause a shoplifting suspect's arrest and prosecution by summoning a peace officer to the store and supplying the probable cause evidence to that officer. There is more flexibility where the security employee is a private citizen than where he holds a regular or special commission. There is no *best approach* to staffing the merchant's security department. The answer is that "it depends" on the needs of a particular company and sometimes on the location of a particular store.

AUTHORITY OF MALL SECURITY OFFICERS

Department stores in a mall always have their own security staffs. As a consequence, they have no need to rely on the shopping center security people to handle shoplifting situations. Specialty stores, by contrast, do not have a security person on their sales floors. These specialty stores must rely on their managers to handle shoplifting cases. When a specialty store manager "calls mall security," the person responding could be any of the following: (1) an off-duty peace officer, (2) a specially commissioned mall security officer, or (3) a contract security guard service employee. The regular and special officer both have full powers of arrest. The employee of a contract guard service company has no more authority to make a warrantless arrest than the store manager who called mall security. It is important for specialty store managers and owners to know if the mall security officer they summon has full powers of arrest or is a private citizen wearing a uniform. There is just one way for the specialty store manager to find out and that is by asking the mall management office. A good topic for regular discussion at mall merchants association meetings is what help a specialty store manager can expect from the mall security staff in a shoplifting case.

Mall companies have different security responsibilities from those of the specialty and department store tenants. They must provide both safety and security protection for the common areas, including parking lots. Mall security people are not as preoccupied with shoplifting as the merchants. Since mall companies are not owners of merchandise, they generally feel their duty is only to assist merchants with shoplifting situations. Mall companies know one thing about shoplifting in specialty stores—they can be sued along with the specialty store if a shoplifting situation is mishandled and a mall security officer is involved. Since mall companies are not owners of shoplifted goods, the merchant's privilege statutes will not provide them with a defense in a civil action. For this reason, mall companies may be reluctant to permit their security staff members to become actively involved with specialty store managers in detaining and investigating the facts.

CASE	Mall security guard case

Here a specialty store, the mall company, and the Indianapolis police department were all sued by a woman after she was acquitted—not of shoplifting—but of disorderly conduct. The woman and her infant son were shopping on the mall. The shopping center security officer who responded was an off-duty Indianapolis police officer. Consider the facts as set forth by the court:

> Very shortly after she entered the Paul Harris store, a lessee of the Mall, an alarm sounded at the front of the store. The alarm is designed to sound when tagged merchandise is removed from the store without having been deactivated by a store employee. When the alarm sounded, a man was observed leaving the store carrying merchandise, and two

employees gave chase; the shoplifter eluded his pursuers and was never apprehended. An employee told the store manager, Mrs. Edie, who was apparently at the rear of the store when the commotion developed, that the shoplifter had entered the store at the same time Mrs. Conn [the woman with the infant] had, and pointed out the latter to her.

Meanwhile, Donald E. Kryter, an officer of the Indianapolis Police department who was working part-time as a security guard for the Mall, was told by an unidentified person that there was trouble at the Paul Harris store. He arrived several minutes later and spoke to Mrs. Edie. She told him that an employee related to her that Mrs. Conn and the shoplifter had entered the store together. Officer Kryter, who was in uniform, approached Mrs. Conn, asked if she knew the shoplifter and requested her identification. She denied knowing the shoplifter, but refused to identify herself. The officer explained he was investigating a felony and persisted in asking her name. She walked away and exited the store. Out in the Mall Mrs. Conn became loud, uttered an obscenity and accused the officer of picking on her because she is black. Mrs. Conn then was placed under arrest for disorderly conduct. She was later acquitted of that charge.

Mrs. Conn then instituted this action against Paul Harris and the others. She ultimately achieved a settlement with the Edward J. DeBartolo Corporation, owner and operator of the Mall, and the Consolidated City of Indianapolis. Paul Harris is the only extant defendant.

She sued the specialty store, mall company, and city police department for false imprisonment, slander, and malicious prosecution. Her theory of recovery was that the specialty store manager had summoned mall security and suggested she might have been the companion of an unidentified and unapprehended shoplifting suspect. Eventually she negotiated an out-of-court settlement with the mall company and city police department. The case went to trial with only the specialty store as a defendant. The trial court found in favor of the store, and the woman appealed the case.

The store defended by saying that its employees had never detained the woman; therefore the question of whether probable cause existed did not arise. The essence of the defense was that one who merely relates facts to a peace officer is not liable for the subsequent actions of that officer, which in this case was an arrest for disorderly conduct. The court agreed, saying she was never arrested for shoplifting so the specialty store was not civilly liable.

Conn v. Paul Harris Stores et al., 439 N.W.2d 195 (Indiana, 1982)

This case is an example of a preventable loss—the loss of dollars paid out to defend civil actions arising out of mishandled shoplifting situations. The mistake was made by the specialty store manager who identified the woman—not as a shoplifter—but as a possible companion of a person who activated an electronic article-surveillance warning device. The person activating the alarm was never detained. The woman charged with disorderly conduct was never seen in wrongful possession of unpurchased merchandise, yet the mall security officer said he responded to a "felony shoplifting" situation. Malls and specialty stores should read this case in its entirety because these situations will come up.

Mall companies generally view their role as one of assisting the specialty store manager. This could mean several things, depending on the policy of the mall security personnel:

1. The specialty store manager actually detains the suspect under the merchant's privilege and then calls mall security, who responds to assist with the investigation of the facts. No shoplifting charge is filed unless the specialty store manager wants to sign the complaint.
2. The specialty store manager calls mall security before detaining. The suspect is not stopped until the mall security officer arrives at the store and confronts the suspect. As in situation 1, a charge will be filed only if the specialty store manager, as owner of the property, signs the complaint.
3. The specialty store manager calls mall security to say a specific person has left with unpurchased merchandise and now is in the mall. This could be on the strength of only a sensor warning device's being activated or on the strength of a personal observation by the store manager or an employee. Under these facts, the specialty store would be supplying probable cause to the mall security people, who may or may not possess the authority to make a warrantless arrest.

These specialty store–mall security staff shoplifting situations contain three fundamental problems:

1. Who detains?
2. Who investigates the facts?
3. Who is covered by the merchant's privilege in case of a civil action?

These questions were not well considered in the Mall Security Case. Part of the answer to the problem is whether the mall security staff has the authority to make a warrantless arrest on information supplied by the specialty store manager or employee. How these cases are handled is entirely a policy matter but one that requires understanding of both the law of warrantless arrest and the merchant's privilege.

DETENTION UNDER THE MERCHANT'S PRIVILEGE DISTINGUISHED FROM A CITIZEN'S ARREST

The retailer is advised to have employees (those not holding any type of commission) detain for investigation of the facts under the merchant's privilege rather than make warrantless citizen's arrests. The reason is that a merchant making a citizen's arrest can defend the stopping only by showing the person was actually guilty. This means going to court on every case. By making a citizen's arrest, the merchant loses the option of stopping the suspect, recovering the merchandise, and electing to release the person without formal prosecution. Under a detention statute, the merchant can detain, investigate the facts, recover unpurchased merchandise, and release the suspect without losing the availability of the statute as a defense if later sued. Said another way, a merchant who detains under the privilege can follow a selective prosecution policy; a store that makes citizen's arrests cannot.

A well-written law review article says the following about the difference between detention and a citizen's arrest: "But not every detention is an arrest in the technical sense of the word. The merchant who halts a suspected shoplifter with no intention of turning him over to the police or prosecuting him in court may be imprisoning the suspect but he is not arresting him."[6] A simple way to remember the difference is this: the act of detaining can be converted into one of deciding to cause an arrest after the store manager or security completes the investigation. Then and only then does that retail employee possess enough facts to determine whether a prosecutable case exists. In the typical shoplifting situation, a private citizen store manager or security staff member makes observations of a suspect on the sales floor. There are no police in the store, and no call has been made to a law enforcement agency. In strict legal terms, one private citizen is about to detain temporarily another for a private purpose.

The word arrest brings to mind thoughts of the police taking a person into their custody and heading off for jail. The purpose of the arrest is to charge the suspect with a crime. By contrast, a detention under the merchant's privilege is a temporary restraint for a private purpose: to investigate the facts and recover unpurchased merchandise. When detaining a suspect, the merchant's purpose is not to call the police automatically and cause a shoplifting charge to be filed—not at all. Under the merchant's privilege, the retail employee is not required to prosecute the case but is given a legally reasonable time in which to investigate the facts and make a decision. Detention statutes are neutral about how the case is ultimately handled.

---

[6]"Shoplifting and the Law of Arrest—the Merchant's Dilemma," 62 Yale Law Journal 788 (1953).

CASE	Two radios case

The case is interesting because the store manager did not call his initial
stopping an arrest. About 11:00 A.M. a drugstore manager saw a woman
standing behind the counter in the photo department. Customers were not
ordinarily permitted in this area because expensive merchandise was located
there. He briefly stepped off the sales floor into the storeroom. When he
returned to the sales floor, the woman was gone. A customer came up and
said to him, "A lady just took two radios and put them in her purse." The
description given by the customer matched the woman the manager had just
seen in the photo department.

Observing the woman in aisle 16, he approached her and said, "Will you
please come with me to the back room, Ma'am? I would like to see what you
have in your purse." Without saying a word, she opened her purse and took
out a radio, one belonging to the drugstore. According to the manager, she
threw it at him; according to her, she handed it to him. While her purse was
open, he could see a second radio inside. She then ran toward the checkout
counter. Now accompanied by two other employees, he caught up with her at
the checkout counter. He told the woman she would have to come with him
to the rear storeroom. When she refused, he advised her "she was under
citizen's arrest for shoplifting and that she will have to go back on her own or
we will have to force her back." The two other employees took the woman by
the arms, and the store manager pushed her to the rear of the store. He then
asked her to produce the other radio in her purse, which she did, handing it to
him. Both radios still had the store's price tags affixed to them. She had no
sales receipt.

When asked if she had any money to pay for the radios, she replied she did
not. She was asked to fill out a form used by the store, which she did using a
false name. A deputy sheriff was summoned to the store. She gave him the
false name, also telling him she was returning the two radios. When booked,
she had $1.17 in cash with her.

At trial, her testimony was different from her explanation given in the store.
She testified she came into the store for ice cream and saw the radios on sale.
She said she put them in her purse, all the time intending to pay for them. She
said the sheriff's booking records were wrong; she had had $120 cash and a
valid credit card in her possession. She was found guilty and appealed. As to
the evidence produced by the store manager, the higher court affirmed the
conviction. There was no doubt the evidence showed she intended to shoplift
the two radios owned by the store.

People v. Buonauro, 170 Cal. Rptr. 285 (California, 1981)

One of her legal grounds for appeal was that the store manager made
an illegal arrest; therefore the evidence (the cameras and her explanation)

should not have been used at trial against her. In overruling her point, the court clearly distinguished between detaining pursuant to the merchant's privilege and an arrest made by a private person. Consider the comments of the court:

> Mr. Ramos [store manager] did not act unlawfully. After having observed the woman behind the counter where customers were normally not allowed, and then being alerted by another customer that the woman had placed two radios in her purse, Mr. Ramos had a merchant's privilege under Penal Code Section 490.5(e) to detain her for investigation of shoplifting.

Notice that the court is citing the merchant's privilege contained in the California detention statute as the source of authority by which the woman was first stopped. The court continued:

> When Mr. Ramos first approached the woman about this matter she voluntarily handed or threw one of the radios to him, then fled with the other radio he observed at that time. Evidence of the first radio was obviously not the product of any illegality.
>
> When Mr. Ramos again caught up with her near the checkstand he advised appellant she was under citizen's arrest (Penal Code Section 837). The arrest was valid. A private person may arrest another "for a public offense committed or attempted in his presence." Appellant committed an offense in his presence when she fled from him with the second radio which he had already seen. When he took her into custody and asked her for the other radio she handed it to him.

The facts of this case show the difference between a detention and a citizen's arrest. As the court points out, the initial encounter with the woman was a detention; the second was a citizen's arrest. Notice the language used by this store manager. During the initial encounter with the woman, he said nothing about her being under arrest, clearly demonstrating that the stopping was a detention under the merchant's privilege. Only when he was sure the woman was in wrongful possession of a radio and was trying to leave without paying for it did he tell her she was under arrest. At this point the offense had been committed, as evidenced by her flight.

Merchants, and particularly their sometimes overzealous security staffs, like to use the word *arrest* because it smacks of authority. A security person can be heard to say things like, "Yesterday I arrested two shoplifters at our Blueview Mall store." What actually happened was this: the private citizen store detective, not holding any type of commission, detained under the merchant's privilege, investigated the facts, and decided to cause a warrantless arrest to be made by summoning a peace officer to the Blueview Mall store. The peace officer did the arresting based on evidence supplied to the officer by the security person.

In most shoplifting situations, the suspect will not flee but rather will remain and make some type of explanation. The merchant is better off legally in these cases to call the stopping a detention for investigation of the facts and not tell the suspect he is under arrest. At the time the suspect is detained, it is apparent to the store manager or security person *but not legally certain* that the suspect intends to shoplift merchandise belonging to the store. The prudent approach is to inquire if the suspect has a sales receipt, which is a way of beginning the investigation of the facts. Once the investigation is concluded, the merchant can decide whether to prosecute.

DETENTION STATUTES DO NOT GRANT POLICE POWER TO OTHERWISE PRIVATE CITIZEN MERCHANTS

The merchant's privilege has been incorporated into the provisions of detention statutes in all states. Law review articles and courts examine civil cases to see if a store manager or security person violated or complied with the provisions of detention statutes in determining if civil liability exists. What is sometimes overlooked is the fact detention statutes *do not* grant merchants any police powers of arrest, use of force, or the right to make unlimited searches. The store manager or security person detaining pursuant to the merchant's privilege remains a private citizen at all times during the encounter with a shoplifting suspect. In passing these detention statutes, the state legislatures did not intend to make otherwise private citizen merchants into agents of the state, county, or city. The intent was to grant merchants conditional and limited immunity from false imprisonment liability so they could more easily recover unpurchased merchandise from shoplifting suspects.

These statutes strike a balance between the rights of the person detained and the right of the retailer to recover unpurchased merchandise in that person's possession. The suspect's right to freedom of movement in the store is protected because a retail employee must meet the objective test of probable cause to justify detention. The statutes are specifically limited to shoplifting. They do not give merchants the right to detain people for other offenses. The suspect's right to proper treatment during the investigation of the facts after being detained is ensured. All investigations must be legally reasonable in manner, method, and time. The suspect's right to privacy is protected because the merchant is not given an absolute right to search for the unpurchased merchandise. The suspect must consent or agree to produce concealed merchandise for examination by the detaining store manager or security person. The merchant is not given the right to detain and search for contraband such as narcotics.

It is important for merchants to remember they are only private citizens. Too often security personnel (with law enforcement backgrounds) forget this fact when entering the world of retail security. An untrained store manager also may want to show some authority and call a detention a citizen's arrest. It is crucial for a retail employee—be it a store manager or the director of loss prevention—to understand the difference between detaining on probable cause under the merchant's privilege and making a warrantless citizen's arrest. The case that follows demonstrates how the courts have concluded that detention statutes do not grant police power to private citizen retail merchants.

| CASE | Fitting room case |

A department store security guard saw a man enter a fitting room with two shirts and two pairs of pants. The store detective was a private citizen. He did not hold a special officers' commission nor was he an off-duty police officer moonlighting in security for the department store. When the man left the fitting room, he was carrying a shopping bag, one the store detective had not seen him with before. A check of the fitting room revealed no store merchandise. The man appeared to have left without paying or offering to pay. He was detained outside the store and taken to the security office, where the shirts and pants were recovered with the price tags on them. He made no explanation.

Following his conviction for retail theft under the Pennsylvania statute, the defendant appealed, claiming the store detective was not a private citizen. He argued the detention provisions of the Retail Theft Act made the private citizen store detective an agent of the state. This meant, according to the defendant, that the acts of detaining and recovering the pants and shirt were done "under color of law," as the courts call it. The defendant further argued that the search was without a warrant, making it illegal, so the recovered merchandise should not have been used as store prosecution evidence at his trial. The court rejected this argument, noting it was the first time it had been raised in Pennsylvania. In affirming the conviction, the court mentioned other states had reached the same conclusion under similar facts. The court said:

> Those courts, finding that such statutes are a codification of the common law's shopkeepers privilege, have held that such statutes do not create police authority in private persons. Such statutes authorize merchants to act without being subjected to civil liabilities for so acting reasonably. We agree and hold that store employees who stop, detain and search individuals they reasonably suspect of retail theft do not act under the color of state authority.

Commonwealth v. Martin, 446 A.2d 965 (Pennsylvania, 1982)

A similar result was reached in the Scarf Case discussed in chapter 3. There the defendant argued that her incriminating statement should not have been used against her as store prosecution evidence because the store detective failed to give her a *Miranda* warning. The defendant also was saying that detention statutes conferred police power on private citizen merchants. The court rejected her argument and made the following comments about the merchant's right to detain temporarily as found in the statute:

> The effect of a similar statutory privilege has been discussed in at least two cases from other jurisdictions. In those cases the courts reasoned that the limited detention rights extended by such statutes do not place store security guards in the category of law enforcement personnel for Miranda purposes. In the instant case we are not confronted with a situation where the security guards are acting in a coordinated effort with the police. As a general rule merely acting pursuant to a state statute does not in and of itself constitute "state action" requiring constitutional guarantees. In sum, we hold that under the facts of this case, the statements given to the security guards were not rendered inadmissible by the alleged failure to give the warnings outlined in Miranda.[7]

In both cases, the defendants were trying to limit the private citizen merchant's ability to gather evidence under these detention statutes. In the Fitting Room Case, the issue was the search and seizure. In the Scarf Case, the issue was an incriminating statement. In both cases, from different states, the security people were private citizens. These two courts held that detention statutes do not grant police power to private citizen merchants but give them only the right of temporary detention and the right to plead compliance with the statute if sued civilly.

The Merchant's Privilege and Miranda Warnings

In 1966 the U.S. Supreme Court handed down its decision in Miranda v. Arizona. The court established a conclusive presumption that all confessions or admissions of guilt made during custodial interrogation by the police are in violation of the person's Fifth Amendment right against self-incrimination. Constitutional protections of the Fourth, Fifth, and Sixth amendments apply only to actions by the state, meaning the federal, state, county, or city government. It is generally held that a person who is not a law enforcement officer and who is not acting in concert with a law enforcement officer is not required to extend constitutional warnings before eliciting an incriminating statement. The admission can generally be used later in court as prosecution evidence.

In the Scarf Case discussed in Chapter 3, the court held that merchant's privilege statutes do not place retailers in the same category as law enforcement officers when it comes to giving Miranda warnings to shoplifting suspects. After detaining on probable cause, a private citizen

---

[7]People v. Raitino, 401 NE2d 278 (IL 1980).

merchant has the right to ask the suspect questions and to receive answers without first having to give that suspect a *Miranda* warning. The reason is that these statutes do not grant any arrest power to merchants but confer only powers of limited detention for a private purpose. As shown in Chapter 4, the explanation a merchant receives from most shoplifting suspects is not a confession anyway, therefore, it cannot be used in court as evidence to prove one of the elements of the offense. The explanation is generally a denial of intent to shoplift (the "I forgot to pay" statements) or a claim of ownership (the "I bought it earlier" statements). Legally speaking, these explanations are denials rather than admissions of guilt.

A few years before the ruling in the Scarf Case, retailers received an unfortunate decision from the California Supreme Court which said security personnel must give *Miranda* warnings. The irony is that the case did not involve a shoplifting prosecution but one for possession of a controlled substance, heroin. The case did not involve an incriminating statement but a search that went too far after the woman had been detained on solid probable cause to believe she was in the process of shoplifting. In the actual *Miranda* decision, the Supreme Court was concerned about in-custody tactics of the police to extract coerced confessions in violation of a person's Fifth Amendment right against self-incrimination.[8] In *Zelinsky*, the issue was the Fourth Amendment's prohibition against unreasonable searches and seizures of physical or real evidence. In *Zelinsky*, the court did not consider the distinction between a citizen's arrest and a detention for probable cause under the merchant's privilege. The court reversed the conviction for possession of heroin, because the search was held to be in violation of the California constitution. The court found that the private citizen store detective was acting "in aid of law enforcement officers" even though he did not know she had heroin in her purse when she was detained on solid probable cause for shoplifting. Fortunately, this *Zelinsky*[9] decision has not been followed in other states. It is discussed here, so merchants can see the mistake the store detective made and learn from it.

Bad Facts Make Bad Laws—the Zelinsky Case

There is an old adage in the law that goes like this: "Bad facts make for bad law." It certainly applies to *Zelinsky*. The bad fact was the store detective's unauthorized search of the woman's purse and recovery of heroin. The search and seizure clearly exceeded the authority of a private citizen merchant's stopping people under either the citizen's arrest statute or the

---

[8]*Miranda v. Arizona*, 384 US 436, 86 S Ct. 1602, 16 LEd 2d 694 (1966).
[9]*People v. Zelinsky*, 594 P2d 1000 (California, 1979).

merchant's privilege. The store detective crossed over the line from protecting his employer's property to enforcing public criminal law. The bad law coming out of this case was that California merchants were required to give *Miranda* warnings because the court found this store detective was acting "in aid of law enforcement authorities." Because he acted as a police officer, the California Supreme Court treated him as a police officer, saying the heroin could not be used as evidence in the woman's prosecution for possession of a controlled substance. Her right to a reasonable expectation of privacy was violated under the California (not the federal) constitution by the unauthorized search and seizure.

This case started out as a garden variety concealment situation. A male store detective watched a female suspect put a blouse in her purse, a pair of sandals on her feet, and a hat on her head and then drop her purse in a straw bag, one that belonged to the store. She left without paying for any of the four items of store merchandise. At the time he stopped the woman, the store detective did not know she had the heroin in her purse. In the security office, she was searched for weapons by two female security officers, neither of whom had a commission. They found no weapons. The male store detective then reentered the room and made his legally fatal mistake: without obtaining her permission or consent, he reached inside the purse to recover the blouse. He found not only the blouse but the heroin.

A footnote to the case said the store detective had worked undercover narcotics operations in the past with the police and unnamed private agencies. Forgetting that his authority was limited to consent searches *only for unpurchased merchandise*, he recovered the heroin and gave it to the police, who had been called regarding the shoplifting situation.

The woman was found guilty in court of possessing a controlled substance. The heroin recovered by the store detective was introduced into evidence against her at trial. On appeal her conviction was reversed. In holding her right to privacy under the California constitution was violated by the search and seizure, the court said:

> In the present case, instead of holding the defendant and her handbag until the arrival of a peace officer who may have been authorized to search, the employees instituted a search to recover goods that were not in plain view. Such intrusion into defendant's person and effects was not authorized as incident to a citizen's arrest pursuant to section 837 of the Penal Code, or pursuant to the merchant's privilege subsequently codified in subdivision (e) of section 490.5. It was unnecessary to achieve the employees' reasonable concerns of assuring that defendant was carrying no weapons and of preventing loss of store property. As a matter of law, therefore, the fruits of that search were illegally obtained.[10]

---

[10]People v. Zelinsky, 594 P2d 1000 (California, 1979).

The irony of the case is that there was no need to search her purse, even for the blouse. As the court pointed out, the officer could have searched the purse on his arrival incident to a lawful warrantless arrest made based on evidence supplied to him by the store detectives. The real problem was that store policy did not require security people to limit their consent searches to ones for unpurchased merchandise. If contraband such as narcotics is discovered, it should be left alone. When the officer responds to make the shoplifting arrest, he should be told in a factual and neutral way about the existence of the drugs. *The retail employee should express no opinion whatsoever about whether possession of the contraband violates any criminal law.* The store is not the owner of the drugs or weapon that may be found. As a consequence, the merchant has no standing to initiate a criminal complaint. This is particularly true when the stopping, in the first place, is a detention under authority of the merchant's privilege statute which is specifically limited to shoplifting situations. Of course, merchants will want to cooperate with the peace officer who responds to handle the shoplifting case, but merchants should leave the decision about filing any other charges concerning possession of drugs or weapons up to the officer. It is the officer's job to make prosecution decisions about a shoplifting suspect's possession of contraband—not the job of the store owner, manager, or security person.[11]

The quote from *Zelinsky* shows that the court recognized there were two separate sources of statutory authority by which a merchant can stop a shoplifting suspect. The problem is, the court does not analyze the facts and decide whether the store detective made a citizen's arrest or detained for probable cause. The court ignored the distinction between an arrest (under one statute) and a detention (under another statute). The court also ignored the existence of a then three-year-old study of California merchants showing that they release more shoplifting suspects than they prosecute.[12] It is hard to see how the court overlooked these two things and jumped to the conclusion that merchants routinely act "in aid of law enforcement personnel" in shoplifting cases.

> At the time of the incident at Zody's, merchants were protected from civil liability for false arrest or false imprisonment in their reasonable efforts to detain shoplifters by a common law privilege that permitted detention for a reasonable time for investigation in a reasonable manner of any person whom the merchant had probable cause to believe had unlawfully taken or attempted to take merchandise from the premises. [citing Colyer v. Kress]

---

[11]Merchants are entitled to conduct a patdown search for weapons in most places. In a New York case, a shoplifting suspect was searched and a pistol found. It was given to the police and used as evidence to convict the man for carrying a concealed weapon. The conviction was upheld. (People v. Horman, 292 N.Y.2d 874, 239 N.E.2d 625 (New York, 1968.)

[12]28 *Stanford Law Review* 589 (1976).

> That privilege has since been enacted into statute as subdivision (e) of Penal
> Code section 490.5.
>   Thus, pursuant to the Penal Code or the civil common law privilege, store
> personnel Moore and O'Connor had authority to arrest or detain the defen-
> dant. The question remains, however, whether they exceeded their authority
> in their subsequent search for and seizure of evidence.[13]

From this quote, it is obvious that the court wanted to zero-in on the
search of the woman's purse. A couple of years later, the California court
properly analyzed the facts in a shoplifting case, one not involving the
suspect's possession of drugs or a weapon. In the Costume Jewelry Case,
the court distinguished between a citizen's arrest and detentions under
the merchant's privilege. The court did not engage in undocumented
editorializing about how merchants handle shoplifting cases but cited the
California study omitted in Zelinsky.

CASE	Costume jewelry case

In this case, a juvenile was seen palming some costume jewelry. There was no
question that the private citizen store detective had probable cause to detain
under the merchant's privilege as incorporated into the California detention
statute. In the security office, he asked the suspect why she had failed to pay.
Her response was that friends had said it was "easy to shoplift at this store."
This incriminating statement (an admission she intended to shoplift) was used
against her as prosecution evidence in a juvenile court proceeding, one that
terminated adversely to the young woman. There was no dispute that the store
detective had asked the question and received the answer without first giving
her a Miranda warning. The court held that failure of the store detective to
give a Miranda warning before asking the question did not violate her
constitutional rights.

Her lawyer appealed the case, arguing that the conviction should be reversed
because the explanation was made to a security person who admitted he had
given no Miranda warnings. The court asked the following question: "Does
Miranda govern custodian investigations by store detectives?" and found it did
not. Confronted squarely with the issue of detention by security personnel in a
shoplifting case, the same California court made the following comments:

> A private citizen is not required to advise another individual of his
> rights before questioning him. Absent evidence of complicity on the part
> of law enforcement officials the admissions or statements of a defendant
> to a private citizen infringe no constitutional rights. . . .
> Nongovernmental security employees that act without police
> cooperation have been regarded as private citizens unaffected by

---

[13]People v. Zelinski, Supre p. 1006.

> *Miranda*. . . . There is no evidence that McGinnis [the store detective]
> acted under any arrangement with the authorities at their direction or
> with their approval.
>
> In Re Deborah C., 635 P.2d 446 (California, 1981)

The California court astutely pointed out that the *Miranda* decision
prohibited use of answers later in court as prosecution evidence where the
answers were obtained involuntarily from a suspect in police custody.
The court said asking of questions is not illegal when done by private
citizen store detectives acting under authority of detention statutes. Such
a ruling is only common sense. The asking of nonaccusatory questions as
part of a reasonable investigation following a detention on probable cause
is what these detention statutes authorize. In distinguishing custodial
interrogation of a person by the police as found in *Miranda* with the
conduct of private citizen store detectives, the court commented:

> We think routine detention and questioning by plainclothes store detectives
> presents a substantially different situation than the facts of the actual
> *Miranda* case. Unless they represent themselves as police they do not enjoy
> the psychological advantage of official authority, a major tool of coercion.
> Moreover, there appears little evidence of abusive techniques by store
> detectives similar to those that Mr. Miranda charged against the police.[14]

A 1982 law review article discusses how the California court clari-
fied the *Zelinsky* holding. Consider the comments of the author of this
article about the Costume Jewelry Case:

> After recognizing that *Miranda* governs custodial interrogation, the Court
> noted that California courts have primarily limited its application to cases
> concerning law enforcement officials, their agents and agents of the court
> while the suspect is in official custody. The court further noted that *a private
> citizen is not required to advise another individual of his rights before
> questioning him.*
>
> By engaging in a policy analysis of the *Miranda* Decision, the court found
> that routine detention and questioning by plainclothes store detectives
> present a *substantially different situation* than was present in *Miranda*.
> *Miranda* responded to historical problems created by misuses of police
> authority to extract confessions through force, duress and lengthy incom-
> municado interrogations. In California, store employees have only *limited
> powers of detention*. Unless they represent themselves as police officers,
> these employees do not have the psychological advantage of official author-
> ity which *Miranda* and its progeny sought to avoid.
>
> Another reason the court felt that the underlying policies of *Miranda* did
> not warrant its application in this situation was the presence of evidence that

---

[14]In Re Deborah C, 635 P2d 446 (CA 1981).

retailers generally exercise restraint and release most shoplifters without police involvement [citing a study on this point].

A major part of the court's policy comparison between *Miranda* interrogation and detention by plainclothes detectives concerned the nature of the detention. The court ruled that *Miranda* criticized police preference for confessions over independent investigation . . . since shoplifting convictions most often depend on eyewitness testimony and physical evidence rather than on statements made by the suspects, the court noted that store detectives have less incentive to extract confessions from their suspects. This lack of incentive to extract confessions was a major policy reason influencing the costume jewelry court not to extend the *Miranda* requirements to store detectives in California. Finally, in refusing to extend *Miranda*'s applicability, the court noted that other jurisdictions have also refused to extend *Miranda* to privately employed personnel. [emphasis supplied][15]

As the article points out, the California court is now properly recognizing that retailers are granted only limited powers of detention under the merchant's privilege, no longer blurring the difference between a detention and a citizen's arrest. Furthermore, the court said merchants do not detain just for the purpose of causing a shoplifting charge to be filed but do follow a selective prosecution approach. This was a complete turnabout from the holding in *Zelinsky* that merchants routinely act in aid of law enforcement officers when they handle shoplifting cases. The California court now recognizes that private citizen merchants handling shoplifting cases are not in the same category as the police. They detain under the merchant's privilege, a statute that does not grant police power to otherwise private citizen merchants.

Finally, the article comments on the court's finding that merchant's do not need confessions in shoplifting cases to obtain convictions. As pointed out in Chapter 4, almost all convictions in shoplifting cases are based on testimonial evidence coupled with real or physical evidence. Confessions are not needed in shoplifting cases. Also, most explanations made by suspects are denials, which cannot be used in court as store prosecution evidence to prove any of the elements of the offense.

CASE	Electric blanket case

A security officer, working for a major national department store in Anchorage, Alaska, used an admission of guilt as prosecution evidence. He saw the

---

[15]"California Supreme Court Survey—A Review of Decisions." Set K—the Miranda Policies and Requirements as they Relate to Department Store Detectives: In Re Deborah C. *Pepperdine Law Review* 9 (1982): 1015–1017.

suspect, whom he knew from previous encounters, enter the store. He watched while the man picked up an electric blanket and woman's purse. The suspect then left; he was detained just outside the store. In the security office, he asked the suspect what he was going to do with the electric blanket. The man's response was, "Sell it." When asked how much he could get for it, the suspect said, "About ten dollars." This explanation was used at the shoplifting trial as evidence showing the defendant intended to shoplift. After being convicted, the defendant appealed.

In affirming his conviction and the use of the explanation as prosecution evidence, the appellate court stated the issue succinctly:

> Louis Metigoruk was convicted of shoplifting. He appeals arguing that a statement he made to a private security guard, employed by the store whose property he allegedly stole, should not have been admitted into evidence against him because the security guard did not give him *Miranda* warnings before questioning him. The municipality concedes that no *Miranda* warnings were given. The trial court held *Miranda* to be inapplicable to private security guards. Under the circumstances present in this case we agree. We hold that a private security guard who is not acting as an agent of the police need not give *Miranda* warnings prior to interrogating a suspect. We therefore affirm the judgment of the trial court.

The court rejected the defendant's argument that the stricter *Miranda* standards applicable to law enforcement officers should be applied to private citizen store detectives, citing cases from several other states as authority for the holding. The Alaska court specifically commented on the California decision in the Costume Jewelry Case:

> Consequently, the California court concluded that the traditional standards govern admissibility of voluntary statements were sufficient to protect a suspect's Fifth Amendment rights when confronted by a store detective so it was not necessary to extend the greater protections established in *Miranda*. We are persuaded by these reasons and hold that store security guards, unless acting as state agents, need not give *Miranda* warnings before questioning suspects.

Metigoruk v. Municipality of Anchorage, 655 P.2d 1317 (Alaska, 1982).

The Scarf Case (Illinois), the Electric Blanket Case (Alaska), and the Costume Jewelry Case (California) are all consistent. They hold that private citizen merchants, whether they are store owners, managers, or security personnel, need not give *Miranda* warnings before asking shoplifting suspects questions about their wrongful possession of merchandise. These cases recognize that merchant's privilege statutes do not grant retailers any police power of arrest and that the retail community does not routinely act in aid of law enforcement officers when they detain shoplifting suspects on probable cause. The retailer detains initially for a private purpose—to prevent loss of merchandise and to recover the goods. After investigating the facts, the merchant may (but is not required to) summon a peace officer and cause the suspect's arrest and prosecution.

RECOVERING THE PHYSICAL EVIDENCE AFTER DETAINING SUSPECTS ON PROBABLE CAUSE

In the following cases, the courts are not concerned with explanations made by suspects but rather with searches for and seizures of merchandise in possession of persons detained. The courts talk about whether recovering unpurchased merchandise violates a suspect's right to privacy—or expectation of privacy as it's sometimes called. This is a traditional Fourth Amendment problem. The general rule is that because there is no police involvement when the private citizen merchant detains and obtains consent to examine the goods, the Fourth Amendment does not apply. This means there is no unreasonable search and seizure by a private citizen, so the merchandise can be used at trial as store prosecution evidence.

| CASE | Five cigarette lighters case |

In this case, the Illinois court considered the question of whether a search by a private citizen security guard violated the suspect's right to privacy. The suspect was detained pursuant to the detention section of the Illinois Retail Theft Act. The court held that because there was no police involvement in the store at the time of the detention, the Fourth Amendment did not apply to the actions of this store detective. Thus, the suspect was not entitled to have the five lighters and box of soup suppressed as store prosecution evidence later at the shoplifting trial.

In this case, a store employee watched the suspect from a catwalk about twenty feet above the selling floor. She saw the suspect tear open a package of lighters and put them in his pocket. She notified her supervisor. The man was stopped after passing through the checkout counter without paying. He was immediately taken to the security office and searched by a male guard. Five lighters and a box of soup were found in his pocket. The police were notified and on their arrival made the warrantless arrest, based on evidence supplied to them by the store employees. Neither the store employees nor the responding police officers had a search warrant.

The court is clearly holding that searches by the security people do not constitute state action. Consider the following comments from the case:

> Even though the statute does not expressly authorize store personnel
> to search someone reasonably believed to be guilty of theft, the law is

> clear that evidence which would be inadmissible if seized by the police
> is admissible if seized by a third-party who is not acting as an agent of
> the police [citing cases]. Because there was no police involvement in
> the search the Fourth Amendment is clearly not applicable.

People v. Tolivar, 377 N.W.2d 207 (Illinois, 1978)

There was no evidence in this case that the merchants violated the reasonable manner provision of the detention statute by forcing a search without the suspect's consent. The search was limited to one for the lighters, the merchandise the suspect was seen concealing minutes earlier. In cases like this one, the courts are inclined to agree that no privacy violation took place. There was no police involvement either in the detention or the search and recovery of the unpurchased lighters. This merchant detained and then conducted an investigation independent of the police. Based on the facts produced, the merchant formulated a reasonable belief that the evidence established a prosecutable case *before* informing the police. The defendant attacked his conviction as an invasion of privacy but was not successful. Privacy in the abstract is one thing, but as all know, shoplifters thrive on privacy. If a merchant watches a person remove goods from a rack, counter, or shelf and then conceal them and walk out without paying, it is difficult to see where that person has a claim of privacy in regard to unpurchased merchandise. To say the suspect in this Five Cigarette Lighters Case has a reasonable expectation of privacy borders on the absurd.

CASE	Four sweaters case

The Pennsylvania court held in this case that store detectives do not act under color of law when they detain on probable cause, search for, and recover unpurchased merchandise belonging to the store. The suspect was seen entering the store with a cardboard box in hand. The security officer watched as he placed four sweaters in the box and left without paying. He was detained and searched. The recovered sweaters were used as store prosecution evidence at the shoplifting trial, where he was convicted of retail theft. In affirming the conviction, the court cited an earlier Pennsylvania case that detention statutes are a codification of the common law's shopkeepers' privilege to recover unpurchased merchandise, so they do not create police power in otherwise private citizen merchants.

The court clearly held that retail employees who detain and search those they reasonably believe are committing shoplifting do not act under color of state authority. The court concluded:

> Accordingly, because the Clover security guards were acting in a

private capacity, rather than under color of state law, they were entitled, upon probable cause, to search appellant without applying for or receiving a search warrant. The record clearly supports the fact that security guards had probable cause. Appellant was seen by a door guard entering the store with a box and was then observed by another guard taking four sweaters off the rack and stuffing them in his box, closing the box and walking out of the store. These observations were more than sufficient to support the guards' belief that appellant was committing theft.

Commonwealth v. Lacy, 471 A.2d 888 (Pennsylvania, 1984)

| CASE | Blazer case |

In a store in Alaska, a woman was seen putting a blazer and a skirt in her purse. Her companion was also seen concealing unpurchased merchandise. When both were detained, a struggle took place, with the woman assaulting the store detective. She was charged with and convicted of both assault and shoplifting. On appeal, she argued that the security employee of a private business was acting under color of state law in searching her purse and retrieving property. She said because the store detective had no search warrant, her Fourth Amendment right to be free from unreasonable searches and seizures was violated. Finally, she said the recovered merchandise should not be used at trial as prosecution evidence because to do so violated both the state and federal constitution. To support her claim, the woman relied on *Zelinsky*.

The Alaska court rejected the defendant's argument and in so doing distinguished the *Zelinsky* case by saying:

> *People v. Zelinsky* is distinguishable. In Zelinsky, the store detective searched the defendant and discovered illegal drugs. Zelinsky was prosecuted for possession of those drugs. Here the store detective searched for his employer's merchandise and recovered it. Jackson [the defendant] was prosecuted for the theft of the merchandise.

Jackson v. Alaska, 657 P.2d 405 (Alaska, 1983)

The Blazer Case makes it clear that when merchants detain, search for, and recover unpurchased merchandise (rather than drugs or other contraband) the courts have held there is no constitutional violation. The recovered merchandise can be used in the shoplifting trial as prosecution evidence.

| CASE | Split decision case |

Here a man was convicted of disorderly conduct out of a shoplifting incident. The case is of value because the Michigan court split four to two in affirming the conviction. The defendant, in the company of two other men, was seen handing tape cassettes to his friend, who put them in his pants. All three were detained. The defendant signed an incriminating statement and was charged with disorderly conduct. The security people admitted they did not give him *Miranda* warnings before reducing the statement to writing for his signature. There was no evidence the security people used coercion, duress or made threats in obtaining his signature on the written admission.

Four members of the court affirmed the conviction, noting the merchandise had to be excluded as prosecution evidence only if governmental involvement can be shown. Statements made to private individuals need not be preceded by *Miranda*, citing several court decisions to support this ruling. The defendant had argued that the conduct of the three security officers in detaining and questioning him amounted to state action so a *Miranda* warning should have been given before obtaining any statements, oral or written. In rejecting the defendant's contention, the court stated:

> We do not believe that the activities of the store security guards and the city police in this case demonstrated the coordinated effort necessary to constitute state action. The Meijer security people were working with the view of furthering their employer's interest only; they were not acting as police agents. Their role may be viewed as an extension of the common law shopkeepers' privilege to detain for a reasonable period of time a person suspected of theft or failure to pay. There was no complicity with the police department or any indication that their acts were instigated or motivated by the police.
> The security guards did not exceed the scope of their power to detain and question the suspected shoplifters. The security guards were in plain clothes; the detention did not last an unreasonably long time. While there was some indication that the suspects were nervous, the acts of the security guards did not present the kind of psychological coercion and threatening environmental custody addressed by *Miranda*.

City of Grand Rapids v. Impens, 327 N.W.2d 278 (Michigan, 1982)

Two judges dissented, saying the conviction should be reversed. Retail and security executives are urged to read this opinion in full because it sets forth both positions. The dissent admits that the facts in shoplifting cases are not like those in the actual *Miranda* case where Mr. Miranda was questioned by police officers at the station about a felony. The dissenting judges would argue for an extension of the "*Miranda* Concept," as he calls it, to shoplifting cases.

The dissent noted that the Michigan constitution has a provision saying no person shall be compelled to testify against himself in a criminal case. The provision is at least as broad as the Fifth Amendment privilege against self-incrimination in the U.S. Constitution. The court began by saying the following:

The People contend that in this case it was not necessary to advise the defendant of his rights or to employ other procedural safeguards because defendant was taken into custody and questioned by private persons and not by the police. We disagree. We are satisfied that the People's classification of private security guards as "private persons" for *Miranda* purposes disregards the significance of, and the role played by private security personnel in today's society. While we recognize that *Miranda* did not deal with the private security guard situation, in order to effectuate Michigan policy we must extend this *Miranda* concept to apply to private security guard interrogation in a custodial setting.

To document the scope of the problem, the court quoted from *The Task Force on Private Security of the National Advisory Committee on Criminal Justice Standards and Goals* of 1976 as follows:

There are more than 1 million people involved in private security in the United States. The private security industry is a multi-billion dollar a year business that grows at a rate of 10 to 12 percent per year. In many large cities the number of private security personnel is considerably greater than the number of police and law enforcement personnel. Of those individuals involved in private security, some are uniformed, some are not; some carry guns, some are unarmed; some guard nuclear energy installations, some guard golf courses; some are trained, some are not; some have college degrees; some are virtually uneducated.

Apparently the issue of training had come up at the trial. In a footnote in the dissenting opinion, the judge pointed to testimony from a store security person that guards receive forty hours of training. The subjects cover such areas as search and seizure, arrest, detention, and employee theft. The fact that this store had a training program for security people did not impress the judge:

Unlike the little old lady next door who has a desire to assist in law enforcement, private security guards are in the business of law enforcement. It is the nature of the activities of private security guards that distinguishes them from private persons. When private security guards "perform functions that are traditionally governmental in nature, their action is tantamount to state action." The court then quoted from another case involving shoplifting—"A retail store security guard, who does more than protect his employer's property full-time but who pursues, apprehends and detains criminals, who performs custodial searches (consensual or nonconsensual) or seizes and preserves evidence, and who interrogates and refers the criminal for prosecution is performing a police function exclusively reserved to the state."[16]

This judge is discussing the public function aspect of the state action

---

[16]*Harvard Civil Rights-Civil Liberties Law Review* 15 (1983): 649, 657–658.

theory. It holds that when a private person performs tasks and exercises, powers that are traditionally governmental in nature, he will be treated as a government actor. Under this theory, the private person will be subject to the same restrictions as the government, even in the absence of direct contact between the private person and a governmental official or agency. This doctrine logically should apply to private security guard cases according to its proponents. They say that policing is one of the most basic functions of the sovereign. When security people are employed to protect private assets (such as a retail store) and question, search for evidence, and arrest, they are performing traditional public police functions.[16] The court now applies this public function theory to the case and holds that the signed statement was not admissible as store prosecution evidence in the disorderly conduct prosecution:

> In the instant case defendant and his companions were apprehended by Meijer security guards and taken to the security office. The guards conducted a "normal search" of the suspects up against the wall and questioned them about the shoplifting incident. One of the guards wrote out confessional statements and requested the defendant and his companions to sign them. The Grand Rapids Police were called. A Meijer security guard testified that "it is up to the security personnel as to whether a shoplifting suspect is prosecuted or just warned and released." He estimated that 20 to 40 suspects are detained for questioning each month.
>
> We find that in the instant case the Meijer security guards were acting as substitute police officers rather than merely as protectors of private property. The confession elicited by the private security guards should have been preceded by *Miranda* warnings and without them is inadmissible as evidence.

The dissenting opinion would make private citizen store detectives agents of the state because of the nature of their duties. But the majority of the court did not find any coordinated effort between the security people and the Grand Rapids police; hence, no state action was present. The majority opinion reflects the law where this question has been directly litigated. The courts have held that detention statutes do not grant police power to otherwise private citizen merchants. To avoid situations where a court could apply this public function theory to shoplifting cases, a merchant must set policy to comply with the merchant's privilege as incorporated into the detention statute in each state where stores are operated. As *Zelinsky* in California showed, where private citizen merchants act like the police, the courts are inclined to treat them like the police.

Most detention statutes make no reference to searching a suspect who has been detained on probable cause. Some detention statutes, like those of Iowa (Section 808.12), Oklahoma (Section 1343), and Wisconsin (Section 943.50) mention circumstances under which a merchant may search. As a practical matter, however, they are of little value in setting policy. These statutes do not distinguish between merchandise in plain view and concealed merchandise. The overwhelming majority of shoplifting cases involve situations where a person has concealed items and then is detained by a retail employee. California has recently amended its detention statute to include a provision dealing with recovery of the merchandise. One section says the detaining retail employee may examine goods that are in plain view in an effort to determine ownership. Another section covers the problem of when the merchandise is concealed, which is most of the time. It says the merchant may ask the suspect to surrender the concealed merchandise for examination voluntarily to determine ownership. This well-drafted statute should be consulted by merchants in any state for it will help them in setting company policy. (This California statute is reproduced in Chapter 6.)

The basic rule is that merchants are not permitted to conduct a full or unlimited search following detention on probable cause. A peace officer making a lawful warrantless arrest can, incident to that arrest, search the suspect without having to obtain consent or permission to do so. Since merchants can only detain temporarily for the specific purpose of recovering unpurchased merchandise, they are not given authority to search without consent. A buzz word around retail security circles is the *consent search*. It implies that store detectives can initiate a search into a purse, shopping bag, or pocket simply because they have probable cause to detain in the first place and ask their suspect for permission.

Merchants would be better off if they forgot about initiating a search and viewed their role as one of obtaining consent by asking for it. The California statute says the merchant "may request the person detained to voluntarily surrender the item." Security people (many with law enforcement backgrounds) tend to be aggressive. Untrained store managers may not fully understand the rule. In either situation, it is easy to force a search, thereby violating test 2 under the detention statute. By requiring all employees to ask the suspect to produce concealed merchandise (as opposed to rummaging around in purses, shopping bags, or pockets), the detaining employee will avoid even the appearance of forcing a search. The fact that a private citizen merchant is not required to give a *Miranda* warning should not be taken as a license to search without first asking the suspect to produce the goods for examination.

The cases have shown how the courts handle the admission of evidence from searches conducted by merchants following detentions on probable cause. Store policy and training programs must take into account that employees will find suspects in possession of the following:

1. unpurchased merchandise belonging to the detaining store
2. merchandise that the suspect can show has been purchased

3. drugs
4. weapons
5. unpurchased merchandise possibly belonging to other stores
6. stolen credit cards
7. false identification

If the California store in *Zelinsky* had taken time to think the problem through, the store detective would never have reached inside the purse in the first place. Remember that bad facts wind up making bad law. Forcing a search not only violates the merchant's privilege statute, but it can have an effect on the prosecution of the case itself. Always ask the suspect to produce concealed merchandise for examination concerning ownership. If the suspect refuses—which the suspect has a right to do—continue the detention until the arrival of a peace officer and complete the investigation with the officer's assistance.

Above all, remember that the large majority of persons detained for shoplifting will be the average citizen types. They do not carry weapons or have drugs in their possession. Most will not try and run out of the store. If given a chance, they will explain the circumstances surrounding their possession of the goods and produce those goods for examination without incident. As those with experience in handling shoplifting cases know, most people will cooperate. They will try and talk the merchant out of calling the police and having them prosecuted. Let them explain, because with the explanation they will hand the merchandise back to the store manager, owner, or security person and say, "I forgot to pay" or "I bought it earlier." When this happens the merchant has established the defense and is on the way to conducting a legally reasonable investigation of the facts.

OBTAINING A WRITTEN CONFESSION

Merchants generally do not need to obtain written confessions to secure convictions in shoplifting cases. The store can rely on observations made by the employee (testimonial evidence) along with the recovered merchandise and price tag (real or physical evidence) at the trial. None of the merchants in the cases in Chapter 3 needed written confessions to convict their suspects. Veteran retail security people realize most of the shoplifting cases they file do not involve these confessions. As the Two Televisions Case will demonstrate, obtaining a written confession gets the merchant into a voluntariness question at trial. Most of the time the merchant is better off just to note any explanation made by the suspect, whether admission or denial, on the offense report and show the statement to the prosecutor before trial.

CASE	Two televisions case

In this case, the store's use of a preprinted form was the crux of the problem. The form had a section containing the following: "I voluntarily admit I took the articles from the store," followed by an area where the employee wrote in a description and value of the recovered merchandise. Here a department store security employee saw two men place two television sets in a shopping cart. They pushed the cart past an area with a large overhead sign reading "No Merchandise Beyond Here Without Receipt." The pair then separated. One suspect pushed the cart outside to the sidewalk, where the security man and another employee detained him. In the security office the suspect explained that his companion went into the store to pay for the televisions. This explanation was clearly a denial of intent to shoplift because it was obvious the department store owned the sets. Investigation revealed that his companion did not return to the store and make any effort to pay.

This store detective had all the evidence he needed to prove the elements of the offense later in court. He knew that the suspect's formal courtroom defense to the charge would be a denial of intent to shoplift. The testimonial and real evidence would combine at trial to prove the suspect intended to shoplift two television sets owned by the store. There was no need to obtain a written confession, though this case was filed as felony theft.

Hunter v. Colorado, 655 P.2d 374 (Colorado, 1979)

In this case, the trial judge made a mistake. He did not hold the voluntariness hearing out of the presence of the jury but let them hear the testimony about the signing of the statement. The defendant testified that the security man took his driver's license and said he would return it only if the confession was signed. The security employee disputed the defendant's account, saying he told the man he did not have to sign the confession form. The jury heard this evidence along with the other prosecution and defense evidence and then convicted the man of theft.

In reversing the conviction, the Colorado Supreme Court said the defendant's objection to letting the jury determine voluntariness of the confession was proper. The failure of the trial judge to excuse the jury and listen to the evidence regarding the signing of the confession himself triggered a due process question. The prosecutor had argued that no due process violation had taken place because there was no peace officer involved in obtaining the confession. Since there was no state action, the due process clause was not violated. The court disagreed, finding there was no state action in the obtaining of the confession because the security man was clearly a private citizen, not acting in concert with the police. State action was found in the trial judge's mistake of letting the jury hear the evidence about the circumstances under which the confession was signed.

The decision was not reversed because of evidence-gathering mistakes made by this store. If anything, this store had too much evidence. The question to ask is whether it was even necessary to obtain the confession. Since the prosecution *always* has the burden of proving that the signed confession was voluntarily obtained, merchants should check with local prosecutors for their opinion as to whether confessions will help or hurt in shoplifting cases. The bottom line is that merchants, and particularly their security departments, should have the ability to determine if a prosecutable shoplifting case exists without using a signed confession. They should not rely on the fact that the suspect will sign a confession but rather rely on the testimonial and real or physical evidence. In any state, a prosecutable case exists with this evidence alone. Obtaining confessions might be fine for employee theft cases where merchants have time to investigate the facts. In shoplifting cases, as the Two Television Case demonstrates, confessions can cause merchants prosecution problems by injecting a nonevidence issue into the case.

CONCLUSION

Much of this chapter has been about just two words: state action. In most shoplifting cases, the only state action is on the part of the peace officer who responds to the store. The officer (not the merchant) makes a warrantless arrest based on evidence supplied by the merchant, who is also the victim and the owner of the goods in question. A home owner can report a residential burglary by summoning the police. So can the owner of a car that has been broken into. No one would say either of these two private citizens was an agent of the state. All they did was make an effort to protect their property. It is the same with a retail merchant. The only difference is that shoplifting takes place every day in malls and in stores across the country. Shoplifting is highly predictable.

The public function doctrine mentioned by the dissenting Michigan court overlooks three basic facts: (1) detention statutes do not grant police power to otherwise private citizen merchants; (2) these detention statutes do not require that any merchant file a shoplifting charge against anybody; and (3) retail industry statistics demonstrate that merchants follow a selective prosecution approach. The property is recovered if the suspect is warned and released or if the suspect is prosecuted. Merchants do not hold themselves out to be quasi-public law enforcement agencies. The job of retail store detectives is to protect private assets, not to fight crime.

The California court's "in aid of law enforcement personnel" statement in *Zelinsky* applied not to a shoplifting case but, as the Alaska court correctly pointed out, to a case where the defendant was prosecuted for possession of heroin. The store detective obviously made a mistake by reaching inside the woman's purse. He did not err by detaining after seeing her obtain wrongful possession of four items of store merchandise. He had established probable cause to detain for investigation in any state, a fact the California court did not dispute. He wore no uniform. He carried no weapon. He used no excessive force. He made no threats of prosecution to obtain a confession or a civil liability release. He made no accusations of shoplifting. He did not detain the woman for an unreasonably long period of time.

In *Zelinsky* the store detective did his job. He protected his employer's property by detaining only after meeting the probable cause test contained in the California detention statute. The court blurred the distinction between a citizen's arrest (under one statute) and a detention for investigation of shoplifting based on probable cause (under another statute). Rather than analyzing the facts, the court zeroed in on the obvious: the search was unauthorized under either statute. Rather than coming to grips with the difficult issues involved in shoplifting cases, the court handed down a ruling in a possession of heroin case, which it applied to all shoplifting situations. Fortunately the court in subsequent decisions, such as the Costume Jewelry Case, is now properly analyzing the facts as they exist in shoplifting cases.

The crux of the problem is this—if store owners, managers or security people act like the police, the courts may well treat them like the police and apply the *Miranda* concept to shoplifting cases. It is incumbent on retailers in their training programs to teach employees to comply with all provisions of detention statutes. The purpose of detaining a shoplifting suspect is not automatically to put the case through the court system but to investigate the facts. The primary facts are ownership of the merchandise and the suspect's intent to shoplift it. There is no state action involved in recovering merchandise that belongs to the store in the first place. This is true whether the merchant elects to release the suspect or to prosecute the case.

Most retailers set policy well within the provisions of detention statutes because they realize civil actions can result if a mistake is made in handling the case. Merchants know they must be more diplomatic when protecting private assets than the police who are fighting crime. Retail employees may detain only those they see obtaining wrongful possession of merchandise and leaving their stores without paying. They do not have a license to detain temporarily persons for other offenses under provisions of the detention statutes. Generally, retail security people do not wear uniforms and do not carry weapons. Retail management wants to avoid the armed camp atmosphere because it is not conducive to selling. Because they do not wear uniforms and do not carry weapons, the courts have recognized that a private citizen store detective does not enjoy the same psychological advantage of commissioned peace officers.

Conscientious retailers conduct regular training programs emphasizing loss prevention. The whole thrust of retail security is preventive. When a shoplifting suspect is detained, the merchant has prevented a loss. If the suspect was not stopped, the merchandise would go out the front door. Industry statistics show that retailers follow a selective prosecution policy. They do not detain and put every case through the court system. The purpose of detaining is to recover merchandise. The goods are recovered if the case is prosecuted or if the suspect is released. To say merchants "act in aid of law enforcement personnel," as the California court did in *Zelinsky*, ignores the evidence found in trade association and other studies. The statement that retail store detectives are "in the business of law enforcement" (as was made by the dissenting Michigan judge in the Split Decision Case) is not supported by industry statistics.

State legislatures have not given merchants authority to arrest anybody. They have given retailers the privilege to detain, investigate the facts, and recover unpurchased merchandise without incurring civil liability *if retail employees comply with the merchant's privilege.* The privilege exists so merchants can prevent loss, both the loss of merchandise to shoplifters and the loss of dollars paid out when a store is sued civilly.

8

Civil Actions Most Commonly Filed against Retail Merchants

THE MERCHANT'S DUTY TO USE REASONABLE CARE DURING THE ENCOUNTER WITH A SHOPLIFTING SUSPECT

The driver of a car has the duty to use reasonable care under all circumstances while operating a car—such as backing, turning, or staying on the right side of the roadway. If the defendant driver backs into, or turns left in front of, or crosses the center line and runs into the plaintiff driver, the defendant has violated the civil tort law duty to use reasonable care. In a civil action for negligence in the operation of a car, the injured driver (the plaintiff) must prove a breach of duty occurred. For example, the civil action may allege a breach of duty by failing to yield the right of way before turning left, thereby causing the accident. If the plaintiff proves the allegation to a jury, the defendant is found to be negligent—meaning the defendant did violate the civil tort law duty to use reasonable care. Said another way, the defendant is found to be liable to the plaintiff for money damages because the breach of duty resulted in an injury to the plaintiff. These automobile accident situations are the most common example of how a person can violate the civil tort law to use reasonable care.

The civil tort law duty to use reasonable care under all the circumstances also applies to retail merchants handling shoplifting situations. It applies *before* and *during* the encounter with a shoplifting suspect. A store owner, manager, or security person violates the civil tort law duty to use reasonable care by failing to meet the tests in the merchant's privilege statutes. By breaking a shoplifting situation into three phases, the merchant can better see how the duty to use reasonable care applies during all aspects of the encounter with a shoplifting suspect (Table 8.1).

TABLE 8.1	Three phases of handling a shoplifting situation	
1: Detention phase	**2: Investigation of facts phase**	**3: Decision-making phase**

Detention on probable cause in any type of shoplifting situation
  Concealment
  No concealment
  Fitting room
  Aiding and abetting
  Price tag switching
  Container stuffing
  Cash refund schemes
	While investigating the facts, avoid mistreatment of the suspect such as the following:
	  Use of excessive force
	  Making threats of prosecution to obtain a confession or a civil liability release
	  Accusations of shoplifting
	  Forcing a search without obtaining consent of the suspect
	
	Conduct a logical and systematic investigation of the facts by doing the following:
	  Obtain suspect's explanation
	  Translate it into the defense of a denial of intent to shoplift or a claim of ownership
	  Verify or disprove the merits of the suspect's explanation
	  Recover the merchandise in question and a price tag
		Review store prosecution evidence to make sure it will establish the elements of the offense at the shoplifting trial
		
		If the decision is to prosecute, summon a peace officer to the store. Based on the evidence presented, that officer will make the formal warrantless arrest of the suspect
		
		If the evidence does not establish intent to shoplift or store ownership of merchandise, release the suspect without formal prosecution

The issue in any civil case is the conduct of the store employee handling the shoplifting situation. The employee's conduct can violate the civil tort law duty to use reasonable care at any time during the encounter with a shoplifting suspect. In the Discarded Sweater Case in Chapter 6, for example, the department store security man made a mistake in all three phases of his encounter with the suspect. First of all, he detained the young woman without establishing probable cause to justify the restraint of her freedom of movement. This mistake exposed the store to false imprisonment liability. During the investigation of the facts phase, he conducted no investigation. He simply detained her and called the police to come out and make the formal arrest. His failure to investigate the facts set the stage for the filing of a nonprosecutable case. During the decision-making phase, he did not review the evidence to see if it would establish the elements of the offense at the trial. The result was the filing of a nonprosecutable case, followed by an acquittal and a civil action.

In other situations, the conduct violating the civil tort law duty to use reasonable care takes place *after* the suspect has been properly detained. This is what happened in the Aspirin Case in Chapter 6. The detention was justified because the contract security guard saw the man drop a bottle of aspirin in his jacket pocket and leave without paying for it. The failure to use reasonable care took place during the investigation of the facts phase. The guard did not look for the ditched box, nor did he and the food store manager investigate the man's claim of ownership by prior purchase. In essence, no investigation of the facts was conducted before calling the police to have the man formally arrested and prosecuted. The result, just like that in the Discarded Sweater Case, was the filing of a nonprosecutable case followed by an acquittal and a civil action.

It is important to understand the exact type of employee conduct that can violate the civil tort law duty to use reasonable care during the encounter with a shoplifting suspect. Consider Figure 8.1, which shows what type of conduct can create civil liability exposure.

FIGURE 8.1	Action and conduct of the merchant in the store that creates liability

Detaining without probable cause	Use of force	Accusations of shoplifting	Failure to investigate and review the facts
False Imprisonment	Assault and Battery	Slander	Sets the Stage for Filing of weak or nonprosecutable cases An acquittal A malicious prosecution action filed against the store

The two most common examples of evidence-gathering mistakes are (1) detaining without probable cause and (2) failing to investigate and review the facts before filing the shoplifting case. There are four common mistakes involving mistreatment of a shoplifting suspect: (1) using excessive force, (2) making accusations of shoplifting, (3) forcing a search without obtaining the suspect's consent, and (4) making threats of prosecution to obtain either confessions or civil liability releases. The case law is clear that where civil liability is found to exist, a jury has decided a retail employee made either an evidence-gathering mistake or mistreated the suspect. Sometimes both types of mistake will be made in the same case, thus creating two different types of civil liability exposure. (See the Flea and Tick Spray Case in this chapter where the food store assistant manager detained without establishing probable cause [False Imprisonment liability created] and then accused his suspect of shoplifting [Slander liability created].)

A universal rule applies to handling shoplifting cases in all states—*the response of the merchant dictates the result of the case.* A merchant in any state who responds to a shoplifting situation without the skills to comply with the five tests in the detention statutes will—sooner or later—make a mistake. That mistake will violate the civil tort law duty to use reasonable care. That mistake will permit the shoplifting suspect to turn the tables and sue the store civilly for actual and punitive damages. That mistake is preventable if the responding merchant's conduct stays within the scope of the statutory privilege to detain, then investigate and review the facts before deciding how to handle the case.

In reading these cases, *forget about shoplifters* for a while. Learn to identify the mistakes made in these cases. The next time a shoplifting situation comes up, do not make the mistakes found here—the big mistakes. In reading these cases (and in rereading the ones in other chapters), put yourself in the place of the store manager or security person who is responding. Always remember that the response dictates the result. By improving the ability to respond to a shoplifting situation, you will prosecute more effectively and reduce the store's exposure to civil liability.

FALSE IMPRISONMENT ACTIONS

In the civil tort law, a restraint or detention is not an arrest since it is made under authority of the merchant's privilege statute. If the detention or restraint is not justified by probable cause, the store can be sued successfully for false imprisonment. Freedom of movement is the personal interest invaded by a false imprisonment. No peace officer need be present when the restraint is made. The merchant need not even touch the suspect to commit a false imprisonment. All that is required is for the suspect's freedom of movement to be restrained by the merchant without a legal excuse for so doing. Consider the following definition of a false imprisonment:

> The wrong [false imprisonment] may be committed by words alone, or by acts alone, or by both. . . . It is not necessary that the individual be confined within a prison or within walls; or that he be assaulted or even touched. It is not necessary that there should be any injury done to the individual's person or to his character or reputation. Nor is it necessary that the wrongful act be committed with ill-will or malice or even with the slightest wrongful intention. Nor is it necessary that the act be under color of any legal or judicial proceeding. All that is necessary is that the individual be restrained of his liberty without any significant legal cause therefor, and by words or acts which he fears to disregard.[1]

Another definition finds the court placing emphasis on the fact that threats of force or conduct implying use of force to effect the restraint can constitute a false imprisonment. This court also stresses the fact that the suspect must actually believe he is being detained:

> A person is restrained or imprisoned when he is deprived of either liberty of movement or freedom to remain in the place of his lawful choice; and such restraint or imprisonment may be accomplished by physical force alone, or by threat of force, or by conduct reasonably implying that force will be used. If the words and conduct are such as to induce a reasonable apprehension of force and the means of coercion are at hand, a person may be as effectually restrained and deprived of liberty as by prison bars.[2]

Generally surveillance alone is not sufficient to establish a restraint, even if the person knows he is being watched. As the definition above says, the courts will look at three factors:

1. if physical force itself is used to cause the restraint;
2. if a threat of force was to effect the restraint;
3. if the conduct of the retail employee reasonably implied that force would be used to prevent the suspect from leaving the store.

Normally the plaintiff in a false imprisonment action will testify that under all the circumstances (words, conduct, tone of voice) he felt he was not free to leave the store but had to accompany the retail employee to an office. This is true even where the retail employee did not touch the suspect on the sales floor.

---

[1]Perry v. Kress, 358 P. 2d 665, 667 (Kansas 1968).
[2]Moore v. Pay 'N Save, 581 P.2d 195 (Washington, 1978).

To recover for false imprisonment the plaintiff must prove the elements of the tort action. They are as follows:

1.   A retail employee restrained the plaintiff's freedom of movement.
2.   The restraint was committed without a legal reason.
3.   The plaintiff did not consent to the restraint.

| CASE | New blue purse case |

This case demonstrates a situation where the restraint or detention was supported only by an employee's opinion that the woman was in wrongful possession of unpurchased merchandise. As the facts will show, no store employee observed the woman remove the purse from its place of display. A woman and her female companion entered a national department store, the woman carrying a purse over her arm. She was also carrying a new blue purse which she had just won in the course of her employment as an Avon sales representative. Her reason for bringing the purse into the store that day was to find some shoes that matched the new purse. First, she and her friend went to the shoe department. Finding no shoes to match the purse they then went to the clothing department. A female employee noticed the woman with two purses, one of which "appeared" to be of a type offered for sale by the store. This employee never saw the woman remove the blue purse from a place of display. The customer had it in plain view and over her arm the entire time.

As the two women were about to leave the store, the female employee notified a male employee, one authorized to detain shoplifting suspects. He stopped the woman outside the store, producing a badge telling her she was under arrest for shoplifting. About that time, an assistant manager arrived. The woman showed the two men the Avon card in the purse, explaining that she won it in a sales contest. Instead of releasing her, the men insisted that she come back into the store and discuss the matter. The shopper was released about twenty minutes later, after the assistant manager made some additional inquiries. There was no use of excessive force, no threat of prosecution, and no accusation of shoplifting made. The manner of the investigation was legally reasonable in every way.

She sued for false imprisonment. The court succinctly pointed out that liability for false imprisonment existed in this situation: "The only basis for the detention was the opinion of the female store employee that the blue purse looked like a purse offered for sale by the department store."

Stewart v. J. C. Penney, 267 S.O.2d 925 (Louisiana, 1972)

In this case, the plaintiff established all three elements of the civil tort action. She proved she was restrained and did not consent to it. She proved the restraint was not justified by probable cause but was based on nothing more than the opinion of an employee that her purse looked like the ones offered for sale by the store. The store could not defend this employee conduct by showing the detention was supported by probable cause as required by the merchant's privilege. This case presents a classic example of why merchants cannot detain shoplifting suspects on the basis of suspicion or opinions. No employee saw this woman obtain wrongful possession of the purse, yet she was detained for possible shoplifting.

The term "probable cause" (sometimes called reasonable grounds) is used by courts when referring to evidence sufficient to justify a detention in any type of shoplifting situation. To establish probable cause, the merchant's observations made on the sales floor must show that a particular person has obtained wrongful possession of unpurchased merchandise under circumstances indicating that the person intends to shoplift rather than to pay for it. In the New Blue Purse Case, the store employee's observations did not establish wrongful possession of merchandise.

| CASE | Wrong woman case |

Here the court was confronted with a situation involving mistaken identity. Consider the facts as set forth by the court.

> On October 16, 1980, at approximately 5:15 P.M. Thelma Powell, an Albertson's employee, observed a young black woman tearing cellophane wrappers from cosmetics packages and secreting the contents in her purse. After surveying the woman's movements throughout the store, Powell saw her stop at the magazine counter. At approximately 5:45 P.M. the plaintiff, also a black woman, entered the Albertson's store and proceeded to look at the gospel record album display located on the opposite side of the magazine counter.
>
> Meanwhile, Powell informed her supervisor, Miles Durrant, about her observations of the woman she believed had been shoplifting cosmetics. In an effort to apprehend the suspect, Durrant accompanied Powell to a location in the store where Powell could identify the woman. The two employees concealed themselves behind an aisle within viewing range of the magazine rack. Powell then peered around the corner, witnessed the suspect positioned at the magazine rack, and advised Durrant that the alleged offender was the black lady standing by the magazine rack. She did not mention that there were two black women standing opposite each other at the counter. When Durrant looked around the corner he observed only the plaintiff standing at the album display which abutted the magazine rack. Unknown to Durrant the suspect apparently had evaded the Albertson's employee by disappearing from the magazine area after Powell had seen her.
>
> At that point Durrant took over the surveillance. He kept watch over the plaintiff (instead of the true suspect) while she finished her shopping. She purchased some grocery items. When she attempted to leave the store Durrant stopped her, accused her of shoplifting and asked her to

accompany him to an upstairs office for questioning. Morris [the woman wrongfully detained] professed her innocence and urged Durrant to verify that she was not the wrongdoer with the clerk who allegedly identified her. However, in order to avoid a further embarrassing scene, Morris agreed to Durrant's request to accompany him to the office. He then telephoned the police and requested they come to the store to assist in the investigation. After contacting the police he paged Powell and directed her to come to the office to check out Morris' story. When Powell arrived she promptly informed Durrant that he had detained the wrong person. Subsequently Durrant apologized and told Morris that she could leave. Morris declined to leave and telephoned the police to insure that they were on their way to the store. After the police and Morris's husband arrived and discussed the incident, Morris departed the store. Morris brought this action against Albertson's claiming damages for false arrest. Albertson's denied liability on the grounds it was immune from suit under Florida statute Section 812.015 [the detention statute].

At trial, the parties stipulated to these facts. The court found that Albertson's had probable cause based on the identification supplied by Powell to Durrant. The court reasoned that Durrant had probable cause to believe the woman had shoplifted cosmetics because he received that information from a reliable source, his fellow employee. The court said further that since Morris was the only black woman at the magazine rack when Durrant arrived on the scene that he was justified in detaining based on this eyewitness information provided to him by Powell. The woman appealed. The higher court said it could not agree that Albertson's was shielded from liability under these facts.

In reversing the trial court finding of no liability, the appellate court stated the following about probable cause under the detention statute:

> The Florida shopkeeper's immunity statute protects a merchant from a false arrest claim only when the merchant has probable cause to believe that the person detained has committed larceny. It is not sufficient for the merchant to have probable cause to believe that someone stole his property; the statute makes it clear that the merchant must have reason to believe that the person taken into custody has committed the theft.

Morris v. Albertson's, 705 F.2d 406 (Florida, 1983)

The point of this case is obvious. Since one store employee may turn the surveillance of a suspect over to another one under the merchant's privilege, it is important that the suspect be properly described. Height, approximate weight, clothing, hair style, and other personal characteristics must be used. The only facts known to the supervisor here were that a black woman was seen putting cosmetics in her purse. The court held this description was not sufficient. The case also shows how many merchants tend to call the police immediately rather than first conducting their own investigation of the facts. The Florida detention statute, like all other detention statutes, gives the merchant a legally reasonable time in which to conduct an investigation concerning ownership of the goods in question. Store policy did not instruct employees to investigate first and make their own determination about whether a prosecutable case exists before summoning a peace officer to the store.

CASE	Store greeter case

The plaintiff, a woman, and her two daughters were shopping. Consider the facts as set forth by the court:

> Plaintiff, Idell Burrow, accompanied by her two daughters, visited the K-Mart store to purchase two lamps. The lamps she selected were the last two of that type. She was unable to get them in the original cartons. The salesman procured two cardboard boxes in which he placed the lamps, leaving the boxes partially opened. According to the plaintiff, two flaps were up and two flaps were down. The salesman carried the boxes to the cashier and gave her the necessary price quotations for the lamps. The cashier rang up the purchase price on the register and gave plaintiff a receipt. She put the receipt in her purse and waited for her daughters to pay for their purchases before leaving. When she picked up her boxes to leave she was approached by Ms. Lewis, the store greeter.
>
> The evidence at trial with regard to K-Mart policies as to packages or boxes may be summarized as follows: K-Mart has a large sign prominently displayed at the entrance that WE RESERVE THE RIGHT TO INSPECT ALL PACKAGES. The K-Mart manager testified that the store greeter's duties were to check all packages coming into the store to make sure they were sealed and if not sealed, she would seal them with a color of the day tape—or the customer could leave the package with the store greeter and pick it up on the way out. The inspection of the packages of persons coming into the store was voluntary and if they did not desire to have their packages inspected they could depart from the store. The store greeter's duty as to persons leaving the store was to insure that sales receipts were visible. If their sales receipts were not readily visible . . . she will ask that the customer show their sales receipts on the way out. The manager stated that all boxes are checked. Open boxes are checked entering or leaving the store because there could be some things concealed in those boxes. The store greeter said that she checked open boxes to insure that the articles therein were the same as those on the receipt.

The woman sued the store for both false imprisonment and slander. The jury awarded her $25,000 in damages on each count. The appellate court held that the conduct of the store greeter did not constitute slander but that the jury properly found that liability for false imprisonment could exist in this situation. The $25,000 award for false imprisonment was affirmed, and the one for slander was reversed. The testimony at trial concerning false imprisonment was somewhat contradictory. The jury chose to believe the woman. She said the store greeter approached her and said, "I got to search your boxes." The woman said she had her sales receipt. The greeter responded, "I still got to

search your boxes," and snatched the boxes from her hands. Plaintiff testified
that the store greeter was talking in a loud and rude manner. Plaintiff said she
began to cry and was humiliated because people were looking at her. She
complained to the store manager. She said the store manager and greeter just
looked at each other and smiled and nothing was done. The store greeter
testified she asked only, "May I check your box, please?" She then opened the
boxes, looked inside, and saw the lamps. When plaintiff produced the sales
receipt, she was permitted to take her purchases and leave the store. The
Georgia court discussed the theory of false imprisonment or unlawful restraint
and concluded that the store was liable.

Burrow v. K-Mart, 304 S.E.2d 460 (Georgia, 1983)

Retailers using this "store greeter" or "package checker" system
must consider whether a detention by their employee is justified under the
merchant's privilege. Since the store greeter in this case did not see the
woman obtain possession of the boxes, the court is saying that no probable
cause was established to justify the detention and search. Under detention
statutes, the merchant, his agent, or employee must possess facts from
some source to justify the restraint. This store greeter did not receive
information from another employee that the woman's possession of the
lamps was wrongful. Since this court did find liability to exist in this
situation, stores using this type of system may want to review their policy.
This store's policy for the greeter was to make sure sales receipts were
visible. If they were not visible, the greeter was to detain the person and
check the contents of packages and boxes. It can easily be argued that the
store greeter did not possess any facts from which to conclude that the
woman's possession was wrongful, thereby justifying the restraint of her
freedom of movement.

A final case demonstrates how merchants can detain in circumstances where it reasonably appears that the suspect has wrongful possession of goods and then mistreat the suspect while investigating the
facts.

CASE	Vest case

A woman went to a department store in Philadelphia to replace some denim
pants of a three-piece suit belonging to her son. She had with her, in a bag,
the vest to the suit and the pants, which had shrunk and faded. She could not
find a satisfactory replacement for the pants and was leaving when two
security employees escorted her off the selling floor. In what the court
described as a "rather unpleasant scene," she was accused of shoplifting the
vest. She testified that the security people were rough and rude and yelled at
her. The store detectives testified they were at all times pleasant, soft spoken,

and mindful of embarrassing the woman. She was released when they were satisfied that the vest was not store merchandise. The jury awarded her $20,000 in actual and $30,000 in punitive damages on her claim for false imprisonment, assault and battery, and defamation.

Daly v. John Wanamaker, 464 A.2d 355 (Pennsylvania, 1983)

There was no question that she was in possession of merchandise that could have belonged to the store. She was seen with the vest and pants along with the paper bag. This department store had probable cause to detain the woman. But its employees violated the reasonable manner provision of the merchant's privilege because the jury believed they mistreated her while investigating the facts. Merchants must remember that there are two separate and distinct requirements of a detention statute. It is not enough just to detain on probable cause. The next step, the investigation of the facts, must be legally reasonable in the manner in which it is conducted. Here the evidence was in conflict, which meant that the jury could believe the woman or the store detectives. The jury chose to believe her, finding liability to exist, and then awarding both actual and punitive damages.

The most common example of violating the reasonable manner provision is when employees detain and then use excessive force, make accusations of shoplifting, force searches, or make threats of prosecution to obtain confessions or releases. The Vest Case demonstrates that sometimes rude and aggressive behavior short of traditional types of suspect mistreatment can violate the detention statute. Detention statutes never tell merchants exactly what type of employee conduct will violate this reasonable manner requirement. For this reason, store policy must teach employees to be diplomatic.

FALSE IMPRISONMENT AND FALSE ARREST DISTINGUISHED

When retail employees detain for investigation under the merchant's privilege, the stopping is not a citizen's arrest. A false imprisonment may be committed by a private citizen who is not claiming any legal authority to make a citizen's arrest. A retail employee may restrain another person's freedom of movement under the merchant's privilege for an entirely private purpose, such as to investigate the facts and recover unpurchased merchandise. When a merchant detains under the privilege, this restraint is an imprisonment or a temporary detention for a specific private purpose. It is not a citizen's arrest. If the suspect is released without any police involvement, there has not been an arrest, only an imprisonment, a restraint or a detention. If the suspect then sues the store, it is not for false arrest but for false imprisonment sometimes called unlawful detention. To convert the detention into an arrest, the merchant must summon the police to make a warrantless arrest based on evidence produced by the merchant.

| CASE | Locking the doors case |

Two women entered a retail establishment. Both were accused of shoplifting by store employees, who locked the doors and called the police. Only one of the women was formally arrested. Both women later sued, alleging false imprisonment, false arrest, and malicious prosecution. The trial court held for the store, finding that a one-year statute of limitations applied so the civil actions were barred. The higher court reversed, finding that a two-year statute for false imprisonment controlled the situation rather than the one-year statute of limitations for false arrest. In distinguishing an imprisonment from an arrest, the court said:

> In this case, the false imprisonment preceded the arrest. . . . Here the merchant falsely accused the suspects of shoplifting and locked the doors to the establishment, thus falsely imprisoning both suspects. The police were summoned and, thereafter, arrested one of the two persons.

Williams v. Joy Shoppes, 422 A.2d 892 (Pennsylvania, 1980)

The facts in this case are easy to analyze. The initial restraint was caused solely by store employees. The police were not present and did not even know about the situation until called. Clearly no false arrest could have taken place until the police arrived and obtained the facts from the store employees. In most shoplifting situations, this is what actually happens: the merchant detains, investigates, and decides to summon the police, who make the formal arrest. For this reason, imprisonment has already taken place by the time the police get to the store.

In some situations, the retail employee may call the police and direct the officer to arrest a particular suspect. The fact that a store employee is not physically involved in the situation but just directs a peace officer to make an arrest is not generally a good defense. The store can be successfully sued for "causing" a person to be arrested without establishing probable cause. As pointed out in Chapter 4, the merchant may not tell the police to arrest and avoid the civil liability consequence if the person arrested is not in possession of unpurchased merchandise belonging to that store.

| CASE | Pocket comb case |

A Washington, D.C. department store, at its suburban Virginia location on a large shopping mall, called the police. A store detective saw a man with a bulge in his pocket. The store detective thought this bulge was a pistol, although all he ever saw was the bulge. The man and his male companion entered the department store a few minutes before closing time and looked at raincoats. The companion used the restroom. Neither man was seen concealing or even obtaining possession of any store merchandise.

The men left at closing time. No store employee had even spoken to either man. The police had responded to the store detective's call. They were waiting out in the mall parking lot, pistols drawn and riot guns leveled. They arrested the two men solely on the information given to them by the store detective. The bulge turned out to be a pocket comb. Both men sued the department store for wrongfully causing their arrest. The jury awarded each man just over $100,000. The reason civil liability resulted was that store policy was not based on the merchant's privilege. The store detective provided the police with nothing more than suspicion about a possible offense not involving shoplifting.

Washington Post, November 11, 1978

This store had not taught its security employees how to comply with the Virginia detention statute, which provides that a merchant shall not be civilly liable for causing the arrest or detention of any person if the merchant has probable cause to believe that person has shoplifted. The observations made by the security man did not produce any facts to support a belief that shoplifting was being committed, yet he notified the police. The store defended the action of its employee by saying they were surprised that the police responded with drawn weapons. The point is this: store policy had not taught its employees the basics of establishing probable cause. The Virginia detention statute, like all other detention statutes, does not provide merchants with a statutory defense if they direct the police to arrest persons for offenses not involving shoplifting.

FALSE IMPRISONMENT AND SLANDER

The merchant's privilege permits a retail employee to detain a suspect on probable cause and then to investigate the facts, provided the manner of the investigation is legally reasonable. Part of any reasonable investigation is talking to the suspect. The more clearly drafted detention statutes, such as that of Illinois, specifically say the merchant is to "inquire" (meaning ask) about ownership of unpurchased merchandise. All would agree that if a store detective detains by saying, "Stop, thief, you just stole those panty hose you put in your purse," such a comment violates the reasonable manner provision of any detention statute in any state. Even if the retail employee had first established probable cause, the store would most likely be sued—successfully—for false imprisonment and slander.

When reading the Flea and Tick Spray Case below, concentrate on the facts as known to the food store assistant manager *before* he responded. It will be seen that he detained based on a conclusion about concealment rather than actually seeing the man put the can of pet spray in his pocket. The decision to detain was not supported by probable cause evidence showing the man had obtained wrongful possession of merchandise. After making an evidence-gathering mistake, this retail employee went on to legally mistreat his suspect by accusing him of shoplifting. The slanderous remark was made on the selling floor and overheard by numerous customers. This case is an excellent example of how the merchant's response dictates the outcome of the case.

| CASE | Flea and tick spray case |

The assistant manager, new to this store, saw a lone male shopping in what he described as an "unusual" fashion. The man would leave his cart at the end of an aisle, walk down the aisle selecting items from the shelf, and then return and place them in the cart.* The customer was seen placing a can of flea and tick spray in his cart. He was seen a few aisles later with no pet spray in the cart. The assistant manager "concluded" the man had concealed it in his jacket because in his opinion, there was not sufficient time for the customer to have replaced it back on the shelf. According to the employee's testimony, he assumed the pet spray was concealed in the jacket pocket. On this evidence, he detained.

The customer, a retired police officer, testified he was stopped in the middle of an aisle, the assistant manager demanding in a loud voice to know what he had done with the spray. When he said he did not have the item, the employee responded by saying, "Don't tell me, you goddamn thief. You got it in your coat." The detention and accusation of shoplifting caused approximately twenty other customers to turn and watch. Traffic in the store was heavy that day. The customer was frisked, and the accusation of shoplifting repeated. A display of canned food was knocked over in the process. The whole situation was described as "circus-like" in testimony. No can of pet spray was found. The man was taken to the office and released a few minutes later. No shoplifting charge was filed because no store merchandise was recovered.

Great Atlantic & Pacific Tea Co. v. Paul, 261 A.2d 373 (Maryland, 1970)

*The customer was a retired police officer and long-time patron of this store. He said he had to examine food articles carefully to make sure they were on his strict post-cardiac diet.

From testimony in the case, it is obvious that the assistant manager knew nothing about the merchant's privilege, because it has not been incorporated into store policy regarding the handling of shoplifting cases. The detention statute was of no value to this national food store. Its employees had not been taught the basics of evidence gathering. Its employees had not been told about the civil tort law duty to use reasonable care during the encounter with a shoplifting suspect. This employee violated both the probable cause to detain and the reasonable investigation tests when he responded. The court made the following comment about the policy of this national food store: "The policy of A&P on shoplifting as testified to by the manager of the store in question was to let each employee *use his own judgment* as to what steps should be taken. He further testified that Parker [the assistant manager handling the situation] was authorized to do what was done in this case" (emphasis added).

Because this food store permitted each employee to use his own judgment in handling shoplifting situations, two mistakes were made, both creating civil liability. This case shows why stores should use an evidence-gathering guide. It shows why store policy must stress compliance with the tests in the detention statutes. The response of this employee was without any guidance from store policy on the dual legal aspects of handling shoplifting cases. The result was a civil action with a jury award of $10,000 in actual damages and $30,000 in punitive damages.

CASE	Bar of soap case

The court recognized that merchants have a qualified privilege to discuss possible shoplifting with persons they detain. Here the drug store manager exceeded the scope of the privilege by accusing the woman of shoplifting, so the store was found liable for both false imprisonment and slander. This store manager saw two women enter the store, and asked them if they needed sales assistance. One woman told him she wanted to purchase some soap, so he directed her to the cosmetics department. The woman found a sales clerk there who helped her find the type of soap she wanted to buy. After purchasing the soap this woman left the store, going out to her car in the parking lot.

The manager testified that before following her outside, he saw her drop a bar of Lowilla soap into a little bag and leave without paying. He further testified that he asked the cashier if she had purchased a bar of Lowilla soap and was told no. The facts are in dispute as to what happened in the parking lot. The woman said he spoke to her in a rude and loud manner saying, "Hey, wait there, you stop. I want to see what you got in that little bag. You stole a bar of soap." He denied accusing her of stealing or of talking in a loud and rude manner. She opened the bag and showed him the soap she had purchased. It was not Lowilla soap, so he apologized. He said it was the woman who insisted they go back inside the store.

She sued the store for false imprisonment by unlawful detention and for slander, receiving an $8,000 jury award, one that was affirmed on appeal. The store argued that the manager had observed her and believed by her actions that she was committing the act of shoplifting a bar of soap. The store said that her actions gave him probable cause to detain and investigate the facts. The store further said that he acted in good faith and upon a privilege to carry out his duties to protect his employer's property. In affirming the existence of liability for slander and the $8,000 jury award, the court disagreed:

> Although the occasion was one of qualified privilege, the privilege was lost by the manner in which it was exercised. . . . Had Mr. Ratliff [store manager] asked the cashier if Mrs. Garner [suspect] had paid for a bar of soap, he would have ascertained that she had. Instead, he asked if she had paid for a bar of Lowilla soap. Then, instead of making inquiry in a reasonable manner, he accused Mrs. Garner of stealing a bar of soap. *When he did so he exceeded the qualified privilege.* In order for the communication to be privileged the person making it must be careful to go no further than his interest or duties require. [Emphasis supplied]

Southwest Drugs v. Garner, 195 S.O.2d 128 (Mississippi, 1967).

As this case clearly holds, the detaining merchant has a qualified privilege to discuss possible shoplifting with suspects. The privilege can be lost if the suspect is directly accused of shoplifting. Many stores require employees to detain and ask a nonaccusatory question about ownership of the merchandise. For example, the drug store manager could have asked the woman if she forgot to pay for the Lowilla soap. His communication is now framed in language designed to comply with the detention statutes which authorize merchants to inquire about ownership. Such an approach does not directly or indirectly imply shoplifting. By giving the woman a chance to respond, the manager would have been investigating the facts in a legally reasonable manner as required by the detention statute. If merchants detain and inquire about ownership, this shows store policy is in compliance with the detention statute and it avoids the possibility of slanderous statements.

| CASE | Men's wallet case |

The court discussed the situation of communicating about possible shoplifting with persons other than the suspect. A nineteen-year-old black female was shopping with her husband. The accounts of what happened in the store differ. The woman said she and her husband had been shopping about ten minutes when they stopped at a rack containing men's wallets. Her husband picked up a wallet, handing it to her for examination. She handed it back to him. The store manager then approached her saying, "Are you going to pay for it or put it back?" She continued by saying the manager (a white female) accused her of shoplifting the wallet by placing it in her pocket. She told the manager to search her, which she did, finding no wallet. A heated exchange then took place between the two women, one overheard by both customers and employees. The manager ordered the couple to leave the store.

The couple went to a nearby restaurant where the woman's mother was eating and told her about the incident. The mother and daughter, leaving the husband in the restaurant, went back to the store almost immediately. Upon inquiry by the mother, the manager said her daughter had stolen a wallet and had been in the store every day for a week shoplifting merchandise. Another heated discussion took place, with the manager ordering both the mother and daughter out of the store. No shoplifting charges were filed.

The store manager's version of what happened was different. She said the couple was looking at men's wallets and she saw the woman put one in her pocket. At this point she told the woman she saw "that" (the concealment) and she could put the wallet back or pay for it. The manager's testimony continued by saying the young woman took the billfold out of her pocket and threw it across two counters, made several ugly remarks to her, and became quite upset. The manager denied searching the young woman or saying that she had been in the store earlier in the week and was shoplifting on those occasions. She testified that after the incident, she told a city police officer she had caught the young woman shoplifting the day of the incident and the woman had been in the store previously, taking things.

The store manager testified that after the incident, she told employees of two other stores in that city she had caught this young woman shoplifting. The young woman testified that after the incident, when she was in those two other stores, she was watched closely by the employees. The evidence also showed that various employees of the store where the incident took place had been told by the manager to watch out for young black women who came into the store to see if they were taking merchandise.

The young woman sued for false imprisonment and slander, receiving $5,000 in actual damages and $100,000 in punitive damages from the jury. The decision was reversed by the higher court, because it felt the trial court made some mistakes in the instructions given to the jury. In discussing the qualified privilege, the appellate court held the statement made by the store manager that the young woman was within the scope of the qualified privilege. The store manager's statement to the police that the woman had shoplifted merchandise was also within the privilege. The court found that the statement of the manager to the young woman's mother was absolutely privileged, but the statements to employees of other stores in that city were slanderous per se.

Brown v. P. N. Hirsch Stores, 661 S.W.2d 587 (Missouri, 1983).

Store policy must be specific on this point of communicating with persons other than the suspect about possible shoplifting. Merchants always have the privilege to discuss theft situations with peace officers. In this case, the conversation with the suspect's mother was privileged, because the mother came back to the store and initiated it. Merchants have an interest in protecting their property, so they may discuss possible shoplifting and shoplifters with employees. Never do what the manager did in this case and tell other merchants that a specific person shoplifted in the store. Even though this case was reversed, it is obvious the $100,000 punitive damage award was based largely on the fact the manager, communicated with other retailers in that city. Keep in mind that most shoplifting suspects, like this nineteen-year-old young woman, are average citizen types—ones with no prior criminal records. They generally have good reputations, a fact which will be brought out at a false imprisonment and slander trial.

In shoplifting-slander cases, the merchant's fundamental problem is one of communicating conclusions. In the Flea and Tick Spray and Bar of Soap Cases, the retail employees both decided the suspect was a *thief* and said so. In court they would not be permitted to testify to this conclusion, so they should avoid communicating conclusions in the store when investigating the situation. Both security and nonsecurity employees are guilty of communicating conclusions. Retailers always want to talk about "what the suspect did" rather than "what the evidence shows." There is a big difference. By talking about what the suspect did, the merchant is expressing an opinion or a conclusion. By discussing what the evidence shows, the merchant is talking about facts. In discussing shoplifting cases, always begin by saying the evidence showed that the suspect obtained possession of the goods by concealing it in her purse, then she left the store without paying. Security personnel particularly should discipline themselves to talk about what the evidence shows rather than what the suspect did.

The case law is clear on one point about slander. Each case will be decided on its individual merits as to whether the merchant's communication constitutes slander. In one case, the statement of a grocery store manager to the father of a teenage girl was found to be slanderous per se, meaning slanderous on its face. The manager said he believed the daughter had "stuffed her pockets full of candy" and asked the father if he wanted to pay for them.[3] In another case involving a national department store, the security man detained an employee outside the store in the parking lot. He said, "Take the stuff out of your pockets," referring to sunglasses the security man thought the employee had concealed and

---

[3]Roper v. Great Atlantic & Pacific Tea Co., 190 A2d 822 (D.C., 1963).

removed without paying for them. The court found this statement sufficiently imputed commission of a crime to constitute slander per se.[4] In a third case, the store manager asked a customer if she had picked up some money that he had left on the counter. The money had actually been misplaced by a store clerk. This statement, considered along with the attendant circumstances, including the manager's insolent behavior, was found to be slanderous.[5]

FALSE IMPRISONMENT AND ASSAULT AND BATTERY

The New Blue Purse Case demonstrated a situation where the only civil action possible was for false imprisonment based on the improper detention. The department store employees there did not legally mistreat the woman in any way so only the probable cause to detain provision of the merchant's privilege was violated. The Men's Wallet and Bar of Soap Cases showed how stores can be sued for both false imprisonment and slander out of an encounter with a shoplifting suspect. There are two basic tests in the merchant's privilege statutes—detain on probable cause and conduct the investigation in a legally reasonable manner, method, and time. The stores in the slander cases violated the reasonable manner provisions of the detention statutes, thereby subjecting them to liability for false imprisonment. They violated this provision by making accusatory remarks, thereby opening the civil liability door to an action for slander.

The After Hours Sale Case which follows is another situation where a store was sued on two counts out of a single shoplifting situation. Here the civil actions were for false imprisonment and assault and battery. As will be seen, the department store security personnel failed to establish probable cause evidence to justify restraining the man in the first place. After detaining him, they too violated the reasonable manner provision by using too much force for the circumstances. They did not accuse the man of shoplifting, so no cause of action for slander was permissible. They did expose the store to assault and battery liability in addition to liability for false imprisonment. Merchants must remember that the primary civil tort action filed is usually for false imprisonment. It can be accompanied by ones for slander or assault and battery depending on the manner in which retail employees treat their suspects once they are detained.

---

[4]Montgomery Ward v. Clisner, 298 A216 (Maryland, 1972).
[5]Gust v. Montgomery Ward 80 S.W.2d 268 (Missouri, 1935).

CASE	After hours sale case

The suspect and his wife, along with other members of the public, were invited to a special sale, one to be held after the normal business hours. All who went into the store that evening were provided a shopping bag by the store to use in placing sale merchandise inside it while they shopped. The husband was in poor physical condition; he had just been released from the hospital where he had been on a kidney dialysis machine. His eyes were bloodshot; his arms were black and blue showing visible needle scars; he walked with a faltering gait; and he appeared nervous and moved in erratic patterns.* He was seen selecting four shirts and several boxes of cufflinks. He dropped one of the cufflinks on the floor. When he bent over to pick it up, the shirts and other boxes of cufflinks fell onto the floor. He then picked up all this merchandise and placed it in the shopping bag that the store had provided. He spent about ten more minutes in the men's department, selecting some additional cufflinks and placing them in the shopping bag. He was detained by two store detectives as he moved toward the belt display, also in the men's department where he had been shopping. He made no effort to leave. Indeed he was in no physical shape to move at more than a slow shuffle, even by the store's version of the evidence. Following the detention, he was taken to a security office and questioned.

In the detention room, he was searched, revealing $3 in cash and a valid shopping charge plate. He was advised of his rights concerning the crime of shoplifting. He was questioned at length, including some questions about his use of drugs and alcohol. He requested to call his wife or his employer. The request was denied although one of the rights explained to him from a preprinted card was the right to make a telephone call. Before the questioning got underway, one of the detectives paced the floor slapping his gun. The shopper was asked to sign a civil release form, being told several times he could not leave until he signed it, and if he refused to sign it, he would go to jail. Initially he refused to sign the form. After continued questioning, he reluctantly signed it. When released, he was cautioned not to mention the detention and questioning to anyone. He requested an apology from security people but received none. The detention and questioning lasted ninety minutes. He wrote a letter to the store requesting a written apology. He also asked the store to repudiate the action, conduct, and statements of the security people and to inform him the company did not ratify the conduct of its employees. A store representative contacted his lawyer, but no letter was ever written.

The jury concluded that the security people did not establish probable cause to justify the detention. The appellate court approved that finding:

> We would note that in this case the suspect had not attempted to leave the store without paying for the merchandise. . . . Had the detectives displayed more restraint and attempted to acquire more

information from the suspect's actions before deciding to act, they might well have concluded he had no criminal purpose whatsoever.

May Department Stores (Hecht Division) v. Devercelli, 314 A.2d 767 (D.C., 1973)
*It came out in testimony during the civil action that he had been under observation by store detectives since his entrance into the store due to his unusual appearance, faltering gait, and nervous mannerisms. His appearance itself was not evidence he was in possession of unpurchased merchandise or that he intended to shoplift. These security people obviously thought he was drunk or on some type of drugs, and that belief was part of their downfall.

The last cash register rule was violated in this case. As the court said, the security people should have displayed more restraint by waiting a while before detaining the customer. Because of his physical condition, the man was not a candidate to run. Here the detention was based more on his physical appearance than any understanding of probable cause. The appellate court recognized the problem:

We recognize that merchants must be permitted to take reasonable steps to protect themselves from the heavy losses arising from shoplifters, and in this case it is not surprising the suspicions of the detectives were aroused by the man's appearance. It is generally recognized that alcoholics and drug addicts frequently steal as a means of supporting their habits. However, the precautions taken by merchants must not offend the basic principles of our criminal justice system.

The evidence regarding the use of force to take the man to the security office was conflicting. The man said he was forced to walk at a pace much too fast for his condition and that he was almost carried despite his request to go at his own pace. He made no attempt to resist. The store detective testified the man was just "escorted" to the detention room. The jury believed that too much force was used, accepting the suspect's version, and found liability existed for assault and battery. The conduct of the security people in the office was also an aggravating factor. It made it easier to find liability existed and to award punitive damages of $90,000.

This case shows that any touching, no matter how slight, can be found to constitute a *battery*, defined as any harmful or offensive touching by the store employee. An assault need not involve actual touching. An *assault* is committed if the actions of the store employee create in the mind of the suspect sufficient apprehension that he is not free to leave and force may be used to effect the restraint. The store employee must also have the apparent means to use force for the assault to be complete. The issue in these assault and battery cases generally refers to the degree of force used to effect the detention. The suspect will always claim excessive force was used under the circumstances, with the merchant countering that the force used was reasonable, therefore justified. Part of the employee's response is deciding under what circumstances force may be used and then what amount or degree of force is justified.[6]

Table 8.2 below shows that the jury in all four cases found the stores violated the probable cause to detain test. Said another way, all four stores made a fundamental evidence-gathering mistake, one which resulted in civil liability exposure. After detaining their suspects, three of the stores legally mistreated them, another mistake that created civil liability exposure. The legal mistreatment in the Flea and Tick Spray and Bar of Soap Cases was to make accusations of shoplifting. In the After-Hours Sale Case, the suspect was legally mistreated by using excessive force under the circumstances. Only in the New Blue Purse Case did the retail employees refrain from legally mistreating their suspect after detaining her. All the evidence-gathering and mistreatment of the suspect mistakes were preventable.

A final point about these four cases is that no store called the police to cause the suspect's formal arrest and prosecution, yet all four stores were successfully sued. These cases demonstrate the difference between false imprisonment and false arrest civil actions. As pointed out in the definition of false imprisonment (this chapter), no peace officer need be present for a store to be sued for false imprisonment, sometimes called unlawful detention. All that is necessary for false imprisonment liability to attach is for the merchant to restrain the customer's freedom of movement without a legal reason or excuse. That reason is called probable cause in the merchant's privilege statutes. To reduce the risk of civil

TABLE 8.2	Evidence-gathering mistakes			
Case	Detaining without probable cause (false imprisonment)	Use of force (assault and battery)	Accusa- tions of shop- lifting (slander)	Calling the police to cause suspect's arrest (false arrest)
Bar of Soap	Yes		Yes	
Flea and Tick Spray	Yes		Yes	
New Blue Purse	Yes			
After-Hours Sale	Yes	Yes		

[6]Review the "Use of Force" section in Chapter 6, which set forth the circumstances in which force can be justified in detaining and during the investigation of the facts. It was the use of offensive rather than harmful force in the After-Hours Sale Case that permitted the suspect to be successful on his assault and battery count of the civil action.

liability, a merchant in any state must learn to establish probable cause to justify the detention. Next, the merchant must conduct an investigation which is legally reasonable in its manner—meaning the suspect is not legally mistreated in any way.

Detaining on probable cause and avoiding mistreatment of the suspect while investigating the facts is only part of the merchant's job. The investigation of the facts must be conducted through a legally reasonable method, which means logically and systematically gathering evidence. The reasonable manner provision refers to mistreatment of the suspect, while the reasonable method provision refers to gathering the evidence. A store, like in the Aspirin Case, can comply with the probable cause and reasonable manner provisions of the merchant's privilege, yet violate the reasonable method provision by failing to investigate the facts. Store policy must teach employees to comply with all three provisions—probable cause to detain, the reasonable manner and reasonable method. As mentioned, the investigation must be completed in a legally reasonable time to stay within the scope of the privilege. Refer to the five tests found in Chapter 6, because they set forth the requirements of the merchant's privilege statutes, the ones store owners, managers, and security personnel must comply with to reduce civil liability exposure.

MALICIOUS PROSECUTION ACTIONS

Elements of the Offense

To establish the store's liability for malicious prosecution of a shoplifting case, the plaintiff must prove the following elements of the offense:

1. The shoplifting case was filed by the store.
2. The store legally caused the person's arrest and prosecution.
3. The shoplifting case terminated in favor of the accused, either by dismissal or by acquittal after a trial on the merits.
4. The store failed to meet the evidence test of establishing probable cause to prosecute the case.
5. Legal malice.
6. Damage to the plaintiff resulted from being prosecuted by the store.

Generally a plaintiff will have no difficulty establishing the first two elements of the offense. There is usually no dispute over the fact that a store manager or security person requested a peace officer to respond to the store. The normal procedure is for a store employee (usually a security person or the store manager) to sign the complaint indicating a desire to prosecute.[7] Since the offense was not committed in the officer's presence, the courts will find the merchant initiated (or caused) the plaintiff's formal arrest by supplying evidence to the officer.

A plaintiff proves element 3 by showing he won the shoplifting case. In any state, the prosecuting merchant must lose the shoplifting case before the store can be sued for malicious prosecution. The case is said to have terminated in favor of the accused if the person is acquitted or if the case is dismissed before trial without a hearing on the merits. In most jurisdictions, a person convicted of shoplifting has the right to appeal the case and have a new trial. In many states the accused may have this new trial in front of a jury rather than being tried by a judge only. If the person is acquitted at this new trial, or *trial de novo* as it is generally called, this acquittal satisfies the requirement of termination in favor of the accused.

The most difficult element for the plaintiff to prove is that the store lacked probable cause to initiate the shoplifting charge. In a malicious prosecution action, the issue is not probable cause to detain but whether the merchant investigated and reviewed the facts after detaining. A plaintiff is successful if he can show that the merchant detained, then failed to investigate and review the facts before summoning the police to have the suspect formally prosecuted. An excellent example of the absence of probable cause to prosecute was found in the Discarded Sweater Case in Chapter 6. In that case, the department store detective made no attempt to talk to his suspect before calling the police to have her prosecuted. The court commented on this policy of failing to review the merits of the case before initiating the shoplifting charge. When merchants detain, then call the police without investigating the facts, they stand a much better chance of losing the shoplifting case. When the store is later sued for malicious prosecution, the plaintiff will point to the fact that no investigation preceded the decision to prosecute. In legal terms, this absence of any investigative activity by the store makes it evident that the store lacked probable cause to prosecute. Much will be said below about establishing probable cause to prosecute a shoplifting case.

Element 5 requires proof of legal malice. Legal malice is different from actual malice. Legal malice does not mean hatred, spite, or ill-will toward a person as those terms are commonly understood. It means the retail employee handling the case was reckless and indifferent about his duty to investigate the facts before having the suspect prosecuted. In most states, the presence of legal malice will be inferred from the absence of probable cause to prosecute. In other words, if a plaintiff proves the store lacked probable cause to initiate the shoplifting charge, the court will infer that legal malice exists without direct proof of any improper motive on the

---

[7]See the summons form in Chapter 3 where the store employee signed as complainant.

part of the store. Using the Discarded Sweater Case again as an example, the court could find legal malice existed, because the security man failed to investigate and review the facts after detaining and before calling the police.

Element 6 requires the plaintiff to establish that damages resulted because the case was prosecuted without probable cause. Generally a plaintiff establishes actual damages by showing he had to pay a bonding company to post bail after being arrested. The money paid to an attorney to defend the person in the shoplifting case can always be shown. If the suspect lost any work, the lost wage dollar amount is easily proved. A personal right has been invaded when a merchant takes a case to court without probable cause to do so. The damage sustained is mental anguish, humiliation, and so forth. Security people can be particularly insensitive to the personal rights of a suspect because they are sometimes overzealous in their quest to protect company assets. The law recognizes emotional damages as well as damage to reputation and standing in the community. Merchants should learn to do the same.

Before discussing the way to reduce the risk of malicious prosecution liability, consider the Flower Seeds Case. It is an example of a store complying with the merchant's privilege and avoiding false imprisonment and false arrest liability but still being found liable for malicious prosecution.

CASE	Flower seeds case

About noon a lone female entered a Florida food store. While shopping, she selected three packages of flower seeds, placing them in her shopping cart. They fell through the wire cart onto the floor. She then placed all three packages in the breast pocket of a shirt she was wearing. She went through the checkout line, paying for $15.67 of grocery items. She did not pay for the three packages of seeds, which were in her pocket the entire time.

Outside the store, she was stopped by a female security officer and taken to the security office. An examination of the cash register tape showed she had not paid for the flower seeds. The woman said a big black-headed man yelled at her, saying she had to sign a combination confession and civil liability release. She refused to sign anything. She told them she felt ill. The man then shoved a wastepaper basket in front of her saying he would call an ambulance. She was detained for thirty to forty minutes until the police arrived. She was then formally arrested for shoplifting.

She testified the seeds were always partially visible, sticking out of her shirt breast pocket. The security officer said they were concealed. In the store, she told them if she had not paid for the seeds, it was an oversight and she had intended to pay for them all along. She had cash on her person and had just bought $15.67 in groceries. In the store, she was denying intent to shoplift. In court, as her formal defense to the charge, she did the same. She was acquitted of shoplifting and filed a civil action.

The jury awarded her $17,500 on her two-count civil action, alleging false imprisonment and malicious prosecution. The appellate court reversed the jury finding of liability on the false imprisonment count, saying the food store employees did comply with the detention statute.

> Under the circumstances the employees of Food Fair had probable cause to believe a larceny had been committed. They were entitled to detain her in a reasonable manner for a reasonable length of time. Mrs. Kincaid was not embarrassed by being accused in public but was politely asked to accompany the store's woman security agent to a private office. There was no suggestion of physical mistreatment. The police were called within five minutes after she was detained and the store cannot be penalized for peaceably holding her for the period necessary for the police to arrive.

(Food Fair Stores v. Kincaid, 335 S.O.2d 769 (Florida, 1976)

The court went on to say that the statute does not provide a defense for the store to use when sued for malicious prosecution. Consider the comments of the court:

> On the other hand, the statute does not offer protection against Malicious Prosecution. . . . As contrasted to the count on False Imprisonment, there were additional facts bearing on the question of whether Food Fair should have caused Mrs. Kincaid to be prosecuted. She gave a plausible explanation for having placed the seeds in her shirt pocket, and according to her the packets were clearly visible. When accosted by the store's security agent, she indicated some confusion over whether she had paid for the seeds but immediately stated that if she had not, she certainly intended to do so. The cost of the seeds was a small fraction of her total bill, she had ample money to pay for them.

In nonlegal terms, the court is saying the store's decision to detain was legally proper, but its decision to prosecute the case was not. The court said there were "*additional facts* bearing on the question of whether Food Fair should have caused Mrs. Kincaid to be prosecuted."

It goes without saying that a merchant possesses more facts about the case at the completion of the investigation than when he detained the suspect. It is these *additional facts* that the Florida court says must be produced before a merchant can initiate a prosecution without malicious prosecution type liability. These facts are produced by following steps 7–11 on the *Sources of Evidence* chart presented in Chapter 4.

Consider the comments of the Florida court in another civil case against a retail merchant. "The probable cause to support a temporary detention of a suspected shoplifter by a merchant or the merchant's employee is less than the probable cause required to support a later prosecution."[8] The court is saying that there are really two types of probable cause. The merchant establishes probable cause to detain for investigation by making observations of a suspect on the selling floor. At the time of the detention, the merchant does not possess sufficient facts to decide if a prosecutable case exists. For this reason, the retailer must produce those additional facts the Florida court mentioned. As the merchant conducts an investigation after detaining the suspect, those additional facts come into his possession. At the completing of the investigative process, the merchant possesses enough facts to decide if a prosecution should be initiated.

Merchants should remember the following two types of probable cause:

1. Probable cause to detain, which is established by watching the suspect; and
2. Probable cause to initiate prosecution, which is established by investigating facts once the suspect has been detained.

Before a merchant can file a shoplifting charge, the observed facts from the selling floor must be combined with the investigated facts. Only then has a merchant produced sufficient evidence to justify prosecution with minimum exposure to malicious prosecution type civil liability.

Reducing the Risk of Malicious Prosecution Type Liability

Most stores are doing business in a state like Florida where the merchant's privilege statute does not provide them with a defense to a malicious prosecution action. Since there is no statutory test to meet in reducing exposure to malicious prosecution liability, that test must come from a store's own policy. In Chapter 6, the merchant was given five tests to meet in complying with the detention statutes. Two of those tests—numbers 3 and 5—are important in reducing the possibility of a malicious prosecution action.

Test 3 told the merchant to investigate the facts in a systematic "method" after the suspect was properly detained on probable cause. Test 5 told the merchant to justify the decision to prosecute by reviewing the facts after completing the investigation. Now the merchant is given the

---

[8]Weisman v. K Mart Corp., 396 S.0.2d 1164 (Fla. 1981).

reasonable belief test, because it cannot be met until the facts are investigated and reviewed. The test demands that a merchant must possess a reasonable belief that a prosecutable case exists before filing it, by first investigating and then reviewing the facts after the suspect has been detained.

Possessing a reasonable belief that a prosecutable case exists is different from "knowing" the suspect is guilty. To say, "I know the suspect is guilty" is nothing more than expressing an opinion about guilt. As pointed out, opinions about guilt are not admissible evidence at a shoplifting trial. To say I possess a reasonable belief that the evidence establishes a prosecutable case indicates the merchant has systematically investigated and reviewed the facts before reaching that belief.

To see how this reasonable belief test is used by merchants as a defense to a malicious prosecution action, assume the shoplifting charge has been filed and lost. Now the store must defend a malicious prosecution civil action. To prove his case, a plaintiff will show two things: (1) the shoplifting charge terminated in his favor, either by an acquittal or by a dismissal, and (2) the store employee handling the case failed to investigate and review the facts before causing his arrest and prosecution for shoplifting. The store will defend itself by showing that both probable cause to detain for investigation and probable cause to initiate the shoplifting charge existed. In other words, the store defends itself by showing that both the decision to detain and the decision to prosecute were supported by facts produced in the store on the day of the plaintiff's arrest for shoplifting.

The fact that the plaintiff won the shoplifting case is not conclusive in showing the absence of probable cause to prosecute. The plaintiff must establish that the retail employee handling the case failed to use reasonable care to investigate and review the facts before summoning the police and having him prosecuted. To counter this allegation, the merchant establishes that his employee met the reasonable belief test by conducting a systematic investigation and review of the facts. The merchant shows that his employee did possess a reasonable belief, based on evidence, that a prosecutable case existed before deciding to file it. The store is not required to prove that its employee was absolutely certain the plaintiff would be found guilty of shoplifting when the charge was filed. The store is required to prove that its employee possessed that reasonable belief. The test for showing the presence of probable cause to prosecute a shoplifting case is reasonable belief, not certainty of guilt.

In most states, the trial judge will let the jury decide whether probable cause to prosecute the shoplifting case existed. This means the jury will hear both the plaintiff's and the store's evidence about how the facts were investigated and reviewed that day in the store when the plaintiff was charged with shoplifting. If the jury concludes that the retail employee met the reasonable belief test, the jury can find that no liability for malicious prosecution exists. On the other hand, if the evidence shows the retail employee handling the case failed to investigate and review the facts, this can become evidence to show the absence of probable cause to prosecute the shoplifter. If the jury finds there was no probable cause to prosecute the plaintiff for shoplifting, then liability against the store is established.

In the Toothpaste Case in Chapter 4, for example, it was easy for the jury to conclude that the food store security man did not possess a reasonable belief that a prosecutable case existed before he filed it. The evidence was that the woman told him her husband was sitting in the car outside with the receipt for the shampoo, hair conditioner, and toothpaste. Instead of investigating and reviewing the facts before calling the police, he ignored the woman's explanation. He did not produce all the evidence available to him before initiating the shoplifting prosecution. Therefore, he did not possess a reasonable belief that a prosecutable case existed. When the store was sued, it could not assert this reasonable belief defense because store policy had not taught its security people to investigate and review the facts before having suspects prosecuted for shoplifting.

In the Aspirin Case in Chapter 6, the food store manager and contract security guard did not investigate and review the facts before calling the police to have the man prosecuted. They did not look for the ditched box, nor did they investigate his claim of ownership. Since they did not meet test 3 and test 5, these two retail employees could not possess that reasonable belief that a prosecutable case existed before they filed it. The court said their failure to investigate and review the facts was reckless and indifferent. Said another way, the failure to investigate and review the facts violated the civil tort law duty to use reasonable care at all stages of the encounter with a shoplifting suspect.

In addition to the Toothpaste and Aspirin Cases, there are eight other cases in this book demonstrating situations where stores could not successfully defend by showing their employees met the reasonable belief test before initiating shoplifting charges. See The Socket Wrench Case (Chapter 4), The Discarded Sweater, Returned Gloves, and Blue Car Coat Cases (Chapter 6), The Credit Card Switch, Hat, and Forty-two Diapers Cases (Chapter 9), and the Snowmobile Suit Case (Chapter 1). In all ten cases, malicious prosecution liability resulted because the employee handling the case failed in one way or another to systematically investigate and review the facts before having the suspect prosecuted. Malicious prosecution liability has nothing to do with mistreatment of the suspect type mistakes. A retail employee can mistreat a suspect, and the store will never be sued for malicious prosecution as long as a shoplifting charge is not filed.

Merchant's privilege statutes do not provide stores with a defense to use in a malicious prosecution. They do not even set forth any tests which must be met to obtain immunity from malicious prosecution liability. For this reason, a store must teach its employees to meet this reasonable belief test in training programs. The only defense a store has to a malicious prosecution action is one found in store policy. If store policy is not specific about following steps 7–11 on the *Sources of Evidence* chart in Chapter 4, a store is increasing the risk of filing nonprosecutable cases and having the store sued for malicious prosecution after the shoplifting case is lost.

There are two ways a store can reduce the risk of having a malicious prosecution action filed against it. First, is to use a selective prosecution policy. If weak or nonprosecutable cases are not filed, the store can never be sued for malicious prosecution. None of the stores in the ten cases just mentioned had to file shoplifting charges yet all ten elected to do so. They all prosecuted suspects in situations where the evidence to prove the element of store ownership or the suspect's intent to shoplifting was weak or nonexistent. By filing these cases, they accomplished only one thing— the store's civil liability exposure was increased from false imprisonment to now include malicious prosecution. They most certainly did not prevent loss. All stores had to pay out money to defend and settle these cases. If the suspects in each case had been released, all stores would have had a defense to assert under the merchant's privilege statute, because their stores could only be sued for false imprisonment. The stores still may have been sued, but the loss would not have been so great because the civil action could not contain a claim for malicious prosecution.

Typically, merchants think of selective prosecution only as a way to save payroll costs because they do not have to take cases to court. Selective prosecution is also a valuable loss-prevention tool in reducing civil liability exposure. Part of any selective prosecution approach is knowing when *not* to prosecute a shoplifting case. Study the ten cases mentioned, because they demonstrate situations where the case should not have been taken to court. More importantly, they explain the evidence reasons why the prosecuting merchant made the wrong decision. Learn from these ten cases how to use a selective prosecution policy as a way to reduce the store's exposure to malicious prosecution liability.

A final point to be made about selective prosecution is that merchants tend to get in a hurry. If they are not sure about the merits of a case they file it, which is a mistake. By filing a questionable case the store is only risking exposure to malicious prosecution liability, a civil tort action to which there is no statutory defense in almost all states. In several of the malicious prosecution cases in this book, the court has commented that the security people or store manager rushed to call the police. This indicates store policy had not taught employees to use a logical evidence-gathering approach as suggested in Chapter 4. Selective prosecution means effective prosecution which means understanding the evidence before making a decision.

The second way to reduce exposure to malicious prosecution actions is by incorporating the reasonable belief test into store policy. Teach employees to justify their decisions to prosecute with evidence. Teach them to take a few minutes and think about how the shoplifting case will be established at trial. Teach them to realize a circumstantial evidence case is inherently weaker than one involving direct evidence. Merchant's privilege statutes give merchants a "legally reasonable time" in which to investigate the facts and make a decision. Merchants who get in a hurry make evidence-gathering mistakes—ones which set the stage for acquittals or dismissals followed by malicious prosecution actions. There is a civil liability consequence to wrongfully filing a shoplifting charge. That consequence is not a civil action for false imprisonment or false arrest, but for malicious prosecution.

In the Flower Seeds Case in this chapter, the court said merchants must produce additional facts after the suspect has been detained, facts which have a bearing on whether a shoplifting charge should be filed. Dean William Prosser, in his universally recognized work on the Law of Torts, says the following when discussing the duty to produce additional facts before initiating a criminal prosecution.

> The appearances must be such as to lead a reasonable man (merchant) to set the criminal proceedings in motion. The defendant (merchant) is not necessarily required to verify his information where it appears to be reliable; but where a reasonable man (merchant) would *investigate further* before beginning the prosecution, he may be liable for failure to do so.[9]

Training programs must teach retail employees to produce those additional facts each time they detain a shoplifting suspect. A merchant who detains and fails to give the suspect an opportunity to explain the circumstances is not producing additional facts. A retailer who detains and fails to investigate a suspect's claim of ownership is not producing additional facts. A merchant who fails to evaluate both the store's prosecution evidence and the suspect's defense evidence before filing a shoplifting case has just made an evidence-gathering mistake—and possibly an expensive one. As Dean Prosser points out, the duty to investigate the facts before initiating a criminal prosecution comes to the merchant from the civil tort law.

Much has been said in this book about the value of the merchant's privilege statutes as a tool in shoplifting loss-prevention. Sometimes merchants think the privilege is to detain and prosecute, so they neglect

---

[9]Prosser, D. W., *The Law of Torts*, 2nd ed. (St. Paul, Minn.: West Publishing Co.) Section 119, p. 841, (197).

learning to investigate and review the facts. The Washington, D.C. department store in the Discarded Sweater Case shows a store policy which did not require security people to even talk with suspects before calling the police. Such a policy is not based on an understanding of the merchant's privilege. The privilege is to detain and then investigate the facts without automatically incurring false imprisonment liability. In discussing the point, the Mississippi court very astutely commented that "it is the stopping, detaining momentarily and questioning which enjoys the privilege, and not the subsequent institution of criminal proceedings."[10] Any defense to a malicious prosecution action must come from store policy, because there is no statutory test to meet in the merchant's privilege laws.

Detaining a suspect based on observations made on the sales floor is only the first step in determining if a prosecutable case exists. The next step is to produce those additional facts the Florida court mentioned and then make a decision about how to handle the case. Those observed facts from the sales floor combined with those investigated facts produced in the office tell the merchant if the evidence will establish the elements of the offense. Once the investigation and review is complete, the reasonable belief test applies. If based on those observed and investigated facts the merchant reasonably believes the evidence justifies initiating a shoplifting prosecution, the charge should be filed. The fact that a malicious prosecution action is possible after an acquittal or dismissal should not be a deterrent to prosecuting shoplifting cases. Consider the findings of the trade association survey mentioned elsewhere in this book about civil liability and prosecution of shoplifting cases.

> In total, out of the 280,000 apprehensions reported, only 16 out of every 10,000 resulted in false arrest suits against the companies, whereas 90% of all prosecutions resulted in convictions. This appears to be significant for the retailer, since previously there seemed to be concern that being aggressive in prosecuting could result in costly lawsuits.[11]

Before filing a shoplifting charge, a store owner, manager, or security person should take a minute and think about this reasonable belief test. Store policy must require employees to formulate this reasonable belief for two reasons: (1) they will file stronger shoplifting cases and release suspects without prosecution when the evidence to prove the elements of the offense is questionable or lacking, and (2) they will be providing the store with a defense to a malicious prosecution action should the shoplifting case result in an acquittal or a dismissal.

---

[10]Owens v. Kroger, 450 S.O.2d 843 (Miss. 1983).

[11]NMRI, *Security and Shrinkage: Third Annual Study of Control and Security Procedures in Retailing* (New York: NMRI, 1982), pp. 6–7.

CONCLUSION

The civil tort law requires merchants to use reasonable care at all stages of the encounter with a shoplifting suspect. Mistakes mean the retail employee failed to use reasonable care. Training programs must teach employees to avoid making mistakes during each of the three phases of the encounter with a shoplifting suspect set forth at the beginning of this chapter. In this way, a store owner, manager, or security person can more easily understand how to comply with the civil tort law duty to use reasonable care, which is another way of saying the employee can better understand how to meet the five tests in Chapter 6 and the reasonable belief test set forth here.

9

Understanding Punitive Damages

Consider the following definition of punitive damages: "Punitive damages may be awarded for conduct that is outrageous because of the defendant's evil motive or his reckless indifference to the rights of others." Typically a jury will not find that a retail employee acted with an evil motive when handling a shoplifting case. More often the jury will find that a store manager or security person was reckless or indifferent toward the rights of the suspect. A jury will award punitive damages if it finds that the conduct of the retail employee demonstrated recklessness or negligence so as to show a conscious disregard of the rights of the suspect.

In the eight cases which follow, the courts are examining the grossly negligent or reckless conduct of retail employees at some point during the encounter with a shoplifting suspect. In these cases, the court ruled that the jury award of punitive damages was proper. In the first three cases (Flea and Tick Spray, After-Hours Sale, and Wedding Rings), no shoplifting charge was filed. In the last five cases (Aspirin, Razor Blades, Credit Card Switch, Hat, and Forty-two Diapers), the retail employees handling the cases filed a shoplifting charge and the suspect was acquitted.

In the Flea and Tick Spray Case, it is easy to see just how the conduct of the food store assistant manager was reckless. There was no doubt that he detained on a conclusion about concealment (an evidence-gathering mistake) rather than seeing the man put the can of pet spray in his jacket pocket. There was no dispute that after detaining the retired police officer, he slandered him (a mistake involving mistreatment of the suspect). Based on the two types of mistakes the jury found that two types of liability existed—false imprisonment and slander. The jury then awarded $10,000 in actual and $30,000 in punitive damages to the plaintiff. The food store appealed the decision, particularly the punitive damage award. The appellate court held that the jury award was proper because the conduct of the assistant manager was reckless to the degree that punitive damages were justified.

The After-Hours Sale Case in Chapter 8 is another good example where a jury found that the conduct of retail security people demonstrated a reckless disregard of the rights of a suspect. All suspects have the right to be detained only on probable cause and then to be treated in a legally reasonable manner during the investigation of the facts. In this case, the department store employees did not establish probable cause to justify the detention. Their conduct after detaining the man was also found to be reckless in several respects: they used too much force to escort him to the security office; they threatened to have him jailed if he did not sign a civil liability release; they refused to let him contact his wife; they asked him about the use of drugs and alcohol; one security man displayed a weapon and they were generally abusive to him. The jury found that two types of liability existed—false imprisonment and assault and battery. The jury also felt the character of the security people's conduct was reckless and awarded actual and punitive damages as follows:

Civil action	Actual damages	Punitive damages	Total award
False Imprisonment	$25,000	$50,000	$ 75,000
Assault-Battery	$40,000	$40,000	$ 80,000
	$65,000	$90,000	$155,000

CASE	Wedding rings case

In this false imprisonment case, the plaintiff obtained a jury verdict for $41.21 in actual damages and $12,500 in punitive damages. About 7:30 P.M. this seventy-nine-year-old man and his fiancée entered the outlet of a national discount store to purchase a set of wedding rings in preparation for their marriage one week later. A guard desk was set up in front of the store about ten feet from the front entrance. On the side of the desk was a sign: "Please have your packages tagged here by the officer." Neither the man nor his fiancée were carrying any packages when they entered.

The front door guard marked incoming packages with a color-of-the-day tag and checked outgoing packages for either the color-of-the-day tag or a blue and white cash register receipt. If a customer purchased more than one item, the clerk was instructed to attach these tags, which were to be removed by the front desk security person. The security people were instructed never to touch a customer. The plaintiff and his fiancée purchased two rings at the jewelry counter. The rings were placed in two boxes and the boxes placed in a sack to which the blue and white cash register receipt was attached. The man testified that as they reached the front door, the security guard grabbed his arm, took his package, and returned him to the desk, saying he wanted to see the package.

The package had the cash register receipt on it, but the guard insisted there should have been a purple color-of-the-day tag. The plaintiff then took the package back to the jewelry counter, where the sales woman advised him no purple tag was needed. She then motioned to the security guard to let the couple leave the store, which he did. The episode lasted around fifteen minutes. The detention itself lasted five or six minutes. The man was never taken to a security office and questioned about the purchase. The security guard did not accuse him of shoplifting the rings.

On appeal the discount store said the evidence did not justify the submission of the issue of malice to the jury in considering punitive damages. The store said the acts of the security man were in good faith and with an honest belief they were lawful. The store said the plaintiff's evidence did not prove otherwise. The court set forth the following definition of malice:

> Malice, as used in these cases which allow recovery for exemplary damages where the imprisonment is actuated by malice does not necessarily mean anger, or a malevolent or vindictive feeling toward the plaintiff; but a wrongful act without reasonable excuse is malicious within the legal meaning of the term.

The court went on to say the jury could have believed that the security guard's action in detaining the plaintiff under the circumstances was a wrongful act intentionally done and without just cause or excuse. The wrongful act, of course, was detaining without actually seeing the man fail to pay for the rings. The security guard did not establish probable cause, so he did restrain the man's freedom of movement without a legal reason for so doing.

Garvis v. K-Mart, 461 S.W.2d 317 (Missouri, 1968)

In the three cases just presented, retail employees made both evidence-gathering and mistreatment of a suspect type mistakes. The court found their conduct was legally unreasonable so as to justify punitive damages. In the next five cases, the primary mistake made was failure to investigate and review the facts before having the suspect prosecuted. These eight cases demonstrate that a merchant can be sued civilly and have punitive damages awarded against the store whether a shoplifting charge is filed or not.

In the Aspirin Case in Chapter 6, the jury found that liability for malicious prosecution of a shoplifting case existed and awarded the plaintiff $175,000 in punitive damages. The appellate court affirmed the award as being entirely reasonable based on the reckless and grossly negligent conduct of the food store manager and security guard in failing to investigate the facts before having the man prosecuted. The quote from the case indicates the court was looking at the conduct of the two employees *after* they detained the suspect. The court was not talking about the probable cause evidence to support the detention, because the decision to detain for investigation of the facts was properly made. The court described the conduct of the two employees by saying they acted with "conscious indifference" toward their duty to investigate and review the facts before initiating the shoplifting charge. Consider the language the court used in characterizing the employee's conduct:

> Mr. Fishel was arrested, handcuffed and held in the back room of a grocery store, accused of a crime he was never shown to have committed. The store manager's conscious indifference and refusal to attempt to ascertain the truth as to whether or not the aspirin had been purchased elsewhere, or to further substantiate the case against Mr. Fishel, justified the award by the jury. The verdict was not excessive.

In the Razor Blades Case in Chapter 4, the suspect was seen putting a package of blades in his pocket and walking just outside the store, where he began smoking a cigarette. He told the discount store security people he was going to pay for the item by check when his wife finished her shopping. They made no effort to find her and verify his explanation before calling the police to have shoplifting charges filed. Consider the comments this court made in describing the conduct of the security people and how it violated the civil tort law to use reasonable care.

> To refuse to verify information easily obtainable and within the confines of the store showed a complete disregard for the exercise of reasonable care in ascertaining all the facts before making a serious accusation against a customer.

This court is clearly saying failure to investigate and review the facts before deciding to prosecute a shoplifting case is reckless, that it violates the merchant's duty to use reasonable care to ascertain the facts. This type of conduct not only establishes liability against the store but then becomes evidence a jury can consider in awarding punitive damages.

CASE	Credit card switch case

The jury found liability to exist then awarded $60,000 in actual and $25,000 in punitive damages. The court described the conduct of the employees who handled this case as "in heedless and reckless disregard" of the woman's rights, meaning her right to be charged with a criminal offense only after an investigation and review of the facts.

In this case, a woman made a purchase at a national department store, using her credit card. Through a mix-up, she was given the credit card of another woman customer and that woman received the plaintiff's credit card. The plaintiff was paged but had apparently left the store after receiving the wrong credit card. The department store entered the credit card now in possession of the plaintiff (but actually belonging to another customer) on its computerized cash register system under code "005," meaning stolen or lost. This meant that any time the card was used, the code would bring to the attention of sales personnel that the person was using a stolen or lost credit card.

Three weeks later she returned to the store, purchasing some infants' wear with the credit card belonging to the other woman. She actually made the purchase from the same clerk who had waited on her three weeks earlier when the mix-up had taken place. When code 005 came up, the clerk called security. The woman was taken to the security office by a store detective. He refused to show her the card she had used, though she insisted it was hers. He refused to let her leave or call her husband. He called the police. She was taken from the store by the police and transported to the station in a squad car, charged with credit card abuse. The entire episode took about ninety minutes. When the error was discovered, the charges were dropped.

Montgomery Ward v. Hernandez, 644 S.W.2d 758 (Texas, 1982)

| CASE | Hat case |

A man was shopping with his mother and sister. No store employee saw him remove the hat from the rack, but he was seen wearing it as he left. Based on this circumstantial evidence of probable cause, he was detained just outside the store. He told the security people he purchased the hat at that store several weeks earlier. His mother and sister verified this explanation, and the store security people recovered no price tag. The man, his mother, and sister all three pointed out that the hat was soiled as evidence that it had been previously purchased and was not a new hat. The shoplifting charge was filed anyway and predictably he was acquitted.

This store did not have a systematic procedure to use in producing, investigating, and reviewing the evidence before making a decision as to whether the evidence would establish the elements of the offense. Firstly, no store employee saw the man obtain wrongful possession of the hat by removing it from its place of display. Secondly, no price tag was recovered. Thirdly, the man claimed ownership, and two adult witnesses, both present in the store, corroborated his claim of prior purchase. Clearly the decision to prosecute was not based on evidence that would establish store ownership of the hat at trial. The mistake made here which created civil liability exposure was an evidence-gathering one pure and simple. The man was not mistreated in any way nor was the time factor found to be unreasonably long.

In affirming the jury finding of liability and the award of punitive damages, the court looked squarely at the investigative procedure used by the security people to make their decision to prosecute this case. The court was concerned that they never realized a mistake could be made about ownership of the hat or that any further investigative activity was needed. Consider the comments of the appellate court in agreeing with the jury that the merchant's conduct was reckless, thus supporting the award of punitive damages.

> Evidence permitted the jury to find malice on the part of employees of the department store who after being told by a customer, his mother and sister that the hat had been purchased at an earlier date never acknowledged that they might have made an honest mistake or that they might have investigated further before filing theft charges on merchandise valued at below $5.00.

This court used the term "malice" to describe the negligent or reckless conduct of the security employees. In fixing the text or criterion of merchant's conduct which will justify the award of punitive damages, the courts use different terms. Whether the courts use the term malicious, reckless, wanton, willful, or grossly negligent they are saying the failure to use reasonable care must be conscious. Here the security people were conscious that by calling the police they were initiating a criminal charge. In other words, there was no uncertainty about what would happen to this man if they decided to prosecute. What made their conduct reckless was the evidence of his ownership which they ignored. The case was aggravated more by the fact that the detention was not supported by direct evidence establishing probable cause.

Gibson Discount Center v. Cruz, 562 S.W.2d 511 (Texas, 1978)

| CASE | Forty-two diapers case |

Another court talked about filing shoplifting charges. The court said malice exists when a charge is made with reckless disregard as to whether it is false or not. Here a lone female testified that she picked up an open package of disposable diapers and put it in her shopping cart. Two diapers had been lying near the open mouth of the package. She picked them up and put them in the package of diapers, where she assumed they belonged. At the checkout counter, she asked the checker to count the diapers to see if the bag contained the correct number. The checker did not count them but told the plaintiff if the package did not contain forty diapers, she could return it and get a refund. She paid for the diapers and left the store.

The security officer, who had been watching her all the time, detained the woman outside the store. They went to his office where he accused her of shoplifting two disposable diapers. A heated discussion followed. A count of the package revealed forty-two diapers. She insisted he verify her account of the conversation with the checker, which he did. He then released the woman. On the way out, she stopped in the front of the store, talking very loudly and still quite upset. At that point the guard told her to return to his office, called the police, and had her arrested. She was acquitted and then sued civilly.

He should not have detained the woman a second time nor should he have initiated a shoplifting charge. He had produced no additional evidence showing she intended to shoplift the two extra diapers. In her cause of action for malicious prosecution, the woman admitted the security officer had probable cause to detain her and investigate the facts. She correctly argued, however, that probable cause to detain ended when he verified her explanation with the cashier. After talking to the cashier, there was no evidence to use in court to prove she intended to shoplift. In fact, the evidence he now possessed showed just the opposite: that he had made a mistake. His later action in causing the charge to be filed was without probable cause, subjecting the store to liability for malicious prosecution. The jury agreed with her argument, finding liability for malicious prosecution existed, and awarded punitive damages.

In this case, the court found that probable cause to detain existed in the first place, but it ceased to exist after the facts were investigated. When the correctness of her explanation was verified with the cashier, the woman should have been released. The security man no longer had probable cause to continue the detention, and he certainly had no evidence to justify filing a shoplifting charge. In the quotation that follows, the court is not talking about the detention or even the manner and method in which the facts were investigated; it is talking about initiating the shoplifting charge:

> Malice exists when a charge is made with reckless disregard as to whether it is false or not. Generally, where lack of probable cause can be shown, malice is presumed. The courts have held that it is not every mistake made that is actionable, but only such mistakes as cannot be reasonably justified by the surrounding circumstances.

Jefferson v. S. S. Kresge Co., 344 S.W.2d 1118 (Louisiana, 1977)

In the Aspirin, Razor Blades, Credit Card Switch, Hat, and Forty-two Diapers Cases, the stores had all filed and lost shoplifting cases, so they were being sued for malicious prosecution of those shoplifting cases. As pointed out and as seen in the Forty-two Diapers Case, the court will infer the presence of legal malice from the absence of probable cause to prosecute a shoplifting case. The courts are inclined to characterize the

conduct of retail employees in these cases as "malicious," because malice
is an element of the civil tort action which the plaintiff must establish. By
contrast, the stores in the Flea and Tick Spray, After-Hours Sale, and
Wedding Rings Cases were sued not for malicious prosecution but for false
imprisonment alone (Wedding Rings Case) or false imprisonment and
slander (Flea and Tick Spray Case) or false imprisonment and assault and
battery (After Hours Sale Case). In these civil actions, a plaintiff does not
have to allege and prove the existence of legal malice to recover and to be
awarded punitive damages. In cases not involving a claim for malicious
prosecution, the courts are inclined to describe the conduct of the retail
employees as reckless or grossly negligent as opposed to malicious. It
really makes no difference as these cases demonstrate, because punitive
damages can be awarded whether a shoplifting charge is filed and lost or
whether the suspect is released without taking the case to court. The
important factor to understand is that conduct of retail employees in
handling the shoplifting situation is the issue. Mistakes, either evidence-
gathering or ones involving mistreatment of a suspect, will furnish a jury
evidence to justify an award of punitive damages.

THE PURPOSE OF PUNITIVE DAMAGES

In the Flea and Tick Spray Case, for example, the jury awarded the plaintiff
$10,000 in actual damages and $30,000 in punitive damages on his claim
for false imprisonment and slander. Actual damages are generally awarded
for "out of pocket" expenses a plaintiff may suffer. Punitive damages, as
the name implies, are to punish a defendant store. They are awarded to
punish the store for the grossly negligent or reckless conduct of its employee
in handling the shoplifting situation. They are also awarded to deter that
store and other stores from similar legally reckless conduct in the future.
Consider the following comment of the court about the purpose of punitive
damages in a false imprisonment action against a retail store.

> The chief purpose of punitive damages, as its name implies, is to inflict
> punishment, and this for the reason the punishment assessed will serve as
> an example and deterrent to anyone considering similar conduct. Included
> in the numerous factors the jury may consider in determining the amount of
> punitive damages to be assessed are the degree of malice, the age, sex, health
> and character of the injured party and the affluence of the defendant. Because
> of the variegated nature and number of the factors that may be taken into
> account there is no precise rule that can be applied with mathematical nicety
> to determine the amount of punitive damages. Each case must turn on its own
> peculiar facts.[1]

[1]Peak v. W. T. Grant, 409 S.W.2d 58 (Missouri, 1966)

As the court points out, each civil action arising out of a mishandled shoplifting situation must be considered on its own merits, because the facts will be different. There is one general comment helpful to merchants about reducing the chances of having punitive damages awarded. Normally the reckless conduct takes place during the investigation of the facts phase. Training programs should teach employees to avoid evidence-gathering mistakes and to avoid mistreating the suspect once he is detained on probable cause. The emphasis should be on conducting a legally reasonable investigation.

Generally, the courts will permit a jury to consider all the circumstances from the point of detention to the time the employee made a decision about how to handle the case in determining if punitive damages are appropriate. As pointed out at the beginning of Chapter 8, the merchant's duty to use reasonable care exists at all times during the encounter with a shoplifting suspect. In some cases (the New Blue Purse Case, for example), the only mistake is detaining on a conclusion about wrongful possession. In that case, the woman was not mistreated, nor was the twenty-minute-period of detention and investigation legally unreasonable. In other cases (the After Hours Sale Case, for example), the detention was not supported by probable cause and the security employees mistreated their suspect after wrongfully detaining him. In that case, the court let the jury consider what happened after the man was released by permitting introduction of the letter he wrote asking for an apology and the fact that the department store made no reply. Because the duty to use reasonable care continues throughout the shoplifting situation, store policy must provide employees with specific information about their conduct in the *detention, the investigation of the facts, and the decision-making phases.*

Evidence of a Store's Net Worth

Since the theory of punitive damages is to punish the store rather than to compensate the plaintiff, the courts will admit evidence of net worth. Consider the following quote, because it is typical of the type of evidence a court will let the jury consider in arriving at a proper punitive damage award.

> On the punitive damage issue, the evidence was that defendant operated 1,087 stores and that its past year's net profits were $9,004,122.00. This evidence along with the evidence bearing on legal malice and other relevant factors was for the jury's consideration in determining whether and in what amount it should award punitive damages.[2]

---

[2]Peak v. W. T. Grant, 409 S.W.2d 58 (Missouri, 1966).

Normally a jury knows the punitive damage award will be paid by the store and not the manager or security person handling the situation. The courts will let the jury consider this "net worth" evidence along with the evidence of mistakes made by the employees which establish false imprisonment or malicious prosecution types of liability. There is generally no requirement that the plaintiff's actual damages bear any relationship to his punitive damages. The net worth of the store is crucial evidence for the jury in this respect. In the Wedding Rings Case, for example, the actual damages were only $41, but the jury awarded $12,000 in punitive damages—a 300 to 1 ratio. The jury is specifically instructed that the purpose of punitive damages is to punish and to deter. Juries take their responsibilities seriously in determining if liability exists and then in awarding actual and punitive damages. The key issues on punitive damages are the conduct of the employee handling the case and the net worth of the store.

The Basis of Punitive Damages

Emotional suffering and mental anguish is the main basis for claiming damages in these false imprisonment and malicious prosecution actions by shoplifting suspects. The person's reputation and standing in the community can be a factor. Sometimes a suspect will submit medical expenses for seeing a psychiatrist or psychologist after being detained, prosecuted, and acquitted, along with the medical evidence of emotional trauma or stress. In one case the award was for over $85,000. The cost of expert witness fees was found to be proper where the plaintiff became confused, dazed, cried, and hallucinated during the detention and investigation. The plaintiff contended that the wrongful detention and improper investigation was the cause of chronic depression and acute anxiety. There was also evidence the plaintiff was unable to function in his former manner.[3] The plaintiff may also claim damage to his career as a result of the shoplifting situation. In these cases, the plaintiff may try to establish that a job loss was due to a personality change or other emotional consequences of the detention, investigation, and trial. If the suspect is prosecuted and wins the case, the damage claim may include the fact that the plaintiff's name was placed in the police computer network and has not been or cannot be expunged.

The merchant must also take into consideration the suspect's condition at the time of the detention. The fact that a plaintiff is sensitive, nervous, or emotionally highstrung will be a factor the jury can consider

---

[3]Landry v. Schwegman Bros. Giant Food Stores, 416 S.O.2d 341 (Louisiana, 1982)

if proved. It is not necessary for the suspect to be physically abused in order to claim damages for mental anguish and emotional distress. The merchant must understand that any harsh, insulting, humiliating, or otherwise traumatic treatment may provide the plaintiff with the basis for a damage claim. The name of the game in detaining and investigating these shoplifting situations is diplomacy—even if it hurts.

RECKLESS AND INDIFFERENT CONDUCT BY RETAIL EMPLOYEES

As the eight cases just discussed demonstrate, the law treats reckless, grossly negligent, or outrageous conduct by a retail employee as if it were intentional. Consider the following definition of gross negligence as it best describes the way a court can describe a merchant's conduct in these civil cases where a jury can award punitive damages. Gross negligence is defined as meaning a callous indifference or a thoughtless disregard for the consequences of one's act or failure to act. If merchants incorporate the five tests to comply with the merchant's privilege statutes set out in Chapter 6 into policy, it will be less likely that the conduct of an employee handling a shoplifting case can fall into this gross negligence category.

In the three cases which follow, liability was established against the stores but the conduct of its employees was not so aggravated, grossly negligent, reckless, or indifferent as to justify a jury award of punitive damages. These retail employees made mistakes during their encounters with shoplifting suspects, but the jury did not award punitive damages. No store wants to be sued in the first place, but if a civil action is filed the merchant may be able to mitigate the punitive damage aspect of the lawsuit.

CASE	Thinning shears case

A woman shopping in a discount drug store was seen by one employee with a pair of thinning shears on the lower level of her shopping cart. She moved them to the basket of the cart, placing them near her open purse. The employee informed a second one to take up the surveillance. The second employee observed that the shears were no longer in sight when she began watching the woman. The suspect went through the checkout line, paying for other items but not for the shears, which the second employee believed were in the woman's purse, though she did not see her conceal them.

When detained, the woman told the security people she had returned the box of shears to a counter and agreed to show them where they were located. When they went to the cosmetics section, no shears in a box were found. The woman was then taken to the security office. According to the woman, she dumped the contents of her purse on the floor at the request of a security officer. No thinning shears were found. She said they next took her to a back room where she was compelled to submit to certain indignities, including the partial removal of the clothing. She also said the employees would not let her go to the restroom. The store security people said she voluntarily emptied the contents of her purse on her floor. They denied any indignities or that she was told to remove any of her clothing.

The police were called. After some discussion, no shoplifting charge was filed. The shears were never found in the woman's possession. That same afternoon, a box, identified as the one that had contained the shears, was found in the ladies' restroom of the store. The woman sued for false imprisonment and slander. The jury found liability existed. The damage award was for $5,000 in actual damages and zero in punitive damages.

Condor v. Toone, 581 P.2d 387 (Kansas, 1978)

This case shows how a store can be sued successfully without punitive damages being awarded. Apparently the jury felt the store's detention and investigation conduct violated the duty to use reasonable care, but the employees were not reckless or indifferent in the way they handled the situation.

| CASE | Sunglasses case |

The security person for a fashionable department store did not check the glasses offered for sale by the store with the ones the suspect had in her possession when detained, though she asked him to do so. The jury found that liability for false imprisonment existed and that the conduct of the security person justified an award of punitive damages. The appellate court disagreed, reversing the case only on the issue of punitive damages. The court said:

> Conduct of security manager in failing to comply with the woman's request to check her sunglasses with types of sunglasses displayed at store counter, if careless . . . did not rise to level of wantonness or maliciousness to warrant an award of punitive damages.

Guion v. Associated Dry Goods (Lord & Taylor Division), 393 N.Y.S.2d 8 (New York, 1977)

The court is saying that the security person was careless in failing to verify the suspect's explanation about ownership of the glasses. In this court's view, however, this conduct was not so serious, reckless, grossly negligent, or outrageous as to justify a punitive damage award. The point is the jury thought the conduct was aggravated enough and did award punitive damages. Clearly the security man failed to use reasonable care. If he had checked her glasses with those offered for sale by the department store, a loss-prevention goal would have been achieved. The store would have prevented the loss of time and money to defend this civil action, including two trips to the appellate court to get the jury award reversed. Because the security person had not been taught to conduct a logical and systematic investigation of the facts after detaining a suspect, the store had to spend time and money needlessly. This is the type of loss that stores can prevent by understanding and complying with the merchant's privilege.

CASE	Lipstick case

A woman and her twelve-year-old daughter were shopping in a drugstore. According to the woman, she was carrying a sack belonging to another store. The drugstore merchandise—lipstick, make-up, and cologne—was on top of the sack, between it and her body. She said at the checkout counter she offered to pay with a social security check. The store employees said she placed the three items inside the sack and did not pay or offer to pay. They said she admitted the items were not paid for and offered to pay for them. The woman said she did not check her change when leaving because her sister was waiting at the front door, urging her to hurry up. An arrest warrant was obtained; she was prosecuted and acquitted.

The case was tried twice, and both times the jury could not reach a verdict. The third time false imprisonment liability was determined to exist, and a $75,000 award for actual and a $75,000 award for punitive damages was returned. On appeal of the case by the store, the court reversed the finding as to punitive damages. The court held that where the clerk in good faith believed the woman had concealed some items in a sack that an award of punitive damages could not be justified.

> No vile language or violent threats were made against Mrs. Rice. She was offered the use of a telephone to call any persons she wished. She was permitted to go out through the back of the store to avoid the embarrassment of seeing any friends or acquaintances while in the custody of the police. . . . There being no evidence suggesting that Mr. Rowland [the drugstore employee] did not in good faith suspect that Mrs. Rice had concealed some items in the Rose's sack, we find nothing in the record to indicate that Rowland or any other Super X employee acted in bad faith, Mrs. Rice was not entitled to an award of punitive damages.

Super X Drugs of Kentucky v. Rice, 554 S.W.2d 903 (Kentucky, 1977)

INSURANCE COVERAGE AND PUNITIVE DAMAGES

Security directors and retail executives in charge of loss prevention should check their insurance policies because the store may not be covered for punitive damages. Not all states permit an insurance company to write coverage for punitive damages. The civil action used to demonstrate the problem involved a plaintiff receiving $35,000 in punitive damages against a large discount store chain out of a situation involving the switching of price tags. Now the merchant is suing the insurance company to determine if its policy includes coverage for punitive damages. It was the first time the Oklahoma court had considered the question. The Oklahoma court found that coverage existed under the discount store's insurance policy, so the carrier and not the merchant had to pay the $35,000 punitive damage award handed out by the jury.[4]

In this case, the relevant part of the merchant's policy said:

> The company [the insurer] will pay on behalf of the insured [the merchant] all sums which the insured shall become legally obligated to pay as damages because of injury (herein called personal injury) sustained by any person or organization and arising out of one or more of the following offenses committed in the conduct of the named insured's business:
>
> Group A: False Arrest, Detention or Imprisonment or Malicious Prosecution.
> Group D: Mental Injury, Mental Anguish, Shock and Humiliation.

The court first stated there was no Oklahoma case law on the point of whether a policy calling for payment of "all sums" is sufficiently broad to include punitive damages. The court's research, including decisions from other states, found a split of authority, with the majority holding that such policy language does cover punitive damages. In deciding the insurance company should pay the punitive damage part of the jury award the court said:

> The policy provisions in the case at bar make no distinction between actual and punitive damages. Punitive damages are not specifically excluded. Under the plain language of the policy the company promises to pay on behalf of the insured all sums which the insured shall be legally obligated to pay as damages because of injury arising from false arrest. The law is clear in Oklahoma that insurance policies are to be construed most liberally to favor recovery. . . . Hence, the policy provision "for all sums which the insured might become legally obligated to pay" is sufficiently broad to include liability for punitive damages.

Merchants should not take this case, and its result, to mean that all

---

[4]American Mutual Liability Insurance Company v. Dayton-Hudson 621 P2d 1115 (Oklahoma, 1980).

policies with similar language will be found to include coverage for punitive damages. Litigation concerning insurance policies is always about the language used. The result could be different in another false imprisonment, false arrest, or malicious prosecution case where the insurance company denies coverage for punitive damages. Merchants must always consult with the company lawyers.

The second aspect of this insurance coverage problem is whether a state's policy will permit the merchant to shift the punitive damage award to an insurance company. In discussing the question, the Oklahoma court talked about the leading case, one involving a drunken driver which held that no coverage of punitive damages is permitted:

> Where punitive damages are awarded for punishment and deterrence, policy considerations would seem to require that the damages rest ultimately on the party actually responsible for the wrong. If that person were permitted to shift the burden to an insurance company, punitive damages would serve no useful purpose. . . . If the liability could be shifted to the insurer, the burden would ultimately come to rest not on the insurance company but rather on the public at large, since the added recovery would be passed along to premium payers. Society would then be punishing itself rather than the actual author of the wrong.[5]

There is an exception to the rule that a merchant cannot shift the punitive damage award to an insurance company. Consider again what the Oklahoma court said on this point:

> In almost all jurisdictions which disallow insurance coverage for punitive damages, an exception is recognized for those torts in which liability is vicariously imposed on the employer for the wrong of his servant. In that class of litigation, public policy does not inhibit a shift in liability incidence to the insurer unless the employer's volition was either directly or indirectly an element in the commission of the harm.

An employer is vicariously liable for the intentional wrongful conduct of his employee. This means the company will be held liable for any false imprisonment, slander, malicious prosecution, or other acts caused by a store manager or security person. Since vicarious liability normally is found to exist in these shoplifting cases, the merchant-employer may be entitled to purchase punitive damage coverage.

If the merchant is sued, most states hold that the insurance company is required to defend the store at its own expense even if the carrier says it is not liable to pay the punitive damage award. The legal relationships between the merchant and his insurance carrier are beyond the scope of this book. Suffice it to say that a periodic review of insurance coverage is always sound business practice. This is particularly true for retailers

---

[5]Northwestern National Casualty v. McNulty, 307 Fed 433 (5th Cir., 1962).

operating stores in different states, because the law on this punitive damage coverage could change by court decisions from time to time. The best rule is never assume punitive damage coverage exists, but always check to be sure.

A final point is understanding who must pay the jury award should one be returned for actual and punitive damages. The general rule is that the employer pays, not the store manager, security person, or other retail employee who may be involved in the mishandled shoplifting situation. Sometimes a false imprisonment or malicious prosecution petition may name the security officer along with the store as parties defendant. The plaintiff in any civil action always wants to sue the party with the "deep pocket" as it is called. Since these cases may involve six figure awards, the plaintiff knows an individual employee does not normally have the resources to pay. Even though the security officer or store manager is named as a party defendant along with the retail corporation, the plaintiff is looking to the company (or its insurance carrier) to pay the jury award or an out of court settlement.

10

Miscellaneous Aspects of Civil Liability and Shoplifting

Merchants must remember the universal rule in dealing with shoplifting situations: *the manner and method of the response dictates the result.* Improper responses violate the merchant's privilege and result in false imprisonment and malicious prosecution actions being filed against the store.

The civil liability cases in this chapter involve legally improper responses made by retail employees. They are not the ordinary shoplifting situations; in fact some do not involve shoplifting at all. Training programs should always contain a "miscellaneous" prosecution and civil liability segment. By understanding the situations presented in these cases, a store manager or security person is in a position to avoid making the mistakes found here. By preventing mistakes the store is preventing loss—the loss of dollars paid out to defend civil actions and to pay awards handed out by juries.

PEACE DISTURBANCE AND DISORDERLY CONDUCT SITUATIONS

CASE	Lay-a-way battery case

In this case, store security was not responding to a theft situation but just the opposite: the person was trying to purchase merchandise rather than shoplift. The result was a successful civil action back against the store rather than a sale. For reasons not fully set out in the case, the sales clerk had the security people come to the department and charge the man with disorderly conduct.

He was acquitted and filed a two-count civil action against the store alleging false arrest and malicious prosecution. The Jury found both types of liability existed. The damage award for false arrest was $500 in actual and $10,000 in punitive damages. On the count alleging malicious prosecution, the damage award was $500 in actual and $5,000 in punitive damages. The jury award was approved as reasonable when the store appealed the adverse decision to the higher court.

Consider the facts of the case as set forth by the court:

> On the night of September 22, 1972 plaintiff sought to buy a battery from one of defendant's salesmen. He wanted to use lay-a-way to take advantage of the battery's sale price, but after paying $5.00 down and being handed a sales receipt the salesman told him there was a $.75 lay-a-way charge. The man asked if there would be an extra charge if instead of putting it on lay-a-way he used his Sears Charge account. Being told no, an argument followed when the man asked to have the battery put on his charge account. The salesman jerked the sales slip out of his hand and left, but returned with two security guards, one telling the man he was under arrest for peace disturbance.
>
> The officers, one of them armed, handcuffed the man and took him upstairs where he was ordered to enter a room. When he refused a guard pushed him against a wall, causing him to strike his head. He was kept in the room for an hour until police arrived and cited him for peace disturbance. He was not allowed to use the phone. While so confined he was read his rights by one of the store's employees. His head and eye began to ache after the injury and later he was treated at a local hospital. He still had head aches at the time of the trial. He lost several days from his place of business in preparing his successful defense of the disturbing the peace charge.

Walker v. Sears, Roebuck & Co., 536 S.W.2d 169 (Missouri, 1976).

Sometimes merchants will encounter situations where filing of a disorderly conduct or peace disturbance charge may be appropriate. These offenses, like shoplifting, require the merchant to produce evidence in the store which in court establishes the elements of the offense. Here the man was acquitted because the security people did not present sufficient evidence to prove the charge. These situations do not come up very often, so evidence-gathering skills can become rusty. The Mall Security Officer case in Chapter 7 shows how a merchant and the mall company can both be sued when disorderly conduct charges are filed in a shoplifting situation.

| CASE | Honking horn case |

A woman successfully sued a discount store after being charged with disorderly conduct. In the store, she had been detained for investigation about possible theft of baby clothes. She was taken to the office. The investigation revealed no store merchandise in her possession, so she was released. According to a security man, she used loud language in the store. Outside in the parking lot, she drove her car in front of the store very slowly for about one-half a minute, honking the horn and yelling loudly. Based on this evidence, having nothing to do with shoplifting, the security man obtained an arrest warrant for disorderly conduct. The charge was dismissed and she sued the discount store. The merchant's privilege statutes do not apply when a store is sued civilly after losing a disorderly conduct or peace disturbance case. This means the store cannot plead compliance with the detention statute in situations demonstrated by the last two cases. The merchant's privilege applies only when a merchant detains for possible shoplifting. Training programs must take this legal fact of life into consideration when instructing employees about the circumstances in which these types of charges should be filed. Mall security personnel have responsibility for the common area and generally, though not always, for the parking lots. Merchants may want to check with the mall security department about situations when it is appropriate to file peace disturbance, disorderly conduct, criminal trespass, and destruction of property charges. Since mall security people have a broader responsibility than merchants, they will normally have more experience with filing these nonshoplifting type charges.

CALLING THE POLICE WITHOUT FIRST DETAINING AND INVESTIGATING THE FACTS

The following case is important, because it could have happened in any specialty store—one without a full-time security staff. If your store has this type of "call the police" policy, it should be reviewed and most likely changed, because civil liability exposure risk is high.

| CASE | Satin sandals case |

This was a circumstantial evidence case, which means that no store employee actually saw the person obtain wrongful possession of the merchandise. All the shoe store employees knew was they found an empty box of size 7 sandals on the floor right after the woman left. She had been trying on size 7 shoes.

When it was determined the pair of satin sandals was missing, the manager told a sales clerk to go outside and get the woman's license number. The woman was easy to identify because she was dressed in a distinctive style: a red blouse, high-heeled shoes, earrings, and blue pants. A police officer responded, taking a written report using a preprinted form. When he completed his investigation, he handed the form to the sales clerk, asking if she wanted to prosecute. The store manager was present at this time and said the store wanted to prosecute. The clerk signed the form in accordance with the manager's directions. There were two places on the officer's report for the complainant-victim to sign. One was to indicate the victim desired to prosecute; the other was to sign if the victim did not want to prosecute.*

The police obtained the woman's name and address by running a license plate check on the number provided them by the sales clerk. They went to her home, finding the woman described to them by the shoe store employees. She was formally arrested for shoplifting. No satin sandals, size 7 or otherwise, were found. The case contains no record of any statement made by the woman to the arresting officer.

She was acquitted of shoplifting and filed a civil action against the shoe store. The jury awarded her $13,000 in actual damages and $74,000 in punitive damages. The finding of liability and award of punitive damages was affirmed as appropriate when the store appealed the adverse decision.

The store defended the malicious prosecution action by saying its employees only reported the facts to the police, leaving it up to them whether to prosecute and whom to prosecute. The court flatly rejected the store's contention. The court said the shoe store employee gave the police a license number and a specific description of the woman they said shoplifted a specific pair of shoes belonging to the store. The clerk, with the manager's approval, had signed the officer's report form in the space designating a desire to prosecute. The court held that the jury could have found from the facts that the store set the legal machinery in motion, thereby causing this woman to be formally arrested and prosecuted. In other words, the decision to prosecute and the decision whom to prosecute was not left up to additional investigative activities of the police. This store did not just report facts to the police but rather directed the officers to arrest a specific person for shoplifting a specific pair of shoes. The only problem was that no store employee had actually seen her obtain wrongful possession of those shoes in the first place, and the shoes were not recovered by the police at the time of formal arrest.

Laparl v. Volume Shoes, 664 S.W.2d 953 (Missouri, 1984)

*It is obvious that the store manager had not been taught the difference between a direct and a circumstantial evidence case, and that circumstantial cases are inherently weaker in court. No employee saw the woman actually obtain possession of the shoes. This store's policy was *not* based on the merchant's privilege statute because no effort was made to detain the woman and investigate the facts before deciding how to handle it. Finally, no merchandise was recovered, which compounds the evidence-gathering mistake of detaining on a conclusion about concealment.

Here the evidence to establish wrongful possession and intent to shoplift was entirely circumstantial. No store employee even attempted to detain and investigate the facts. Instead, based entirely on this circumstantial evidence, the store manager summoned a police officer to the store and instructed him to make a warrantless arrest. No merchandise had been recovered and examined. No explanation had been obtained from the woman. The civil action could have been prevented if training programs had been based on the merchant's privilege statute.

The following case is another example of a charge being filed without recovering the merchandise.

| CASE | Baby clothes case |

An employee in the infants department became "suspicious" of a woman customer when the woman refused an offer of sales assistance. She was carrying a box belonging to another store in that city. For reasons not explained in the case, the sales clerk thought the customer had put some baby clothes inside the box she was carrying and called security. The security officer testified he saw the woman put some infant garments in the box and leave the department without paying. He followed her out of the store and watched as she entered another store on the mall. He obtained permission from the security people in that store to detain her and investigate the facts.

She refused to let him examine the contents of the box. Knowing not to force a search without consent, he continued the detention for the arrival of a police officer. After hearing the security man's evidence about what happened, the officer told the woman she was under arrest. This meant the officer now had legal authority to search the box without the woman's consent or permission. He had made a warrantless arrest based on probable cause evidence supplied to him by a private citizen store detective who had detained the woman pursuant to the merchant's privilege. Up to this point everything was perfectly proper. She opened the box, and no department store merchandise was found. For reasons not stated in the case, the store detective signed a complaint causing her formal arrest and prosecution for shoplifting merchandise he had not recovered. She was acquitted of shoplifting and then filed a civil suit against the store for malicious prosecution. She received $10,000 in actual and $7,000 in punitive damages, the award being affirmed when the store appealed the case.

Sestrich v. R. H. Macy & Co., 493 S.W.2d 52 (Missouri, 1973)

Initially the security officer did the right thing. He did not force a search but rather continued the detention for investigative assistance by the police. Under the merchant's privilege, he had a legally reasonable time in which to conduct a legally reasonable investigation of the facts—the fact of ownership of the merchandise. There was no mention in the case that calling the police and continuing the detention violated the reasonable investigation or reasonable time provision of the detention statute. The woman was not mistreated in any way. But there is no explanation why the complaint was signed.

The security officer handled the situation correctly up to the point of justifying his decision to prosecute. He should have released her, because no merchandise was recovered. Had he released this woman, the only civil action she could have filed was for false imprisonment, to which the store had a defense under the merchant's privilege. One can speculate as to whether she ditched or dumped the goods or whether he was mistaken about observing her conceal it in the box. In either event, it makes no difference. The decision should have been to release the woman rather than to file the charge. By filing a nonprosecutable case, the store's exposure to civil liability was increased from false imprisonment alone to false imprisonment and malicious prosecution.

ALERTING OTHER STORES ON THE MALL

There are two fundamental points to learn from the following case. First is that the statutory privilege to detain and investigate the facts belongs to the store that owns the merchandise. Secondly, these merchant's privilege statutes do not apply to credit card situations as a general rule. As the facts of this case will demonstrate, the credit card pickup order was put out by the store's credit department for reasons not having anything to do with shoplifting or fraudulent use of a credit card.

The Plaza Alert was an information-dispensing system used by a major mall to broadcast security information to all stores on the mall. According to the case, a merchant receiving the alert was not required to detain or take any action just because the alert was broadcast. When an alert was put out, all stores on the mall and the local police were notified. The case contains no description or account of what type of situations were considered serious enough to justify broadcasting the alert. As the facts of this case show, the department store security people putting out the alert had no probable cause from any source to believe theft by credit card or by shoplifting had taken place.

In this case, the suspect was detained not by the store initiating the alert but by one receiving it. Both department stores were sued civilly. Liability for false imprisonment was found against the department store initiating the alert. The jury found in favor of the department store receiving the alert, the one whose security person (an off-duty police officer) actually detained the female suspect. Any malls using these alert systems would do well to read this case in its entirety. It contains serious probable cause and merchant's privilege questions, ones that must be thought through when reviewing policy with regard to the alerts.

CASE	Plaza alert case

A college student entered a major national department store on the mall and made some purchases using a credit card. It had belonged to her father, who had died some four years before the day in question. She was accompanied by a friend. The card, issued by the national department store, was an older one. The plaintiff (the young woman) signed her name, address, and telephone number as requested when making the purchases. The clerk ran a check on the card, giving the credit department the information. She then completed the sale and returned the card to the plaintiff, who left the store. The time was around 8:00 P.M.

The credit department had called the plaintiff's home, talking to her mother who said her daughter was authorized to use the card. The credit office then notified the security office that the regional credit office (located several hundred miles away) wanted the card picked up. The security officer talked to the sales clerk, obtaining a description of the young woman, and then contacted the mall security dispatcher. The plaza alert was then issued. The information was simultaneously relayed by telephone to each store on the mall and to the local police department. When advising the mall dispatcher to issue the alert, the security officer said he wanted to get the credit card back.

The two young women had now entered another national department store on the mall where they were spotted by the off-duty policeman working as a security officer. He detained both women and also contacted the police department, probably twice.* He testified that he had been told by the store sending out the alert that they wanted to talk with both women. The officer ordered both women to go through the warehouse section of the store to the security office. The evidence was conflicting on the amount of force he used to require the women to make the trip. In about ten minutes, the security officer from the store initiating the alert arrived. He asked for the woman's student ID card and his store's company credit card. He kept the credit card and returned the ID card. After about fifteen minutes, both women were released with "apologies" for the inconvenience. No attempt was made to recover the merchandise the young woman had purchased with the credit card.

Vaughn v. Sears Roebuck & Co., 643 S.W.2d 30 (Missouri, 1983)

* There was no probable cause evidence from any source to justify detaining the companion. Now civil liability exposure had extended to a nonsuspect because of the alert.

The alert went out because of the credit department's policies—not because of any facts observed by any employee of the department store that established probable cause. Because of the alert the police were notified. In other words, the store sold the woman the merchandise, and then put out a call for that credit card and because of the plaza alert, this became police business. She had done nothing illegal, a fact the department store knew because they called her mother.

The college student sued both department stores. The detaining store successfully defended the actions of its security officer in stopping the women. The department store initiating the alert was found liable for false imprisonment. It defended the actions of its credit department and security staff by trying to plead compliance with the detention statute. The store said probable cause existed based on the pickup order by the credit department. The court disagreed.

In all states, probable cause must support a reasonable belief that the suspect is committing theft of merchandise. By his own admission, the security man for the store initiating the alert said his purpose was only to pick up the credit card. He was acting on information given to him by the store's credit department several hundred miles away. He had already called the young woman's mother and established that she was authorized to use the credit card. Neither the credit department nor the security officer possessed facts sufficient to establish probable cause that theft by unauthorized use of credit card was taking place. There was not even a hint that either woman was attempting to shoplift.

CREDIT CARD PICKUP POLICIES

The real problem, in this case, was the credit card pickup policy of the department store initiating the plaza alert. Credit personnel furnished the authorization to the security department who put out the alert that resulted in another store detaining the young woman and her companion. To aggravate the situation, the police were notified because of the way the plaza alert system operated on that mall. In this case, the woman was using one of the department store's credit cards. In other situations, people may be using bank credit cards or ones issued by private credit card companies. Sometimes these institutions instruct merchants, hotels, restaurants, and other retailers to pick up *bad cards*. A "bad card" has no legally defined meaning, either in criminal or civil law. If a credit card company or the merchant's own credit department says to pick up a card without further explanation, this could invite civil liability. Security personnel must work with the credit department when setting credit card pickup policies to avoid civil liability situations as found here. The real culprit, in this case, was the credit department. They did not realize that picking up the cards involves a restraint of a person's freedom of movement which exposed the store to false imprisonment liability.

Nonsecurity personnel, such as those in a credit department, normally do not give much thought to the civil liability consequences of their policies. Security personnel should meet with the credit people to help the latter formulate policy regarding picking up a credit card for nontheft reasons. They should make private credit card companies be specific about why they want a card picked up; the fact a card is "bad" means nothing legally. Make them tell the retail employee why the card is to be picked up: stolen, over the limit, expired, unauthorized use, and so on. Also merchants should request an opinion from the legal department as to whether detention statutes provide a defense in credit card situations. These credit card cases are much like those involving peace disturbance and disorderly conduct; the merchant's privilege may not be available as a defense if the store is sued.

New York has a statute providing merchants with a defense of lawful detention when they detain persons concerning ownership, possession, validity, or use of a credit card. The statute is broad, covering situations where the card is lost, stolen, revoked, cancelled, or forged. It mentions the purchase or lease of both property and services, as well as obtaining cash advances. It says a reasonable time is that time necessary for a person to make an explanation or to refuse to make an explanation and the time necessary for the merchant to examine records relative to whether proper use is being made of the card.

| STATUTE | New York credit card theft statute |

Improper use of credit card; defense of lawful detention (Section 516)

In any action for false arrest, false imprisonment, unlawful detention, defamation of character, assault, trespass, or invasion of civil rights, brought by any person by reason of having been detained on or in the immediate vicinity of the premises of a seller, lender or issuer, for the purpose of investigation or questioning as to the ownership, possession, validity or use of a credit card, it shall be a defense to such action that the person was detained in a reasonable manner and for not more than a reasonable time to permit such investigation or questioning by a peace officer, or by a person acting on behalf of or by such seller, lender or issuer, and that such peace officer, person, seller, lender or issuer had reasonable grounds to believe that the person so detained was using or attempting to use a stolen or forged credit card or was making or attempting to make unlawful use of a credit card. As used in this section, "reasonable grounds" shall include, but not be limited to, knowledge that the credit card has been, or has been reported to be, lost, stolen, revoked, cancelled, or forged and knowledge that the person had used or attempted to use the credit card to purchase or lease property or services or to obtain a cash advance, and a "reasonable time" shall mean the time necessary to permit the person detained to make a statement or to refuse to make a statement, and the time necessary to examine employees and records of the seller, lender, issuer or holder relative to whether improper use was being made of the card.

Most larger malls have some type of security information dispensing system as found in the Plaza Alert Case, because a need for it exists. Malls and their tenants must research the law of merchant's privilege in states where they operate stores, especially with regard to credit card situations. Any restraint based on broadcasted information should be reviewed to insure that somebody—the merchant or the mall—possesses facts sufficient to restrain the suspect, because there is always a civil liability consequence. Policy should always consider ways to minimize this exposure whether the detention is made by a merchant or a mall security employee.

CIVIL LIABILITY WHEN MERCHANTS HIRE CONTRACT GUARD SERVICES

The central legal question here is whether the contract security guard is an agent of the merchant or an independent contractor. Store managers or security executives in retail operations using guard service employees should always check with the law department about the legal status of guards. The merchant will want to have the security company carry its own insurance and present a certificate of insurance before any contract is signed. The merchant may want to be named as an additional insured party on the guard service policy. Some merchants require the guard service to provide them with a *hold-harmless agreement*; this means that the guard service agrees to defend the store and hold it harmless for any civil tort actions filed as a result of wrongful acts of the guard service employees. Often there is substantial negotiation with guard services before they are employed by a retailer. The most prudent approach is to discuss the civil liability possibilities with guard services before entering into any contractual agreement with them.

In the two cases discussed below the courts found the merchant civilly liable. In the Complaining Customer Case, the food store manager called the guard over and involved him in the discussion with the customer. In the Necklace Case, the reverse happened: the guard detained the suspect and took her to the specialty store manager. In the first case, the court found both the store and guard service liable for false imprisonment and assault and battery. In the second case, only the merchant was liable for false imprisonment. These two cases are not intended to demonstrate that stores are always found liable in guard service situations. They do show that as a practical matter, courts are reluctant to let merchants escape liability by hiring a guard service and calling them an independent contractor. In one Texas case, the court said if a merchant was liable for wrongful detentions, investigations, and prosecutions of suspects when caused by their own employees, the merchant could not avoid liability for the same wrongful acts when committed by a guard service under contract to the store.[1]

CASE	Complaining customer case

A national food store had a contract with a security company to provide guards for its sixteen stores in the Washington, D.C., area. The chief security investigator for the food store testified that the merchant did not hire or train the guards.* He said there was an oral understanding they were to be paid monthly in lump sum and they were under the general direction of the store manager, who had operational control of all aspects of the store. The manager could set the hours the guards worked and if dissatisfied with the performance of a specific guard could request that he be replaced.

In this case, a customer, after purchasing groceries, complained about the front door, which apparently did not work well. He contacted the manager, and a somewhat heated discussion began to develop. The manager summoned the guard. The customer testified the guard approached him from the rear and grabbed him around the throat. He said the police became involved; he was pushed to the ground and handcuffed. He was then taken to the rear of the store and required to stand there, handcuffed, for about fifteen minutes, where he was seen by others in the store. He was charged with unlawful entry. The charge was dropped.

He sued both the store and guard service, receiving $40,000 for false arrest and $25,000 for assault and battery. The trial judge has the authority in most jurisdictions to reduce a jury award before either the plaintiff or defendant files an appeal. The judge reduced the award to a total of $15,000, but an appeal was still taken.

The appellate court ruled the grocery store exercised sufficient control over the guard so the store was liable for his wrongful acts of false arrest and assault and battery. In so ruling, the court stated the issue as follows:

> The threshold determination is whether Safeway is liable for the alleged assault & battery and false inmprisonment of the plaintiff by a security guard who was working at a Safeway store and employed by an independent security service. Safeway argues that it avoids liability since the guard service company was an independent contractor and not a servant (employee) of Safeway.

Safeway v. Kelly, 448 A.2d 865 (D.C., 1982)

* Always check about what type of training the security agency provides guards under the contract. Some companies do not train guards at all.

---

[1]Dupree v. Piggley Wiggley Stores, 542 S.W.2d 888 (Texas, 1976).

The court emphasized that no single fact is ever conclusive in these cases as to whether the guard is an independent contractor or an agent or employee of the merchant. The general rule is that a person hiring an independent contractor does not control the specific duties or the exact way in which the work is performed. Consider the following definition of an independent contractor as set forth by the American Law Institute:

> Restatement of Agency, 2nd—Section 2(3)
> An independent contractor is defined as a person who contracts with another to do something for him but who is not controlled by the other nor subject to the other's right to control with respect to his physical conduct in the performance of the undertaking.

As a practical matter, it will be difficult for merchants to prove they do not have control over (or the right to control) the specific conduct of contract security guards. The guard will normally be required to comply with store policy on detaining suspects and investigating the facts. If a shoplifting charge is filed, it is usually with the approval of the store manager. It would be civil liability folly for a merchant to hire contract security guards and give them no specific instructions. Guards must become familiar with the store's merchandise, its inventory control system, and policy about when to initiate prosecutions.

The court will look closely at the facts of each case to determine if the guard is an independent contractor or an agent of the store. Some of the factors to be considered are these:

1. selection and hiring of the guard
2. payment of wages
3. power to discharge the guard
4. power to control the guard's conduct
5. whether the work is part of the merchant's regular business

The most important factor is the power to control the guard's conduct. In the Complaining Customer Case, the evidence was undisputed that the manager summoned the guard and caused him to become involved in the discussion with the unhappy shopper. To the court, this right to control the guard was demonstrated sufficiently. The guard was found to be an agent of the store rather than an independent contractor.

CASE	Necklace case

In this case, the contract security guard detained a teenage girl, accusing her of shoplifting a necklace she was wearing. The girl told her she had received the necklace as a gift (an ownership defense). She did not have a receipt but told the guard her mother was on the shopping mall and would verify the fact it was recieved as a gift. The guard took the girl to the office, explaining to the manager (who had no previous knowledge of the conversation) that she had seen the girl take the necklace. The girl repeated the explanation about receiving it as a gift and asked if they could find her mother. All three went outside to the parking lot and found the girl's mother, who told them the necklace was a gift. The security guard then produced a civil liability release, asking it be signed, telling the mother it was not store policy to prosecute juveniles. The mother refused to sign anything, telling both employees she was going to prosecute the store, which she did. The necklace was returned to the girl. Both the mother and daughter left.

At the trial for false imprisonment, the plaintiff produced evidence tending to show the specialty store did not stock necklaces of the same quality as the one she wore in the store that day. The jury found that only the store was liable for false imprisonment. The court said the following in affirming the jury finding and reversing the judge's rule that the store could not sue the guard service:

> The evidence in this case is undisputed that the assistant manager's actions with respect to the plaintiff were taken in reliance upon the guard's representation that she had seen the plaintiff take the necklace. There is no indication that the assistant manager's actions with respect to the plaintiff were anything other than innocent and reasonable responses to this representation. Ordinarily, if one person (the store) is compelled to pay damages because of liability imputed to him as the result of a tort committed by another (the guard), he (the store) may maintain an action over for indemnity against the person whose wrong has thus been imputed to him. We hold it was error to deny Casual Corner's cross claim under the evidence presented.

U.S. Shoe Corporation v. Jones, 225 S.E.2d 73 (Georgia, 1979)

ELECTRONIC ARTICLE SURVEILLANCE SYSTEMS

These systems, called EAS in the retail industry, are in use particularly in apparel stores. Most merchants who use them feel they do have a deterrent effect, especially on the average citizen shoplifter types. Much of this book has been devoted to defining and explaining the term "probable cause" as found in both criminal law and in the merchant's privilege statutes. The legal problem with EAS systems is that no retail employee has observed a person obtain wrongful possession of the merchandise when the alarm system activates. Shoplifting is an offense involving a person who obtains wrongful possession of merchandise and intends to shoplift rather than pay for it. When an EAS alarm goes off, this is evidence only that the customer is in possession of merchandise. The possession could be lawful, such as when a sales employee fails to remove the tag. The possession of merchandise could be wrongful. The legal dilemma is that probable cause to detain and investigate for possible shoplifting has not been established.

Consider the following sign, because it is typical of ones posted at exits of stores that use EAS systems.

> Merchandise in this store is protected by an electronic inventory control system. If the alarm sounds, please take merchandise to the cashier and have the inventory control tag removed.
>
> > Thank You
> > ABC Department Store

From a legal standpoint, this sign is well-thought-out. It recognizes the possibility that the alarm may be activated by reason of an employee's failure to remove the tag after a valid sale. The sign clearly implies that failure to remove the tag and not shoplifting is the reason the alarm may go off. Since the merchant normally is required to post a notice that inventory control tags and warning devices are in use, the message contained in this sign is a good one. In the two cases discussed below, retail employees failed to remove EAS tags and the court found this fact to be important.

EAS systems have been on the market over ten years, but only a few states—as few as three or four—have passed antishoplifting device statutes. The Georgia statute is typical.

| STATUTE | Georgia antishoplifting device statute |

105-1006 Detention of persons leaving mercantile establishment equipped with anti-shoplifting or inventory control device

(a) As used in this section, "anti-shoplifting or inventory control device" means a mechanism or other device designed and operated for the purpose of detecting the removal from a mercantile establishment or similar enclosure, or from a protected area within such an enclosure, of specially marked or tagged merchandise.

(b) In the case of a mercantile establishment utilizing an anti-shoplifting or inventory control device, the automatic activation of the device as a result of a person exiting the establishment or a protected area within the establishment shall constitute reasonable cause for the detention of the person so exiting by the owner or operator of the establishment or by an agent or employee of the owner or operator. Each such detention shall be made only in a reasonable manner and only for a reasonable period of time sufficient for any inquiry into the circumstances surrounding the activation of the device.

(c) The provisions of this section shall apply only with respect to mercantile establishments in which a notice has been posted in a clear and visible manner advising patrons of the establishment that an anti-shoplifting or inventory control device is being utilized in the establishment.

(Acts 1979, pp. 762, 763, eff. July 1, 1979.)

Section (b) says automatic activation of the alarm shall constitute reasonable cause for detention. It requires each detention to be reasonable in manner and only for a time to "inquire into the circumstances" surrounding the activation. As pointed out, one circumstance could be failure of a sales clerk to remove the tag. The other could be the person's failure to pay for unpurchased merchandise. This statute does not say that activation of the alarm constitutes probable cause to detain and investigate the facts about possible shoplifting as does the merchant's privilege statutes. This statute does not give the store a statutory defense to use in the event that a civil action for false imprisonment or unlawful detention is filed.

As pointed out, there are two types of cases merchants present in court—direct and circumstantial evidence cases. In each one, a retail employee has made some observation to justify his decision to detain for investigation of the facts. In EAS cases, the retail employee detaining the customer has not made any observation. All that employee knows is the antishoplifting device sounded an alarm. Some systems have voice-activated alarms while others use bells, buzzers, or other types of signals. Stopping the person is a restraint of that person's freedom of movement. The courts will always want to know what source of evidence justified or supported the merchant's decision to detain.

CASE	Sensor device case

In this case, there was no EAS statute on the books when the woman was stopped. The court held that the activation of the antishoplifting device did not constitute probable cause to detain and search the woman. In essence, the court found that a false imprisonment or an unlawful detention took place. The store had recently installed a sensor system. To inform the public of the installation, the merchant posted notices in its stores and publicized the fact in newspapers and on television. During the first three days of operation, the alarm was activated five to ten times because employees failed to remove tags from merchandise. The system could also be accidentally set off by transistor radios. The store was crowded on the day in question. As a woman went out, the device activated. A number of customers heard the alarm activate and then witnessed the detention and search. The woman was detained outside and asked to return to the store, which she did. It was discovered that a sales clerk had forgotten to remove the tag when her shopping bag was searched. The shopper had in fact purchased the merchandise. The woman was permitted to leave with apologies from the management. None of the store personnel accused her of shoplifting or had acted discourteously.

The woman filed a civil action for unlawful detention, alleging humiliation and embarrassment because of the detention and search of her shopping bag. The court said the facts were not disputed, setting forth the following comments:

> Two or three days before the incident occurred, I. H. Rubenstein's installed an electronic anti-shoplifting system in its Baton Rouge Broadmoor store. To inform the public of the installation Rubenstein's posted notices in its stores and caused it to be publicized by newspapers and television stations. The system consisted of devices which emitted an audible alarm upon the passage of a special tag through an invisible electronic field at any exit of the building. The tags were attached to articles of merchandise in the store and Rubenstein's sales personnel were instructed to remove the tags from each item sold. Thus it was intended that purchasers of merchandise would pass through the electronic field without incident, but the sounding of the alarm would alert store personnel to the possibility of a theft being committed. However, during the first three days the system was in operation the alarm was activated 5 or 10 times by an employee's failure to remove a tag. The system was also susceptible to being set off accidentally by transistor radios and other objects as well as the special merchandise tags.

Clark v. I. H. Rubenstein's, 326 S.O.2d 497 (Louisiana, 1976)

The Louisiana Supreme Court reviewed the decision of the court of appeals (a lower court), which had concluded the woman was lawfully detained under the detention statute. The supreme court said it was not clear about the reasoning found in the lower court's decision. The appellate court was saying either that the store had probable cause to believe she had committed theft so detention and questioning was proper or that the stopping did not constitute a detention because she voluntarily went back into the store. In reversing the appeals court finding, the supreme court said, "We cannot agree with either proposition."

The supreme court was concerned that the merchant knew about the previous activations caused by the failure of employees to remove the tags. It found that the merchant did not have probable cause to detain and stated:

> Because knowledge of these facts [the prior activations caused by employee negligence in removing the tags] was attributable to I. H. Rubenstein, Inc., as well as knowledge of the sales clerk's failure to remove the tag on the occasion in question here, the defendant [the store] did not have reasonable grounds to believe that the sounding of the alarm was caused by a theft of goods by Mrs. Clark.

The court reasoned that the woman was certainly subjected to a detention and had only two courses of action available. She could have attempted to leave the store area, thus tending to confirm the suspicions of store employees and bystanders that she had stolen something. This approach would have subjected her to more humiliation and possible restraint by force.[2] Her other choice was to submit to a public inspection of the packages she was carrying. The court left no doubt that her freedom of movement was restrained. The court said, "A restraint was effectively placed upon her liberty."

At the time this case was decided, Louisiana did not have a section in its detention statute covering use of antishoplifting devices. Four years later the Louisiana legislature amended the detention statute by adding the following section:

| STATUTE | Louisiana detention statute (Article 215(B)) |

If a merchant utilizes electronic devices which are designed to detect the unauthorized removal of marked merchandise from the store, and if sufficient notice be posted to advise the patrons that such a device is being utilized, a signal from the device to the merchant or employee indicating the removal of specially marked merchandise shall constitute a sufficient basis for reasonable cause to detain the person.

| CASE | Tag in the bag case |

This statute says activation of the device shall constitute a "sufficient basis for reasonable cause to detain the person." Like the Georgia statute set out above, this one from Louisiana does not use the language of probable cause to detain for investigation of the facts concerning possible shoplifting. It does not provide the merchant with a statutory defense to use in defending the store from a false imprisonment action if an employee detains and mistreats the suspect.

The first reported decision under this statute involves two stores on the same mall. Both the specialty store and the national department store were using EAS systems. A woman bought a purse at the specialty store. The clerk could not find the tag to remove it. She put the newly purchased purse in a bag along with the receipt. When the woman left the specialty store, the EAS system's alarm did not activate. The woman went to have lunch, at which time she transferred the contents of her old purse to the new one. She put the

---

[2]The Louisiana detention statute is one of the few that specifically mentions use of force.

old purse into the bag she received at the specialty store.

After lunch she entered the national department store, carrying the new purse with the live EAS tag in it over her arm. The department store's EAS system did not activate when she entered. She made a purchase at the department store, placing the specialty store sack containing her old purse into the larger sack provided by the department store. When she started to leave, the department store's EAS system activated the alarm. The merchandise she purchased in the department store was not tagged, so no department store employee failed to remove an EAS tag.

She was approached by a saleswoman who explained that most likely a clerk had forgotten to remove the tag when the customer made the purchase. No tag was found on the items she just purchased from the department store. The saleswoman did notice the specialty store sack inside the department store sack. She examined the woman's purse, which was the old purse, and found no EAS tag. At this point the customer explained about the new purse and how it had been purchased at the specialty store. Department store employees then opened her new purse and found the live EAS tag, the one the specialty store employee failed to remove when making the sale.

The woman sued both stores for unlawful detention. Her theory of liability was that the statute should not protect either store. She said the statute was not designed to protect merchants who detain innocent customers because a sales clerk neglects to remove a sensor warning tag. She also claimed the statute could not be used by the merchants as a defense because the equipment was defective. These stores were using sensor warning devices that worked only part of the time. The court found there was no liability against the department store. It held that the detention and search in the department store was legally reasonable, even though the department store employees may have been discourteous.

As to the specialty store, the woman claimed that immunity should not be granted where the detention was caused by the clerk's failure to remove the tag. In holding that the statute did protect the specialty store, the court examined the purpose behind passage of this antishoplifting device statute. In a weakly written opinion, one not addressing the key issue of probable cause to detain, the court said the legislative intent was to encourage use of the detection equipment in combating shoplifting.

Allen v. Sears & Roebuck, 409 /S.O.2d 1268 (Louisiana, 1982)

Although neither merchant suffered liability in this case, it does not help clarify the underlying legal issue involved in use of these devices by merchants. The court did not discuss probable cause but avoided the question.

The two Louisiana decisions seem to be contradictory. In the first one, before the passage of the statute, the court specifically found that failure to remove the tag after selling the merchandise was a key factor in deciding that probable cause to detain did not exist. In the second, it seems that the court is approving employee negligence in failing to remove sensor warning tags and justifying it solely on the basis of legislative policy underlying passage of the antishoplifting device statute. Such an analysis is shallow and misses the legal point.

In analyzing the legal aspects of detaining and examining merchandise after activation of an EAS warning device, merchants should consider the following points:

1. Activation of the warning is not based on an observation of the suspect obtaining wrongful possession of merchandise, so it is different from the evidential test of probable cause found in merchant's privilege statutes.

2. Activation of the warning alarm is the only evidence that the person is in possession of merchandise. It is not evidence that the person's possession is wrongful, because a sales employee may have failed to remove the EAS tag after making a valid sale.

3. Because the merchant does not know if the item is being shoplifted or has actually been purchased at the time of the stopping, the merchant may not have the right to request that the person produce concealed items for examination. Neither the Louisiana or Georgia statutes cited above mention the right to search.

4. Both statutes cited above require the merchant to handle the detention and investigation in a legally reasonable manner, just like the test in the merchant's privilege statutes.

5. Antishoplifting device statutes do not provide stores with a defense to use if sued civilly for a false imprisonment or an unlawful detention. Since they do not contain the probable cause to detain test as found in merchant's privilege statutes, a court may not allow a merchant to use the detention statutes as a defense when a store is sued civilly out of an EAS situation which is mishandled. In all states, the test to detain and investigate the facts about possible shoplifting is probable cause, and this test is not found in these antishoplifting device statutes.

Stores that use these EAS systems must devise training programs to inform employees how to handle detentions and investigations. The safest legal approach is to assume the reason the device activated was an employee's failure to remove the tag. Do not assume the person is in possession of unpurchased merchandise with the intention to shoplift it, because there is no evidence to support that reasonable belief at the time of the detention. Ask the customer if the clerk removed the tag at the time of sale, and see how the person responds. Do not imply the customer has intentionally failed to pay for concealed merchandise. Since these antishoplifting device statutes do not mention the right to ask the suspect to produce concealed merchandise for examination concerning ownership, the detaining retail employee must be diplomatic. Merchants are on legal thin ice if they demand to search purses, shopping bags, or parcels without statutory authority to do so. A merchant's legal position is much weaker when the detention is based on activation of an EAS alarm than when the detention is supported by observations which constitute probable cause under a merchant's privilege statute.

If a store detains and mishandles a situation involving the EAS alarms, the result will be a civil action for false imprisonment. If the mistreatment involves the use of force, the false imprisonment action could be accompanied by one for assault and battery. If the detaining employee accuses the person of shoplifting, the civil action can then include a claim for damages based on slander. In short, the civil liability exposure in these EAS situations is just the same as in situations where a suspect is improperly detained or detained and mistreated in the cases found in Chapter 8.

A final point about EAS systems must be mentioned. Do not neglect sales employee shoplifting alertness training just because the store purchases or leases one of these expensive EAS systems. It is easy for sales employees to feel they can forget about shoplifting because the EAS system will take care of the problem. In most stores, not all the merchandise is tagged, so sales employee vigilance is still the best deterrent. Remember the quote from the California department store manager in Chapter 1 who said tags are good but employees are better than tags.

Index